PROFITABLE PIG FARMING:

A STEP BY STEP GUIDE TO COMMERCIAL PIG FARMING FROM AN AFRICA PERSPECTIVE

By **Yemi Adesina**

PROFITABLE PIG PRODUCTION

Disclaimer

Every reasonable effort has been made to ensure that the material in this book is true, correct, complete and appropriate at the time of writing. Nevertheless, the publishers and the author do not accept responsibility for any omission or error, or for any injury, damage, loss or financial consequences arising from the use of this book. Views expressed in the articles are those of the author and not of the Publisher.

ISBN: 978-1-68638-005-1

1. CONTENTS

2. Foreword

At present, there is a huge appetite towards farming in sub-Sahara Africa and several governments are encouraging entrepreneurs, professionals, diasporas and businesses to venture into agricultural businesses.

The author believes that the recent influx of middle-class farmers into farming in Africa will bring about the much-needed green revolution that has brought about economic growth to Asian and Latin American countries like Brazil and Thailand.

Like many other readers of this book, you are probably an entrepreneur, professional or a diaspora (like I was), who wanted to venture into farming as a business and not as a hobby. However, research on successful farming from around the world has shown one component that is critical to the success of any farm enterprise — and that is, the owner must have a good knowledge of the business and should personally direct his farm operations.

This book was written to help bridge the knowledge gap required by those that wanted to establish and operate a successful commercial farm in Africa. I believe that after reading this book, you will have a good understanding of what you need to do to achieve your goals and aspirations. In addition,

I believe the farmer in you will begin to come out gradually, bringing you closer to the fulfilment of your dream of having a successful commercial farm in Africa.

My motivation to write this book came after receiving hundreds of emails and thousands of texts from some of our 1.5 million YouTube viewers who have watched our 120 YouTube videos but have not been able to physically attend our profitable pig farming training.

This book is a practical and easy to understand guide, a more complete book that will take the conception of your ideas through a step by step process involving planning, implementing, operating and marketing of your product. This book is written to increase the chances of you succeeding in your farming venture.

This book is divided into 3 sections:

1. Business section
2. Farm operations section
3. The marketing section

In the first part of the book (the business section), you will learn the reasons why middle class (and diaspora) like yourself are venturing into farming in Africa, the characteristics of pig that made it the preferred choice of livestock farming for many new farmers and the advantage it has over cattle and poultry farming. You will understand the right mindset and attitude that is required to become a successful farmer in Africa, the business approach and the organisational structure that you need to put in place to run a long-lasting commercial farm.

Whether you have already bought farmland or you are still searching, this book covers how to evaluate and select a good location for your farm. I took the time to breakdown how much it will cost you to set up and operate a medium-size commercial farm and the different sources of funding that are available for your projects.

In the second part of the book (the farm operations), you will learn the advantages and disadvantages of the different pig production system. This will help you to decide which area of pig farming that you wish to specialise in. And how your choice will ultimately determine the product type that your farm will produce and how they will be marketed.

As a farmer and a trainer, people always ask me what breed of pig is the best for their farm? My answer is always "it depends on the goal of your farm", this is not always the answer that people expected from me. However, during my training, I always stress the importance of 'profitability' because I realise that just increasing the physical performance of your pigs on the farm is not enough. And that is why, in this book, my focus is on how to increase the profitability of your pig farm.

There are also specific suggestions on how to set up a commercial pig farm such as building suitable houses for your pigs, selecting the right breed and transporting them safely to your farm. The book also features how to get the best from the different categories of pigs on your farm and how to feed, medicate and keep them in top condition for best production, for example, large litter and high birth weight of your piglets, rapid growth rate of your weaner, timely mating of your sows and gilts to increase the litter size.

The uniqueness of this book is that throughout each section, we tried to look deep into the physiology and anatomy of pigs that are relevant for farmers especially during the pig stressful and critical situations like mating, pregnancy, farrowing, disease attack, etc.

In the final section, you will learn about the various stakeholders who are involved in moving our pigs from the farmgate to the consumer in sub-Sahara Africa and how this relationship affects the market price of your product from the farmgate to the consumer. There are also suggestion methods of increasing the product value of your farm produce and the most effective and efficient means of getting these products to the market profitably.

As a diaspora farmer, I tried to strike a balance between the attractive features of living on the farm and being your own boss, but I also emphasised the unpleasant and tough ones.

When my Chinese friend in the United Kingdom brought it to my attention that 2019 was the Year of the Pig according to the Chinese zodiac, between Feb. 5, 2019 and Jan. 24, 2020. I told myself that this was the right time to publish this book to commemorate the Year of Earth Pig.

It is my sincere hope that this book will help you to avoid failure, delay, disappointment, and mistakes that are typical of people who are new to farming. It should also help you to attain the satisfaction that characterizes personal and well-directed efforts in farming.

ABOUT THE AUTHOR

My experience in farming starts at an early age after relocating from the United Kingdom to Africa with my parents. During my early days in Nigeria, my parents rented an acre of an allotted farm at the back of our house where we planted maize, cassava, tomato, and okra. As a family, we worked together on the farm every Wednesday evening and sometimes, during the weekends — Saturday to be precise.

As a young person, aside from playing football with my friends, the few hours spent on the farm were the most memorable and exciting time of my childhood.

In my sixth form, I chose to study animal health and husbandry at Obafemi Awolowo University, Nigeria. I did my National Youth Service Corps at Bornu College of Agriculture before I finally moved to the United Kingdom. I lived, studied, worked, and raised my family for 20 years in the United Kingdom. I also honed my project management skills and did lots of projects with the UK government before I decided to immigrate back to Nigeria in 2006 to start a livestock farm enterprise with the intention of alleviating the chronic meat shortage in Nigeria.

Upon arriving in Nigeria, I was confronted with the enormity of my ambition and the task required to start farming in Africa.

I realised that most of my initial assumptions and planning about farming that I conceived while in the United Kingdom, had lots of gaps, as the present situation in Nigeria had deteriorated than when I left the country 20 years ago. The basic infrastructures, such as electricity or municipal water had gone down from a few hours a day to few hours a week, the road networks to rural areas were bad. While the old farming practices seemed to have frozen since I left the country, most of the farming activities were still done manually, with little or no use of machinery, equipment, or technology.

Eventually, I resorted to managing the construction of the farm by myself. I had to create a road path through the thick forest jungle to get to my newly bought farmland and clear the thick vegetation on the farmland, coordinated the construction of each of the pens and farmhouse, sourcing, management and recruitment of staff, etc. Over the course of this book, I will share some of the lessons that I learn in more detail and the new mindset that I had to develop to go through to become a successful pig farmer in Africa.

I would like to forewarn the new farmers that have set their minds on being a commercial farmer in Africa: your decision to leave your job or move your family from your existing comfort zone either as a city person or diaspora should not be hastily made. But I can also assure you that this decision you are about to make is a noble one that will improve your health, bring your family closer and, most importantly, it will build up and develop your children's character to deal with all life's challenges that might be thrown at them later in life.

This quote from Thomas Henry Huxley describes what farming does to a young person:

"Liberal education that happens on the farm does not only prepare a child to escape the great evils of disobedience to natural laws, but it trains him to appreciate and to seize upon the rewards which Nature scatters with a free hand as well as her penalties.

A man that had a liberal education is the one who has been so trained in his youth that his body is the ready servant of his will, and does with ease and pleasure all the work that he is capable of; whose intellect is a clear; and ready to do any kind of work; whose mind is stored with a knowledge of the great and fundamental truths of Nature and of the laws of her operations; one who is full of life and fire, but whose passions are trained to come to heel by a vigorous will, the servant of a tender conscience; who has learned to love all beauty, whether of Nature or of art, to hate all vileness, and to respect others as himself.

Where, I ask, can a boy or a girl acquire and develop such qualifications so well but, on a farm, that is well managed by loving parents".

This book was written based on my 20 years of experience of farming and 8 years of training farmers across Africa. Despite the fact that I did my first degree in animal health and production and Masters in business administration in London, I am not just an agricultural theorist who only understood how to do everything verbally, but I have proven what I teach. I had sweat and got my hands dirty and even lost money along the way. So, I understand what is at stake when you invest your life savings on a farming project.

I successfully built my first commercial pig farm starting with 39 pigs and raised over 3,500 pigs and sold over 2,000 pigs to the public within 2 years in 2010. I have trained over 580 farmers in Ghana, Togo, Nigeria and Cameroon. I have also helped to set up 34 successful pig farms in 3 countries, which are still in operation.

The speed and rapidity of this achievement brought lots of media attention to my farm, and I was called upon by the National Television NTA and local TV and Radio stations for interviews to share my achievements. I also went on to do five television documentaries on how to start and run a commercial pig farm and the program was watched by over 55 million people in Nigeria and in Ghana.

As part of my determination to make the pig farming knowledge available to a wider audience across Africa, I posted over 120 training videos on YouTube on pig farming. These videos covered the different aspects of profitable pig production, marketing, and slaughtering. To date, our YouTube videos have been watched by over 1.5 million people from over 36 countries in Africa, making them the most-watched videos on pig farming from African perspectives.

(To view the 120 videos *Enter "papayemo1" to Youtube search engine).

In this book, I shared a lot of my personal experiences, including my challenges, mistakes, and successes, so that you, as the reader, might understand that the journey is not always that smooth. But as the saying goes, "While you may not be able to direct the (unfavourable) wind, you could trim your sail so as to propel your vessel as you pleased, no matter which way the wind blew". What I put in this book is not only what I have learnt but also what I have learnt from other farmers who I was opportune to work with during my career.

ACKNOWLEDGEMENTS

Although one man has written this book, it wouldn't have been possible without a huge number of people who have been so patient and helpful to me during the last 20 years.

I want to thank God Almighty for His grace and protection while I was in Nigeria and for giving me the opportunity to put some of my thoughts about pig farming in Africa into a book.

I also owe much to lots of people that have encouraged me to follow my dream, especially my late dad, Mr Solomon Ola-jide Adesina, who exposed me to my first farming experience and encouraged me to be passionate about farming. He once told me when I was complaining about the high price of meat in Nigeria, to which he replied, "If agricultural graduates like you could get their hands dirty on the farm, abundant animals will be produced and meat will no longer be a luxury item that only a certain class of citizen finds convenient to buy and consume regularly".

To Bola, my wife of 25 golden years of marriage. I would like to thank her greatly for her undying love, support and encouragement, for allowing me to emigrate to Nigeria temporarily to establish one of the fastest and well-run pig farms in Nigeria and for bearing with me through all the different challenges of establishing a farm business in Africa. And also her forbearance for the use of our dining room table and littering of the floor with books and research papers for 9 months while I wrote the book.

To my two sons, Femi and Seun, who prevented my computer from driving me mad and eventually had to buy a new computer for me, so that I could finish writing the book. I also thank them for the lovely chats at 2 am in the morning when I hijacked them on their way from the toilet, to clarify ideas that I was struggling to put into writing.

Next, I would like to appreciate the hard work of my team at Pristine Integrated Farm Resources in Nigeria, Ghana and Cameroon, for organising the profitable pig farming training in their respective countries during my absence, to allow me the time to focus on writing this book.

Since 2014, when I became a pig consultant and trainer, I have had opportunities to help set up 54 pig farms across Africa. Most of these farms have been loyal and persevering. They have generously allowed me to use their pigs and facilities to conduct farm training and have opened their premises to visitors who sometimes criticise too much and praised too little. I owe them a debt of thanks for their trouble and patience. Boyd Farm, the first farm that I set up in Nigeria. How much I have learnt over two decades about pigs — and people.

My appreciation also goes to the over 580 participants that have attended our profitable pig farming training in Nigeria, Ghana and Togo, and I will not forget to mention our over 1.5 million YouTube audience that regularly watches our videos across Africa, for their positive comments on the great work that we are doing.

Finally, there are many academics, veterinarians and scientists who know so much more about pig farming than I do. Where would this book be without them?

I certainly owe them a debt, especially to those whose advice or work are gratefully acknowledged in the references, and in the 'further reading' appendix. Please pardon me if I forgot to acknowledge you.

APOLOGIA

There are bound to be — only a few, I hope — errors and omissions and I apologise in advance. No man knows it all, especially me! I learn new things about pigs every day, important things once a month, and things of revolutionary importance once a year. And you learn more as you get older. One good thing with age is that you are then quite happy to confess you don't know all, and are content to pass the enquirer on to a specialist who probably does.

This book is dedicated to:

Thousands of farmers all across Africa who are hardworking, dedicated, patient, enthusiastic, generally under-recognised and under-rewarded people in food production, and to pig farmers, piggery farmer's associations and cooperatives across Africa, some of whom I've met, encouraged and learnt from — all of whom helped make this book possible. To whom I say in a traditional Chinese saying "May you live in interesting times".

3. Be Forewarned — Word of warning to new farmer

Before you make your final decision to go into pig farming, here are some key things that you should think about before you start committing money to your idea.

1. **Commitment** — Livestock farming is an enterprise that is unlike any other inanimate business that you might have been involved with in the past. It is usually not always easy to stop pig farming at the press of a button. Once you start operating your farm, it can be difficult if not impossible, depending on the size, how much you have invested and how long you have run your farm before you decide to stop. That is why it is important that you are fully convinced before you commit lots of money to pig farming. I would recommend that you start small and be ready to devote the required time, energy and money for the setup and the management of the farm if you want to get the most from it. You might have to employ some staff and a manager to perform the day to day operations of the farm but, as the proprietor, you should try as much as possible to learn and understand the basics of your business. You will definitely learn a lot from this book. But try not to be just a silent listener to

every conversation, rather be ready to ask the right and open questions, practices and to challenge the basis for every action and omission that happens on your farm.

2. **Always start small** — As a trainer, I have been privileged to train many farmers. One key observation with new farmers that I have walked through our main farm is how overwhelmed and eager they are to have the same size of farm and number of pigs on our farm right now, not realising it takes few years to get to this level. I realized that many of us in this generation go about our lives and interact with so many "big corporations, organizations and enterprise" (especially the non-governmental ones) and we rarely take time to comprehend the evolutionary process that the enterprise went through from small to become this big. The second observation is the big aspirations and the incessant urge of many new farmers to become a large commercial pig farm overnight. While I very much understand that some of us may have quit our jobs and we may desire that our farm provides us with the same salary and lifestyle that we have with our current job, but we forget how long it took us to earn this money from our employer in the first place.

   My advice to every new pig farmer is to start small. By this I meant that the size of your farm should be within your manageable limits from all aspects and this should be determined not only your budget but your past knowledge, experience, your education on farming and other life skills and training. Starting small will allow you to expose only a small amount of your capital to the risk of failure which is possible for most new start-ups. With your small capital invested, it will not be the end your world if something goes wrong, you can easily bounce back and put what you have learnt to use. It will also allow you to discover patterns, tricks, things that work and won't work in pig farming. And based on this grass root experience of the business, you will understand better what customers wants, and from your small successes and failures, you can gradually use the knowledge gained to build and increase the size of your pig farm.

Please note, all the knowledge gained from this book or any other sources cannot prevent you from making some mistakes, the goal of this book is to drastically reduce the number of mistakes that you will make before you become successful.

"Experience is the hardest and the most expensive kind of teacher. It gives you the test first and the lesson afterward." Oscar Wilde

3. **Grow your farm organically** (i.e. grow your farm from within) — this advice is similar to the previous advice of starting your farm small. It is important that you start your farm with what I will call minimal viable number of pigs. The minimum viable number of pigs is the total number of pigs you will need to achieve your first milestone (for example to produce the first 1,000 pigs on your farm within two years, you will need to start your farm with a minimum of 25 gilts and 2 boars and no more).

This allows you to focus your initial energy and drive on buying your first set of minimal viable number of breeder pigs from a reliable source and subsequently use the female pigs birthed and raised on the farm to breed and populate the rest of the pigs on your farm. Starting with minimal viable number of pigs will also allow you to focus on achieving your first goal of producing and selling your product out in bulk to the market.

"Success isn't always about greatness. It's about consistency. Consistent hard work leads to success. Greatness will come". Dwayne Johnson

4. **Be market oriented** — I always make this statement into my participants during training

"Until you sell pigs on your farm for money, you are not a farmer, you are just a zookeeper".

To improve your marketing chances, it is important that your farm begins to attract and sell pigs to pig buyers as early as possible. To these effects, I always recommend that along with your breeder pigs you should also buy an additional 20 or more weaners. These weaners should be fattened and sold to market within the first 6 months of operation weighing 85kg or more. The goal of this initial sale is to serve as a pilot test for your pig marketing. In Africa, the most effective form of marketing is word of mouth. As soon as buyers start buying pigs from your farm, they will spread the word around about your farm to the rest of the pig buying community.

From my experience, selling your first set of pigs for money is a confidence boosting exercise for farm owner, it helps to confirm the marketability and profitability of the product produced. Finally, the timing of the sales of the weaners also correlate with the time when your breeder pigs will begin to give birth to lots of piglets, the sale of the weaners will bring a timely and the much needed additional funds to the farm.

5. **Don't get carried away with your farm infrastructure** — except you buy or rent an existing farm. Your first set of activities and expenditures when setting up your pig farm will be clearing land and building farm infrastructure. This will include boundary fencing, farm-

house, breeder pen, grower pen, storage, sinking bore holes, plumbing, etc. As a mentor to farmers, I have witnessed many new entrepreneurs who get carried away and over invested on their farm infrastructure at the expense of their operational cost. As a consequence, when the infrastructure was ready, some of them had to delay the commencement of the operation to raise more capital and drastically cut down on their initial goal for the farm.

As a serious farmer, you need a business plan that details how much you will need to spend on both capital and operational expenditure for the first 2 years and you need to adhere to this budget.

My advice is that during the construction of your farm, focus on the basic and important infrastructure that is necessary to start your farm and ensure the welfare of your pigs. We will discuss this in later chapters of this book when we look at what your pig needs. You should ring fence your operation capital that you will need to source for good quality pigs, purchase feed, health care, management, etc., these are what will help you to achieve your profit.

Health — The health and welfare of your pig is very important and your farm health care measures must not be ignored. You should have a good hygiene system on your farm and regularly consult with veterinarian or an experienced person to learn about the suitable breed, housing system, etc.

Before purchasing pigs and piglets, visit different pig breeding farms in your area to assess the performance and health history of their herds. Your farm should adhere to good pig farming practices, use good quality medication, deworming your pigs periodically and carry out other routine medication. Cleanliness of the farm must be maintained at all times. Make sure your farm is washed daily with soap and disinfectant and the water in your foot dip is changed daily.

Recent research has shown that poor hygiene reduces feed conversion in pigs by 30% and can cost farmers up to $50 per breeder pig per annum. And in addition, sows may also gives birth to fewer pigs per litter as a result of poor hygiene.

6. **Focus on one thing at a time** — Many new farmers are always desirous of implementing many farming ventures e.g. to combine piggery, with poultry and arable farming, they usually want to do all of this at the same time despite the fact that they know very little about what each business entails. Research has shown that doing only one thing at a time is a powerful way to become more productive and is the ultimate path to productivity. The research disagrees with the cultural norm that doing more than one thing at a time is a great way to become productive and to spread risk. The study proves that it is impossible for our brains to focus and learn two different tasks at once. Instead it is actually rapidly switching between them. So when we multitask, we end up doing a mediocre job of everything.

Focusing on one thing at a time gives us the depth and knowledge needed to become an expert in a particular field and it also ensures that we do not spread our time, attention, and energy too thin—these three are the key ingredients of productivity.

The application of this to you as pig farmers is that once you decided to invest in pig farming, you should focus on pig farming long enough to master it well and be productive before you jump into another farming project. This will allow you time to create more attentional space around your farm, and to know your business very well.

7. **Know your farm** — One of the most profitable habits that you can form around your farm as a new pig farmer is to systematically, go over your pig farm premises at least once each week and spend time to observe your pigs and your staff as they go about their daily activities in a leisurely and scrutinizing and thoughtful way. With this habit. You will reap the harvest of observation through a quiet eye and fill your imagination with knowledge of the habits of your pigs when they are well and to note and interpret the behaviour of your pigs under varying conditions of cold and heat, sunshine and shade, drought and wetness, fair weather and foul, rich and poor feeding. You will be able to observe and see a piglet being born with their placenta still hanging on them and their eyes being shut, and through all the stages of growth until they reach puberty and they too are mated and pregnant and are also farrowing. On a pig farm, it is possible to witness all these activities within 6 months of operations. This I believe is the best pig farm school where you can learn the duties that you owe to your animals and yourself for your own best interests.

4. Why you should venture into commercial pig farming

'When purpose is not known, abuse is inevitable'
– Myles Munroe

To be a successful pig farmer, you need to think and be very clear about why you want to venture into pig farming. There is no right or wrong answer, but you must be able to answer the question truthfully to yourself.

As an introduction to this chapter, I would like you to listen to this interesting conversation between Alice and the Cheshire Cat in Chapter 6 of Lewis Carroll's Alice's Adventures in Wonderland.

"Would you tell me, please, which way I ought to go from here?"

"That depends a good deal on where you want to get to," said the Cat.

"I don't much care where—" said Alice.

"Then it doesn't matter which way you go," said the Cat.

The summary of this conversation, is that "If you don't know where you're going, any road will take you there" but it might not be where you originally wanted to be.

4.1   REASONS WHY PEOPLE ARE COMING INTO PIG FARMING

From our years of conducting over sixty profitable pig farming training in countries across Africa, we have had opportunity to ask many of our participants this question, "Why do you want to venture in to pig farming" and here are some of the reasons they gave:

1. A hobby
2. To pilot test if farming or pig farming is for me
3. It is the popular thing — others are doing it, so I wanted to try it.
4. A homestead business at the back of the house
5. A safe investment — to pay unexpected to hospital bills
6. A piggy bank — a planned one-off bill e.g. school fees
7. For meat consumptions — roasting joints, sausages, ham, offal and intestine
8. A new endeavour to escape the dissatisfaction with current job
9. Looking for something significant
10. For profit
11. To build wealth for the next generation
12. To take advantage of the Increase in pork consumption

I am sure that you will be able to relate to at least one or more of these reasons.

Your answer to this question is important because whether you like it or not your motivation for starting a farming business will always influence, direct, and impact you subconsciously in all your decisions.

There is nothing wrong in starting your pig farm as a hobby farm or running it as a side-business at the back of your house, or as a pilot test to see if pig farming is for you. You can later decide to go into commercial pig farming if the pilot test is successful and the financials add up.

I like the quote from Khloe Kardashian, "We all have to start somewhere, and doing something is better than nothing at all. Start small so you don't get discouraged and give up. Remember it is all about consistency."

Whatever your motivation is, starting small is better than doing nothing, and with this book you will be able to learn lots of secrets to successful pig farming. The book should help you to discover and determine if pig farming is for and also help you to clarify why you should invest in pig farming.

Here are some reasons why we believe people should invest in pig farming.

From the left, Mr Yemi and the participants in the classroom and (right) on the farm for the practical session

4.2 KEEPING PIG FOR MEAT CONSUMPTIONS

Majority of the pig farmers in sub-Sahara Africa keep pigs primarily for meat consumption. This is the most popular reasons for keeping pigs especially amongst small scale farmers. Having a small pig farm at home will provide good home-reared pork, roasting joints, chops, sausages, ham and bacon.

Pig meat (Pork) is usually marketed in this form:

- Fresh meat — This is the most important product in Africa in general, as processing facilities are limited. Pig destined for the fresh meat trade are usually slaughtered without refrigeration. In general, pork is sold and used as fresh meat and occasionally, meat is cut into small pieces and roasted as suya

- Offal and intestines — while these might not be regarded as edible in many developed countries, but in Africa these are considered as edible and the liver inparticular is a delicacy.

4.3   RAISING PIGS FOR BREEDING

Breeding pigs can be immensely enjoyable. You can decide to keep a set of good breeding stock of gilts, sow and boar and see them breed from 20 sows to 250 pigs within 12 months. As long as the gilts and sows are promptly mated by boar or through artificial insemination and are pregnant for four months and they farrow piglets. These piglets are then nursed for 6 to 8 weeks until they are weaned. Your weaners will attract new farmers who are stocking their farm for the first time and farms that are replacing their old/sold stock. Weaners bought by farms are then raised into a breeder or fattener.

4.4   KEEPING PIG AS A SAFE INVESTMENT

The majority of the small-scale women pig farmers in sub-Sahara Africa keep pigs as a safe investment that can be sold as a live animal or slaughtered meat during cash shortage. The money generated can be used to pay school fees or emergency hospital bills.

I believe this is probably where the word Piggy banks comes from, according to Collins dictionary "Piggy Bank are usually made of ceramic and serve to teach children the value of money by encouraging them to save money". Money is inserted through a hole in the top and traditional Piggy Banks, but it must be broken open for the cash to be retrieved.

A similar metaphor for investing money on your pig and pig feed so that the pig grows and increase in weight and when you need the money, you sell off the pig.

Participants at the farm for the practical session of the profitable pig farming

4.5 TO ESCAPE THE DISSATISFACTION WITH THEIR CURRENT JOB FOR SOMETHING SIGNIFICANT

Over seventy percent of the participants that attended our profitable pig farm training came to us after watching our YouTube videos "papayemo1". Most of them are middle and senior managers in their profession or successful diaspora that are planning to come back home to invest in farming. Some of them attended our training because they are getting bored or burnt out with their current job. Some of them felt stuck in the same job. For many years the job is no longer bringing them the joy and satisfaction that they expected at this stage of their career. Some came after spending most of their adult professional life climbing up through the corporate ladder and they suddenly came to the realisation that they are about to retire and they want something that is their own.

The description of the circumstances facing these middle-class farmers across Africa that are coming to farming, is best illustrated using Maslow's hierarchy of needs. Maslow reckons that once you have successfully ascended in your career beyond the "physiological", "safety," "belonging and love needs. You next goal is the need to do something that you can call your own and leave as a legacy for the generation to come. However, this is very hard to achieve as an employee.

Here is aquote from one of our training participants, Mr Ben from Edo State, "I have used my knowledge and skills to date to make lots of money for my company and my boss. Mr Yemi, I think it is high time that I do the same for myself and my family"

Jim Rohn, a motivational speaker, put it this way "Your income is better than your salary, while your income will give you a good living, your income will give you fortune or financial independence."

4.6 TO TAKE ADVANTAGE OF THE GOVERNMENT'S CALL FOR PEOPLE TO START UP AGRICULTURAL BUSINESSES

At present, there is an appetite towards farming, several governments in Africa are encouraging middle-class entrepreneurs and businesses to start agricultural businesses.

With the world's market value of crude oil diminishing, many oil dependent countries in Africa are driving their focus to other largely ignored revenue streams such as agricultural commodities as an alternative to maintain a steady flow of income.

Agriculture as a source of income is still highly beneficial for Africa as a continent, because of the abundance of farmable lands and it offers a wide range of employment opportunities for new entrants into job markets because of the multifaceted and multifunctional nature of the sector. The benefits that the industry poses have caused an emergency action by many African governments to introduce several attractive incentives for new and existing farmers in the sector. Entrepreneur investing in agriculture across Africa now have easier access to loans for machinery, land, pens, and a lot more.

The early players will most likely be the greatest beneficiaries, and they also stand a better chance of owning the future large industries. I believe that starting pig farming now, is a smart move beforethe incentives get drastically reduced. The reduction will probably start as soon as reasonable number of agricultural businesses that have be-come successful.

4.7 TO TAKE ADVANTAGE OF THE INCREASE IN PORK CONSUMPTION

There is an acute shortage of dietary animal protein in Africa. The gravity of this problem is magnified in populous African countries, such as Nigeria, due to the rapid growth of the population and urbanization. As a result, animal protein has become a luxury instead of a dietary necessity and only a certain class of citizen find it convenient to buy and consume regularly.

According to of the F.A.O (2003) on an average basis, a man's daily protein intake should be between 65-72 grams per caput per day and 53% (about 35 grams) of this should be animal based. In Nigeria, the daily animal protein intake is below the recommended minimum level of 65 gm per caput per day. The research also revealed that only 8.4gm of the 53.8gm of protein consumption level of Nigerians is derived from animal sources, this is very poor indeed when compared with countries like USA and UK with about 69% of the total protein derived from animal sources.

The deficiency of protein in the diet is increasing the occurrence of disease such as kwashiorkor and miasma, which affects children physical and mental productivity, thus, adversely affecting the future labour force. In adults, it results in weight loss, weakness, fatigue, poor appetite, and anaemia.

Due to this acute shortage of animal protein in the diet of many Africans, there is now the need to increase the production of domestic animals for meat. However, a closer look at the current meat production and distribution in Nigeria reveals that beef accounts for about 70% of the meat consumed this is followed by poultry and fish. This overdependence of over 200 million people on very few conventional sources of meat like cattle, goat, and poultry only has led to high cost of meat and low meat consumption. This has made pig production and pork consumption a better and more attractive proposition for African as it is the most affordable meat for customers who are not forbidden by their religion to eat pork meat.

Pig has some unique advantages over all the other domesticated animal that is used as meat protein source in Africa. Pig is a good species of animals that can be raised extensively to combat protein shortages. Among these advantages are the fact that they have fast growth rate which is only slightly exceeded by broilers from poultry and their prolificacy surpassed any other animals' species except birds.

For those that are entrepreneurial minded, pig farming is a good opportunity that's worth exploring not only to create alternative source of meat but a source of wealth.

4.8   THE IMPACT OF URBANISATION ON PORK MEAT CONSUMPTION

Furthermore, the urbanisation and economic growth in most of the major cities in Africa has led to increasing presence of international and local fast food restaurants across the continent of Africa. Fast food brands, like Dominoes and KFC, supermarket and retail giants like ShopRite and Just rite, these multinationals are introducing a range of pork-dominated Western diets to African middle-class consumers.

In addition, foreign tourists, diasporas, investors, expatriates and their families are also flocking to the shores of Africa for business and pleasure and as a result, more of the hotels and restaurants who have a large customer base of foreigners are now looking for pork meat to serve and serve pork delicacies.

A good example of the surge in pork meat is glaring in countries such as Tunisia and Morocco, two overwhelmingly Muslim countries. Recently, Moroccan pig production has increased annually at an exponential rate to cater to the demand of millions of tourists (especially Europeans) who visit the North African nation every year. This is an interesting and positive trend towards pork meat, and it is sure to spread to other Africa's cities to cater for the growth in tourist.

4.9 THE PIG HAS THE HIGHEST FEED CONVERSION EFFICIENCY

Though pig has been domesticated for over 6,000 years by the Chinese, the recent increase in commercial pig production and pork consumption took a new level in the 1950s after the second world war and the food and meat shortage that came as a consequence. After the second world war and the scarcity of meat that follows, the western world realised that to meet the ever-increasing demand of animal protein for their populace. They needed a livestock that can be produced in accordance to human population growth. Of the production potential of each of the domesticated animal tested, the scientist discovered that pig is one of the fastest growing livestock and the annual growth rate of pig (3.8%) is higher than that of the human population (2.30 − 2.80%).

Pig has the highest feed conversion efficiency i.e.; they produce more live weight gain from a given weight of feed than any other meat producing animals excepts broilers. Not only do pigs convert more feed into body weight (flesh/meat), they also produce more meat when they are slaughtered. For example, unlike cattle, goats and sheep which produce between 50 and 55 percent meat from their bodies, pigs can yield up to 70 percent edible meat because they have a much smaller proportion of bones than meat. In addition to its high meat yields, meat processors and marketers love pig carcasses because they're easier to handle, stored and packaged compared to other types of meat.

4.10 PIG FEEDING REQUIREMENTS IS CHEAPER AND EASY TO FIND

Pig is omnivorous and, in some respect, competes with man for food, but is also a very useful utilizer of the by-products and waste from human food. Pig digestive system is well suited to benefit greatly from non-conventional feedstuff than human because pig has an organ, known as the caecum, that is attached to the large intestine, which allows a longer digestion period for the cellulose from plant cell walls to be properly broken down, digested and absorbed before exiting the pig. This organ is important in herbivore digestive system to break down raw plants, however pigs through evolution, though omnivore, benefit from this organ's presence.

As a result, pig feeding requirements are cheaper than fishery or poultry. Pig has over 15,000 taste buds (compare to humans that have just about 9,000). This enables them to eat everything that humans eat and also utilize wide variety of foodstuffs such as grains, grass, forages, damaged feeds and garbage and other non-conventional foodstuffs and convert them into valuable nutritious meat.

All these facts make pigs the best and the most efficient animals for converting kitchen waste, garbage, leftover food and by product and waste from human food to meat. Considering the high and rising cost of grains and concentrates used to produce livestock feed, the ability of pigs to consume a wide variety of foods reduces their feed cost and increases the farm profit potential.

4.11 PIGS ARE PROLIFIC AND HAS SHORTER GENERATION INTERVAL

As mentioned earlier, pigs are very prolific and have a shorter generation interval. One of the reasons why pig farming is very lucrative is that pigs multiply really fast. A sow (i.e. a mature female pig) reaches puberty and is ready for mating as early as 7-8 months of age and can they produce 8-12 piglets in each farrowing. The gestation (pregnancy) period for pigs is just four months. This means that one sow, which costs about $100, can produce up to $16 - 36$ piglets in a single year. These piglets can reach a market size of 70 kg within six to seven months and be sold for up to $100 each!

4.12 OTHER REASONS FOR RAISING PIGS

a. Research have shown that the role of pig production in converting food waste or factory bye product into animal feed is the way forward to recycle food waste in sub-Sahara Africa rather than for the industrial uses such as (biofuels production) landfill or incineration that are practised by the developed countries.

There is a potential opportunity for the African government to evaluate the opportunities and improve the environmental sustainability of pork production especially in the reduction of post-harvest loss or waste which is currently very high in Africa. Currently, most food waste or post-harvest losses in sub-Sahara Africa are disposed in landfills, which has significant negative impacts on the environment. However, pigs have the ability not only to help Africa's food security but also improve her environmental pollution. It is also important to note that pigs have a better carbon footprint as it produces 90% less methane than other livestock like cattle.

b. Pigs also have a high resistance to diseases (they hardly become sick or die suddenly like chickens or fish) and they also adapt easily to most environments (hot or cold). This makes it possible for pigs to be raised on both a small and large scale in almost every communities in Africa. Pig's adaptability also makes it the best animal for intensified or diversified agriculture that fits a wide range of budgets.

c.   Pig rearing is very scalable. It can be initiated at different levels. A school child can raise 1 boar and 2 sows at the back of his parent's house, a rural woman can raise 1 boar and 5 sows and use the revenue to send children to school and a commercial pig farmer can raise 10 boars and 200 sows producing over 3000 pigs a year.

d.   Pig farming also requires a small investment on buildings and equipment compared to fish and poultry.

e.   Pork is very nutritious with high fat and low water content and has got better energy value than that of other meats. It is rich in vitamins like thiamine, Niacin, and riboflavin.

f.   Pig manure is widely used as fertilizer for agriculture farms and fishponds.

g.   Pigs store fat rapidly (lard) and there is an increasing demand from this for soap, paints and other chemical industries.

h.   Pork is suitable for processing and some of the processed products have a longer shelf life than fresh meat and can thus be distributed to a wider section of the population.

i.   There is good demand from domestic as well as regional market for pig products such as pork, bacon, ham, sausages, lard, etc.

5. Brief history of pig production

"Pig might fly".

This is a humorous or sarcastic remark that many people use to indicate the unlikeliness of some event happening. It is also used to mock the gullibility of a person. However, the reality is that many people do venture into commercial farming with a lack of caution and they wonder why they are not successful.

As a pig farmer, we should be concerned about why pig was selected for this saying, Why not other non-flying creatures such as 'snail may fly', 'cow might fly', etc., I believe it is because pig is the favoured image of an animal that is particularly unsuited to flight. The bulkiness of the creature and their habit of rooting the earth suggests that pig is designed to get all their feed easily by foraging the ground, so with this abilities and capabilities why should pigs waste their time flying.

During our profitable pig farming training, I always challenge our participants that before they invest their hard-earned cash into commercial pig farming, they should learn as much as possible not only about the business of pig farming but also about the nature, the history and the characteristic of the animal that they hope to build their wealth upon. And they should be convinced in their minds why they believe that pig is the most suitable animal that can help them to achieve their goal instead of trying to fit square pegs into round holes or make pigs to fly.

The reality is that pigs are as they are, they can't and would never fly and there is nothing any farmer can do about it however there are some behaviours and characteristics that pig has (not flight) that farmer can benefit greatly from but farmer needs to first of all be aware of these behaviours and characters.

In this chapter, we will start by briefly looking at the history of pig interaction with humans, i.e. by looking at pig from the wild through to domestication and, in the next chapter, we will look at the characteristic, the limitations, the behaviour and the attitude that the animal has acquired during evolution and have retained despite years of domestication.

5.1   BRIEF HISTORY ABOUT THE DOMESTICATION OF PIGS

According to scientists, the first pigs evolved in Southeast Asia from smaller mammals, about two million years ago, and spread out from there all over Eurasia and Africa. Wild boars are very dangerous to hunt. They are smart and they have long, sharp tusks and teeth.

Human beings first met pigs before they emigrated out of Africa; the early men used dogs, spears and nets to hunt wild pigs in the forest. Archaeological drawings show that men in those days hunted pig primarily to look cool and to impress girls.

Wild pigs generally live in forests, with thick undergrowth, especially where there are fruit trees. Pigs naturally look towards the ground due to restricted visibility of the forest. However, they have developed a considerable vocal information system for keeping close contact within the groups. The bulkiness of their body means they are not good at climbing trees but they have developed the habit of rooting and foraging the earth and eat fruits from the ground instead of climbing the tree. They also root the ground to feed on insects, herbs, roots, mushrooms, flesh, and live animals.

People first began to keep tamed pigs about 10000 BC, in Central Asia. From Central Asia, tamed pigs spread slowly east to China, and south-west to West Asia and North Africa.

About 6,000 BC, due to the rapid increase in the population of people in china that needed to be fed and the level of poverty that prevails during the period, the Chinese soon realised the importance of domesticating pigs. Pigs are highly resilient, mature quickly, have large litters and are able to sustain themselves on low-quality feedstuffs. Pigs can fend for themselves pretty independently if neglected, and they will eat fruit cores and rotten meat and peapods. Chinese people tend to feed their pigs on garbage during times of scarcity and they preserve pig meat with salt.

It is very interesting to know that in China, the character 家 of a home, is also used to describe the dwelling for pigs. From my little research about the Chinese culture, the typical concept of a Chinese "home" means a plot of land, a house, and some pigs that help support the family. During this period pigs became so important or so significant for a family that the word "home" is named after it. Although the modern "home" has changed over time, the concept and the Chinese character remain.

With this brief history of pig farming, it is easy to see that human domestication of pigs and human interactions and influence on pigs is very recent evolutionary speaking, unlike other wild predatory animals that attack pigs, pigs have not change their behaviour to accommodate humans and this is why it is important for farmers to understand that the nature of their pigs is still very wild or can revert back to wild very easily.

In an experiment conducted in the USA , where some domesticated pigs were left in the wild on their own for 3 years without any human contact, they discovered that the pigs reverted back to their wild nature very quickly, the pig skin and hair colour (even those with white skin) become darker so as to camouflage with their surrounding and their tusk quickly develop into long sharp tusks and teeth to hunt and defend themselves.

The implication of this history to us as pig farmers is that in order to get most out of our pigs, we need to design both the pig operation and environment around the natural need of pigs. This will not only contribute to the pig's sense of wellbeing and welfare but it will also enable the farmer to avoid unnecessary cost whilst also allowing the pig to yield their best.

In summary, the more you know about the nature and characteristic of your animal the better you are to meet their need.

5.2 WHY SOME PEOPLE DON'T EAT PIG?

Before we look at the different characteristics and behaviours of pigs in the wild, let us look at why some cultures do not eat pork. This is very important for every pig farmer to know as you will often be asked.

In pig production, culture and religion is perhaps the most fundamental and most pervasive external influence that affects both the buyers and the consumers behaviour towards pig. While we will look at this in more details at the marketing of pigs chapter, however, this is a good time to look at why some people don't eat pork meat.

As mentioned earlier, pig consumption was a very popular source of food all through the ancient times, from West Asia all the way west to England and east to China, from Scandinavia to North Africa.

However, from 1500 BC during the period of the Egyptian empire, the Egyptian people labeled pigs as disgusting animals because of the way pigs were herded along the bank of the muddy River Nile (Egypt is situated on an arid desert where rainfall is very scarce so the Egyptian's farmers depended on cultivating their crop on the flooded muddy river bank of River Nile). The fact that pigs tend to disturb the arable farm that are along the River Nile bank, eating everything including the crops that the Egyptian people and civilisation depended on for survival.

To discourage the rearing of pigs across the whole of Egypt and the consumption of pork meat among her empire, the Egyptian labeled pork meat as something dirty and only poor people and slave should eat it. And this belief was spread and left as legacy to all the nations that were conquered by the Egyptians from North Africa through to the whole of the middle east, where they colonised and establish their New Kingdom.

Nowadays, it is easy to underestimate the long and lasting impact that an empire or colonisation can have on the people colonised. I had first-hand experience of colonisation when I lodged in probably a 2-star hotel in a remote village in Ghana during one of the profitable pig farming training to the rural community in Ghana. In the morning, I requested breakfast at the hotel and I was shocked when they told me that the only food on the menu for breakfast was English breakfast with sausage and ham. I was expecting something containing the local dishes such as yam, plantain, sweet potato, maize, millet, sorghum and beans, but I reckon this is an example of British Empire legacy on Ghana long after independence.

The Egyptian Empire legacy on most Semitic people in West Asia included the Jews, the Phoenicians and the Arabs, and as a result they would not eat pig meat. The Bible and the Quran were written not long after the Egyptian Empire both say that Jews and Muslims should not eat pig meat.

However, at the end of the Bronze Age, when the Greeks invaded Israel and settled there as the Philistines, they brought European pigs with them to Israel. This is one of the reasons why the Jews didn't like the Philistines because they kept pigs. The Romans also conquered Israel and they brought European pigs with them.

The earliest Christians, who lived in Israel, like the Jews did not eat pork, but by about 50 AD many Christians that were converted from places where people did eat pork, like Greece, Rome. Those Christians decided that this rule did not apply to them. Especially after Peter's vision in the Bible — the Acts of the Apostle 10:9-16 15 "Do not call anything impure that God has made clean." And from Paul's exposition Romans 14:17, "For the kingdom of God is not a matter of eating and drinking, but of righteousness, peace and joy in the Holy Spirit"

Furthermore, when Mohammed told the Arabs about the new religion of Islam, he also said that Muslims (people who followed Islam) should not eat pork.

Quran 5:3 — Prohibited for you is the carrion, blood, the 'lahm' (flesh) of the pig and what has been dedicated to other than God.

From about 200 AD, pigs became much less common around the Mediterranean and in West Asia after and they are still very uncommon until today. But in Europe and in China, where people were Christian or Buddhist or Taoist and not Muslim, pigs remained very common.

However, in recent times pig farming is now authorised in Tunisia and Morocco, two strict Muslim countries, to cater for the flocks of European and other non-Muslim tourists

Moroccan pig production is increasing annually at an exponential rate to cater to the demand of millions of tourists (especially Europeans) who visit the North African nation every year.as a result of its booming tourism trade.

"Our clientele is 98 percent European. They want bacon for breakfast, ham for lunch and pork chops for dinner," said Ahmad Bartoul a pig farmer in Morocco.

The majority of pig farmers in Morocco are Muslims and Jews (who do not consume pork for religious reasons).

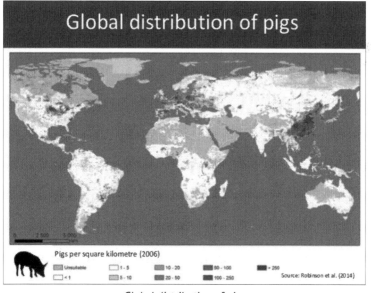

Global distribution of pigs

6. Let's talk about pigs' behaviour and character

In this chapter, we will look at some of the innate behaviours and characters of pigs in the wild. We will also consider how you as a farmer can use this behaviour to your farm's advantage. The list below is not exhaustive, but it will serve as a starting point for you to understand and apply pigs' character.

We recommend that you endeavour to learn as much of this behaviour and characteristic of pigs and incorporate them into the design of the environment and operations of your farm so as to meet pig's natural needs. Not only will this contribute to the pig's sense of wellbeing and welfare, but it will also reduce your farm's construction and operation cost.

Natural behaviour is the collection of different behaviours that pig show when kept in an environment where they can express behaviours created in the evolutionary process. These innate behaviours are essential aspects of the natural and survival behaviour, and research has shown that hindering this behaviour may lead to abnormal behaviour and stress.

According to Lund and Weary, "a good understanding of animal behaviour is required if we are going to achieve our objective of allowing our pigs to express their basic behavioural needs and in return produce their best for us".

6.1 PIG'S DAILY ACTIVITY PATTERNS IN THE WILD

By nature, a pig is an agile, sturdy animal with two activity periods — early morning and early in the evening. Pigs enjoy hunting and foraging. They forage for 7 hours or more per day. Their focus during this active period is primarily to look for food. Moreover, once they find food, they all fight and struggle for food at the same time, though the bigger or stronger might always win.

Consequently, they also have two resting periods per 24 hrs, and after dusk, pigs usually rest or sleep. At night, pigs construct simple nests for sleeping, particularly if the weather is cold.

How to maximise this behaviour to the advantage of your farm?

a. Armed with this knowledge that pigs will naturally seek out food in the morning and evening, it makes sense for farmers to provide feed for pigs during these time periods to match the pig's body clock drives.

b. A pig should be fed at least twice a day to match their biological clock and to improve their feed utilisation. Where possible, it is advisable to increase the frequency of their feeding to at least twice (or two portions) a day as opposed to dumping the whole daily feed at once, as this tend to lead to lots of feed wastage. A pig will always eat anytime you bring fresh feed to them until they are full and, after this, they will move on to forage and might not come back to the same food. The feed can easily get soiled and washed away by staff with the faeces during cleaning.

c. Unlike the dog, there is no social hierarchy among pig during feeding. Farmers should feed all their pigs promptly and avoid unnecessary delay during feeding. Pigs are not used to watching other pig feeding without being able to join them, so farmers needs to make sure that all the animals are served together and promptly and that there is enough feeding space for all the animals in a group house to feed at once, thereby reducing fight at the feeding trough.

6.2 PIG'S DAILY FEEDING' HABIT IN THE WILD

Pigs are omnivorous; they are opportunist and will eat almost anything to survive. Pig food includes grass, roots, tubers, invertebrates, nuts, berries and vertebrates such as frogs, snakes, turtles, young birds, eggs, small rodents. Pigs forage mostly at ground level by sniffing, rooting, chewing and eating for several hours a day to find food. This pig's exploratory behaviour is an essential part of their life, even in situations where they are domesticated and are supplied with the basic necessities (food, water and shelter).

How to maximise this behaviour to the advantage of your farm?

a. Pigs are single-stomach animals and therefore require at least two or three meals a day. It is advisable to divide their daily feed requirements into portions; feed the pigs half the feed in the morning and the rest in the evening.

b. Pigs enjoy seeking out and eating a wide variety of food, especially food high in fibre, farmer should endeavour to raise pig with variety of feed — a mix of concentrates with lots of different local feed ingredients and also fresh green feed that best meet a pigs natural feed need. This should include ingredients such as maize, barley, sorghum, rice bran, fish meal and meat meal, palm kernel cake, groundnut cake, soya meal and root crops like sweet potatoes, cassava tuber and fresh greens such as vegetables, watercress, plantain or papayas can improve pig feed.

c. It is also important to make sure that small or weak pigs are fed separately from the bigger ones, because these stronger pigs will eat all the food. If you have more than four adult pigs, then food should be divided into two lots, so that every animal can have a share.

d. A pig will also express these exploratory behaviours to new environments or objects, so farmers should make sure that the wall and the floor of their pig cell is solid with the right amount of gravel cement and sand, as pigs will root and forage and expose the weak spot on the floor or the wall of their cell.

6.3 ESTABLISHMENT OF SOCIAL ORDER AMONG PIGS IN THE WILD

In the wild, stress is a routine part of a pig's life, and this occurs in the context of social dynamics, especially during feeding and drinking and mating. For example, within a few hours after the birth of piglets, social dominance relationships are formed among piglets. The dominant one (which is usually also the biggest) would bully the smaller pigs for the best of the sow's nipple, usually the teats towards the front of the sow, and the lower ranking pigs will be submissive to higher ranking pigs. However, continuous fighting is widespread among pig-lets especially if social dominance relationship is not achieved on time due to introducing new pigs to the herd or mixing of two sets of piglets or pigs from different sows for the first time.

Pigs also experience stress when coping with the environmental challenges (such as heat, cold or fear of predators loitering around to prey on them). In the wild, pigs are mostly prey though they themselves feed on smaller animals. As a consequence, pigs are usually smaller in size in the wild (compared to domesticated pigs) due to this stress, but where there is less environmental stress pigs grows bigger and breed better.

How to maximise this behaviour to the advantage of your farm

a. Armed with this knowledge, farmers must do all within their reach to minimise stress on the farm. This can be achieved by minimising introducing new pig(s) to an existing group after weaning. You should prevent any form of mixing of different pigs from different batches as this is potentially stressful for pigs, especially among grower or finisher pigs. A good farmer will respect this instinct by ensuring pigs are kept in stable family groups from weaning to slaughter and try as much as possible to avoid remixing.

b. If you have to mix, do so at weaning stage and allow sufficient space, at least +20% more space than normal so as to allow the dominants in each group to get the challenges over with minimal damage and to allow the submissive pigs to run away and avoid the dominant pigs.

c. Where practicable, it is a good practice to withhold 30% of the feed allowance prior to mixing the pigs and immediately after mixing pigs provide ample food for the pigs to distract them from fighting each other. You should distract the pigs with food since most of the mixing fighting or aggressive acts tend to happen during feeding. Also make sure that the feed or the feeding trough is well spread out to minimise physical contact during feeding.

d. Where practicable, always introduce or mix new pigs in the evening just before dusk (just before it gets dark). This will allow the pigs to sleep and wake up together the following morning as good neighbours.

e. Finally, where possible try to spray all the pigs with lavatory freshener aerosol or detergent just before mixing to distract and remove previous bonding so that new bonding can be established

6.4   IN A PIG'S EYE

When compared to human's eyes, pig's eyes are relatively small and the expression 'a pig's eye' has been used to denote small eyes in many cultures. Many of the previous research and observations carried out on pigs reveals that pigs have good vision. The pig's eyes are deeply placed and have a wide angle of vision and as a result they can see 310° out of 360 or 85% of their surroundings. This means that compared to humans, pigs through evolution have prioritised seeing more of the environment around them in black and white (panoramic vision). This gives them greater capacity to detect possible movement or danger such as predators, food, other pigs, etc. while limiting their binocular vision (seeing in detailed colour) to just 35-50°. However, this sacrifice creates greater difficulty for pigs when calculating distances and variation at ground level. That is why pigs sometimes struggle to move forward when there is a change on the floor surface e.g. height, gaps or if they have to go across a gutter, pigs are not able to perceive or gauge this variation properly, so they hesitate to move across.

Pigs also generally prefer lighted areas as opposed to darkness; they tend to move toward more brightly illuminated areas.

How to maximise this behaviour to the advantage of your farm

a. Knowing this means farmers can direct and encourage their pig movement by brightening up the areas where they wanted the pigs to move towards e.g. lightening the interior of a truck to facilitate loading of pigs onto the truck.

b. There should be no gap or variation in height or obstruction on the floor structure that the pig is supposed to walk through as pigs are not able to perceive this properly, so they will hesitate to move forward.

c. Please note that pig's lateral vision means that the pig will always see any opening at the side of the pen and try to escape through small gaps in your pen. But at the same time, if you want a pigs to go to a particular direction or cell, all you need to do is to block all the other escape routes or space with pig board and pigs will naturally go through the only space that is purposely left in the cell.

d. Finally, the eyes of pigs are very sensitive to white colour, so staff uniform should not be of white colour as this colour can induce stress in pigs. It is recommended that staff uniform should be blue or green.

6.5 PIG'S SENSE OF HEARING

Pigs have very sensitive hearing. This is evolutionary important for pigs especially in their natural habitat which is thick forest where they cannot see very far. Their hearing makes up for their poor bifocal vision. Pigs' hearing range is similar to that of humans, but with a shift toward ultrasound. Most communication in pigs is mainly through sound. There are ~20 different recognized sounds. The grunt is one of the most common sounds, given in response to familiar sounds or while looking for food (rooting). A short grunt is given when the pig is excited, whereas a long grunt is a contact call. When pigs are aroused, they may squeal, and they may also scream when agitated or hurt (e.g. when a sow accidentally lay on her piglets). Their sensitive hearing allows them to detect prey for food and identify predators. For survival, it is important for pigs to detect predators quickly and take flight rather than fight.

Loud or high-pitched noises normally startle pigs, as this is how hyena or cheetah will sound in the wild. Your pig will become stressed with prolonged exposure to such noise or disturbance. Pigs show an aversion to sudden loud noise; research has shown that sudden noise or movement increase heart rate and pigs retreat in response to loud noise.

How to maximise this behaviour to the advantage of your farm

a. Staff should try as much as possible to do everything quietly and reduce all unnecessary noise. And open pen doors quietly and listen before entering.

b. Staff should also move slowly not aggressively when moving through the pen or the pen corridor, so that they do not sound like predators.

c. Allowing the public to stand by and watch your pig daily may be good for the farm public image but it is very stressful for your pig. They like to be left alone when you are not feeding them.

6.6 PIG'S SENSE OF SMELL

Smell is very important in a pig's world. Pig's smelling sense is the strongest of all its senses and is one of its best defences against predators and hunters. Pigs rely on their good sense of smell to make up for their weaker sense of vision.

The sense of smell develops early in pigs and is important for survival because piglets are very mobile from birth. They need to be able to follow the odour of their mother.

In the wild a pig's sense of smell is so powerful it can pick up scents from a long distance away. Depending on what scents pass through its nose, a hog will either go towards the source, or keep as far away as possible. In addition, pigs can also smell up to 25 feet below its trotters in order to root up worms, insects, or crab.

There is a fable in some parts of Nigeria that if you want to survey the flow of underground water aqueduct on your farm (to detect the best spot to sink a well), look out for the path that pigs are foraging as they tend to follow the underground aqueduct as this is usually the path where they find most worms.

The large round disk of cartilage at the tip of the snout is connected to muscle that gives it extra flexibility and strength for rooting in the ground and it has as many tactile and sensitive organs as the palms of both hands of humans.

How to maximise this behaviour to the advantage of your farm

a. Since odours are related to eating, farmers can use this knowledge to increase the feed consumed by deliberately improving the pig's feed odour and palatability. For example, we noticed on our farms that the smells of bread, fermented cassava, fish meal and fish oil, vegetable oils or chicken feed can be used to stimulate appetite in pigs.

b. And again, since pigs instinctively trust their nose more than their eye sight, that means during fostering, staff should make sure that the new piglets to be fostered and the host piglets are covered with as much odour e.g. with lavatory freshener aerosol or detergent as possible to prevent the sow from detecting the piglets that are hers and those that are fostered. From our experience, we noticed that sows rarely reject foster piglets because of the colour of their skin or hair but we have seen sows rejecting piglets with a strange smell.

6.7   PIG'S SOCIAL COMMUNITY

Pigs naturally operate in small groups of about six to ten mature females with their offspring and they develop strong social bonds. One sow will remain with the piglets while the others forage. Boars are usually solitary and they only join females during mating season. Pigs also sleep so close together and this is part of their species preservation. Pigs are sound sleepers and they usually packed tightly together like spoons in a canteen of cutlery. There are obvious reasons for this behaviour, firstly, it keeps all members of the group warm during cold days, and secondly, it offers more protection from predators than sleeping apart.

In the wild, areas inhabited by pigs always contain the following: water, feeding areas, resting places and separate sites for defecation. As a social animal, pigs will avoid urinating or defecating in the resting nest of their group. A sow will even avoid soiling her farrowing nest if possible. If she is not allowed to leave the nest, she will rather stop defecating for a number of days than spoil the nest, though this is not good for her.

The idea that pigs are not clean comes from their tendency to wallow in mud when feeling hot. Pigs do not have any sweat glands, so they naturally seek out mud to roll in when the weather reaches high temperatures.

Pigs also cannot swiftly move their necks like goats or wag their tails like cattle to keep away the insect and other external parasite off their body. As a result, pigs tend to roll in mud, not only to protect themselves against the sun and extreme temperatures but also to drown and suffocate the parasites that might be on their skin such as lice and mange. After wallowing in mud, they allow the mud to stay on their body for a while until it dries (sufficient time to suffocate the insects) after which the pig will rub their muddy skin against trees to clear the mud from their body.

How to maximise this behaviour to the advantage of your farm

a. When you are designing a pig cell for a pig or group of pigs, it is important to ensure that there is enough space in each cell to clearly demarcate areas for feeding, resting and defecating.

b. Also, when stocking pigs in groups, especially the weaners or growers, it is important that a maximum of 20 pigs per group be kept together. Grouping pigs in a larger number than 20 pigs will increase fighting and tail biting.

c. It is not necessary for pigs to have muddy water. Their environment and pens should be cleaned regularly to limit the number of flies and other parasites.

d. Pigs must always have clean, fresh water to drink. One pig needs at least 5 to 10 litres of water every day. When they are feeding young, sows need to drink more water because they have to produce milk.

e. Farmers should make sure that there is a water trough especially in the sows' pen for them to wallow or have a shower system to cool the animal down during the heat of the day.

f. Pigs will rub their body against the walls of their cells, so the wall of pig cells should be smooth without any protrusions or else pig skin will get caught and injured while rubbing its skin on the wall.

g. Pigs will turn red and get sunburnt when kept in the sun without shelter or water for too long or die from heatstroke, so make sure there is enough shelter for your pigs to protect them from the external elements.

h. Pigs do not have much hair on their bodies to protect them from the cold or insulate them against heat. Many piglets will die from pneumonia if they are left in the cold, wind or rain or left overnight on a cold floor. And even if the pigs do not die, they will not be as healthy and strong as they should be.

i. Pigs must be able to enjoy the early morning sun for vitamin D and must be able to lie in the shade out of the sun. If the roof is made of metal, it must be covered with grass or tree branches to keep it cool.

j. Pigs do not like a water logged cell, it is important that the floor of the pen is slightly sloppy so that excess water can run off, allowing the pen to stay dry.

k. Pigs always dung in the same place. You should make sure that this mess is cleaned out daily to lessen the risk of disease.

6.8   SOW FARROWING BEHAVIOUR

A sow has a gestation period of 115 days. In the wild, a sow has one of the most elaborate nesting behaviours. Two days prior to giving birth a sow will separate herself from her group of other pigs, work hard for about five hours to build her farrowing nests, using the nesting material (usually dry and wet wood). Having gone through all nesting preparations, she stretches in her nest on her side and undergoes the pains of farrowing.

Naturally, litter size is usually 3 to 6 piglets in the wild and are usually born at approximately 15-minute intervals. The largest first, smallest last and during the farrowing period, a sow spends most of the time lying on her side and does not lick her young to remove embryonic sheath nor try to help the young piglet to stand up.

How to maximise this behaviour to the advantage of your farm

a. Sows are hard wired naturally to build a nest before giving birth. A good farmer should provide a sow nesting material such as straw or wood shavings that will allow her to build a nest prior to giving birth to piglets and give her the freedom to move around without restraint to carry out this vital nest building activity. This in return will help prepare the sow psychologically for farrowing and also improves her maternal instinct to farrow and take care of her piglets. This naturally reduces some of the strange negative post-natal behaviour such as neglecting or eating piglets.

b. As in the wild, a sow should be left to her own devices during farrowing without any interference by man. She is capable of successfully farrowing her piglets by herself. A good farmer should give the sow a quiet and undisturbed space that she needs to do her farrowing.

c. Piglets are very vulnerable during farrowing as sows are not able to protect the piglets during the farrowing process. It is therefore advisable for farmers not to put 2 pregnant sows in the same cell during farrowing.

d. Keeping up to date mating records is also important as it will allow the farmer to know when the sow is going to farrow and hence make sure the nesting preparation is done and a staff is at hand to help if required during the farrowing period.

6.9 PIGLET AND MATERNAL BEHAVIOUR

The relationship between sow and piglets between the first 4 weeks after birth is very important for a pig farmer because studies have shown that more than 40% of pig mortality on a pig farm happens around this period.

In the wild, sows spend more time lying on their side and are relatively inactive during the first few days. She grunts softly to encourage piglets to suckle but after a few days the piglets initiate most of the suckling.

In the wild, young pigs are very active and they can stand up within a few minutes of birth and sample each of the sow's 14 teats and choose one of them. Ideally, each of the piglets will probably drink from this same nipple for the rest of the nursing period. Largest pigs tend to attach themselves to more productive and anterior teats.

Piglets keep warm by huddling together close to the mother's udders for the first few days

A few days after farrowing there is a gradual movement away from the nest site. Before standing and lying down the sow and piglet co-ordinate their behaviour to avoid crushing. There is also the ritual of sow rooting through the nest to disturb the piglets and nudge them out of the way. If a piglet is laid upon, it will squeal loudly, and the sow will instantly adjust her position. The main danger period for crushing is within the first 3 days of birth

During the first week of life, piglets are either nursing or sleeping or playing. Piglets start sampling solid food early and naturally through investigating their environment especially the feed that the sow eats. It's a gradual process.

At the age of one week, the piglets are "house-trained" and urinate and defecate only at the edges of the farrowing nest.

After two weeks of isolation, the sows and their litters regroup with rest of the herd the sows tend offspring together, social interaction continues between litters of pigs. Piglets are gradually weaned between 13-17 weeks, but they remain in family.

How to maximise this behaviour to the advantage of your farm

a. Piglets are active and able to suckle very quickly. A good farmer will allow mother and offspring to relate naturally to each other for the first few days after birth making sure the piglets are taking the colostrum from mum.

b. A sow is always careful when lying down to avoid crushing her piglets. You should ensure that the sow has sufficient space to move and there should be sufficient dry space with insulation in your farrowing cell for mother and piglets to lie down without inadvertently crushing her piglets.

c. Sows take great care to raise their young piglets in a safe protective environment. You should ensure an environment that is quiet and not disruptive.

d. She is naturally highly protective of the piglets. There should also be a good relationship between your sow and the staff. This needs to be established before and during pregnancy so that the sow is not alarmed by keeper presence in the vicinity of her piglets.

e. A sow will naturally re-join the rest of the group within 1-2 weeks of giving birth. A good farmer should avoid separating pigs of any age from their batch for too long or the pig will be treated as a stranger.

f. Piglets start sampling solid food early. You should encourage this process, give piglets creep feed that is nutritious, palatable and easily digestible to aid the transition from milk to solid feed.

g. Weaning naturally starts gradually at 8 weeks and can take as long as 13-17 weeks for piglets to be fully weaned in the wild. You should not overly shorten the natural nursing process timescale and if you do so make sure the creep feed is of high quality, rich in animal protein and easily digestible.

In conclusion, throughout this chapter, we delved into some of the innate behaviours of pigs in the wild and how this can be used to your farm's advantage. There are still many behaviours of pigs to be exploited, but these are good ones to start with. As you observe and better understand your pigs, you will be able to discover better ways of inculcating some of this findings into your farm design and operation, this in return will improve your pig's sense of well-being and welfare and ultimately reduce your capital and operational cost.

7. What do pigs need and how do you meet this need on your farm

Now that you are aware of some of the innate behaviours and characteristics of pigs in the wild and how you can translate some of them onto your farm operations.

In this chapter, we will summarise what your pig needs on your farm not only to survive but to grow and to flourish and how you as a farmer need to prepare to meet these needs profitably. There is a symbiotic relationship between the goal of the farmer and the need of his pigs, the working together of both parties to meet each other needs and goals is very important and will ultimately differentiate a profitable farm from a mediocre farm.

The goal of this chapter is to get you to start thinking about how you are going to address some of the critical questions that is associated with each of your pig's needs and what is available in your locality to meet them as early as possible during the planning stage of your pig farm.

What your pig needs

7.1 FOOD

As pig farmers, we all know that we need to provide quality and affordable feed to our pigs. While this sounds obvious and straightforward, it is not as easy as it sounds.

Participants having a Q and A interactive session with Mr Yemi

Processed feed ingredients (palm kernel cake and minerals)

As a good farmer, you need to start thinking about how and where to source the feed that you will feed your pigs.

- What variety of feed ingredients do you need for your pigs?

- What kind of pig feed ingredients is locally available in your area?

- Are you going to grow the feed ingredients or are you going to buy them?

- If you are growing, do you have sufficient land, funds, expertise and labour to grow the variety of ingredients needed to feed your pigs

- How are you going to make sure that cultivating crop for your feed did not distract you and your staff from your core business which is pig farming? (earlier in this book we talked about the importance of focus and the challenges of multi-tasking).

• If you decide to buy the feed ingredients, where are you going to source them?

• How much will you buy at a time?

• How would you transport the feed to the farm (vehicle and good roads)?

• Where will you store the feed on the farm (warehouse) to prevent from damp and vermin?

• Are you planning to buy compounded concentrate or feed ingredients?

• How will you compound the feed ingredients (hand mixing, grinder and mixer machine), on your farm to meet the need of the different categories of pigs?

• How much and how often will you feed your pigs (staffing, wheelbarrow, feeding trough, weigh scale)?

• How you would maintain the hygiene of the feeding trough?

Throughout the course of this book, we will be answering some of these questions as they apply.

7.2 WATER

Your pig needs clean water to drink and to cool down in the heat of the day. This is especially important in sub-Sahara countries where the weather can be very hot in the afternoon. Your staff also needs lots of water to clean the pen daily.

As a farmer, you need to start thinking about how you will source and provide water for your pigs. There are lots of ways to provide fresh water for your farm:

- We recommend that you check your neighbourhood to see how they get their fresh water.

- Are you going to access to municipal water, dig a well or sink a bore hole?

- Avoid using streams and rivers as you can never predict what has happened at the top end of the river.

- You need to think about the power source to pump the water from the source to the farm (generator, solar system and national grid to power the pumping machine).

- How will you store the water on the farm e.g. storage tank?

- How you will get the water from the storage tank to the pigs (plumbing work to pipe the water).

- What the pigs will drink the water from (bucket, water trough or water nipple).

- How you would maintain the hygiene of the water trough.

- How you would cool the animal down (a fixed wallow or showering system).

Water tanks to store water and Fencing to protect the farm

7.3 SECURITY

Security is more than just protecting your pig from theft or pilfering (, e.g. fencing and solid gate, lightening at night) but it also includes constructing your pig pen in a location on your farm where the pigs will feel safe and secure because they are not regularly disturbed or troubled by the public, those passing by, buyers, dogs or predators.

- You need to protect your pigs from unnecessary remixing new set of pigs, physical abuse from staff e.g., beating, threatening, or intimidating.

- Your pig pen should be located in an area on your farm where they can live and sleep feeling secure.

- Pigs need shelter from rain and from wind, but also from the sun and heat.

- Piglets will also need dry floor and bedding to keep warm.

- Biosecurity means that pigs need to be prevented from pathogens that could make them sick or cause death.

- You need to think about protecting them from pathogens coming from outside e.g. from man or animal or vehicle.

- You need to also think about how and when you will clean the pen.

- You will want to ensure that your pigs are secure, not just to protect them from the environment but also stop them from being attacked by hunter or predators or damaging another person's property.

- You might also want to net the pen to protect them from insects such as Tsetse flies.

7.4 **SPACE**

As mentioned in the last chapter, pigs need space to sleep, eat, dung and forage. You should provide sufficient space for your pig to be able to do each of these activities with ease. Later in the book we will talk about the ideal dimensions for different categories pig pen based on some of the work we have done in Africa.

Pig always fight to establish the dominant and submissive pig in the flock. You should ensure that there is sufficient space for the submissive one to get away from a more aggressive pig in the group thereby reducing the injury inflicted on each other. This is particular important for grower pen when you are mixing new batches of piglets from different sows or when you are returning farrowed or mated sows back to her main herd.

7.5 **AIR**

Air may sound obvious but pigs need a good supply of fresh air, good ventilation and ample shade, no smells, no draft and no dampness. This is extremely important if you are raising your pigs as indoor pigs or in a humid region.

A good airflow is needed in your pig pen, ventilation helps in keeping the cell dry. Your goal is to keep out drafts at lower levels of the cell, however, the wall of the pen should not be too tall to block air flow (the height should be about 3 feet in height) this will allow the air freely just above the height of the pigs. You might want to leave the top half of the pen open and use a see-through door that will allow wind to go through and circulate the cell.

Pigs enjoy a dry cell that is draft free. For beddings use wood shaving or straw to keep the pigs warm in cold periods. especially the piglets.

Ammonia is the most common poison in the pig's environment. Farmers should aim to improve the quality of air in the pig pen to prevent the accumulation of ammonia by increasing the drainage of urine from the house and remove solid faeces daily.

8. Attitude of a successful farmer

8.1 WHY ATTITUDE

This chapter is dedicated to those who are coming to commercial farming for the first time, those who have lived in the city all their life, those who are not used to the pace of life on the farm and for diaspora who has resided outside Africa for a long time but wants to come back to invest in farming in Africa.

The 3 professions that are often used in the Bible to describe life journey are soldier, athlete (entertainer) and farmer.

Bible verses 2 Timothy 2:3 — 7 *Vs 3 Endure suffering along with me, as a good soldier of Christ Jesus. Vs 4 Soldiers don't get tied up in the affairs of civilian life, for then they cannot please the officer who enlisted them. Vs 5 And athletes cannot win the prize unless they follow the rules. Vs 6 And hardworking farmers should be the first to enjoy the fruit of their labour. — New Living Translation*

The first two professions i.e. athletes (or entertainers) and soldiers are well known to many youths in Africa and these professions are regarded as glamorous, very attractive and many youths aspire to become either of the two professions. However, farming profession is considered by many youths as belittling and has a very poor image.

The first evidence of apathy towards farming among youth is apparent in the regional examination such as the West African Examination Council, which showed that less than 3% of those who applied for an admission to Universities wanted to study Agriculture as a course.

Many young people have a stereotyped vision of agriculture and view agriculture as a non-status occupation and as a manual undignified one, which is most suitable for those who are not qualified or intelligent enough for office work.

The media has also played a big role in demonising agriculture and rural areas, and overly promoting a western and urban lifestyle; all of which strongly influence rural youth's aspirations in relation to farming.

However, in the last few years, there has been a paradigm shift in the calibre of people who are investing in farming in Africa. As a farm training consultant, I noticed that the majority of our recent attendees of our trainings in Nigeria, Togo and Ghana, are professionals, diasporas, entrepreneurs and managers from different walks of life who have honed their skills in their profession and these are also the kind of people that are reading this book. This paradigm shift is very significant because these middle-class farmers are what Africa needs to maximise the full benefits of the current green revolution that is taking place in Africa. And they will also serve as a role model and mentor for young people, but will also motivate lots of youth to consider farming.

According to FAO, Africa has never lacked in the number of people that are into farming but what is lacking are the middle-class farmers — professional young men and women that will take farming from subsistence to commercial farming. For example, sub-Sahara countries such as Nigeria, Togo and Ghana have more than 70%, 75% and 79.6% respectively of their populace who are into farming, yet these countries are still struggling to feed themselves. Whereas, Canada, the UK and South Africa has less than 20% and yet they produce more than enough and also export products. The research reckons that the complexity of present-day agriculture is too much for old and primitive practices such as hoe and cutlass that is practiced in most African countries.

The difference in these middle-class farmers is that unlike the previous subsistence farmers, most of them already have access to land (they either buy new farmland close to the city or use their family land in the village). They also have the initial capital to invest in Agriculture (funds that they have acquired from their own savings or from their other business). They have good collateral and credibility (this makes it easy for them to access finance from banks if they ever wish to expand their farm). I sincerely believe that the drive of the middle-class entrepreneur towards farming will ultimately make the needed difference in agricultural commodity production in Africa.

However, for this group of people who have spent most of their career in the city or outside Africa, farming at first is likely going to be a foreign language. They will have to learn nature's alphabet before they can read her messages. At the beginning, the middle class farmers will be at somewhat a disadvantage when compared with those who were born or grew up in the rural areas. Those that grow up in the rural areas have the advantage, as they have knowledge about soils, plants, animals and how to treat each, from their past experience.

The greatest pitfall for middle-class farmers will be to have the wrong attitude towards farming. By this I mean, if they approach farming with the perception that farming is easy, or if they think because they have read books and watch videos they are now expert and with this nonchalant attitude, they turn a deaf ear to the voice of experienced (but uneducated) farmers or mentors and disregard fundamental principles of farming, or ignore the market demands, they will fail.

Pig farming like all other farming is a skill of time, patience and a bit of strategic thinking. It is a skill for those who are dedicated and hard working. It is not for the feeble-hearted and requires a certain level of determination.

As in every other enterprise, pig farming success depends primarily upon the attitude of the man or the woman who owns or is leading the project. Not everybody who starts pig farming in Africa will succeed. On the other hand, those who are able to inculcate sthe right attitudes mentioned in this section will stand a good chance of succeeding.

We know from experience that without the correct attitude, even if farmers have all the money to invest, best staff, best location and best breed or spent many days training and attending seminars, he might still not be very successful.

8.2 WHAT IS ATTITUDE?

Irrespective of the rosy picture that you might have regarding pig farming either from the internet, watching YouTube videos or reading books that depict only the attractive features of farm life in spectacular colours, the reality is that pig farming like any other farming enterprise is indeed a tough profession.

According to Harvey W Wiley, in his book "In the lure of the land" he said, *"Farming is a business which requires the highest business talent and passion for the welfare of the animal; it is a profession which requires the many technical skills. No other profession requires such a variety of learning, such an insight into nature, such skill of technical kind in order to be successful, as a profession of farming".*

Farmer's life is characterised by persevering toil; A farmer is expected to work on their farm throughout the day. Most farmers are up before non-farmers and work longer hours than non-farmers. Pig farmers have to feed, nurture, protect and take care of their pigs' day and night and in all weather. This they have to do every day, not when they feel like it.

Unlike a city guy that works and waits monthly for their salary, a farmer knows that every animal has cycles that cannot be disrupted. For example, after mating a sow, it takes nearly 4 months of pregnancy to see the outcome of the mating, it takes the piglets another 7 months to reach the market weight to sell.

As a pig farmer, you will also have to make decisions in a risky, ever-changing environment. The consequences of some of these decisions will generally not be known when the decisions are made, and the outcomes may be better or worse than expected. You need to have a healthy respect for the things beyond your control (storms, drought, disease, market prices, competition, etc.).

The question is how have farmers throughout the ages survived and endured all of these challenges and still kept on feeding the world. The answer is that a farmer possesses certain attitudes that keep them going and we will look at some of them in this chapter.

8.3 YOU MUST HAVE AN OPTIMISTIC ATTITUDE TOWARDS YOUR VENTURE

"Attitude is the thought process behind something".

Attitude is the feeling you have towards the goal that you want to achieve on your pig venture.

Attitude is the daily "Yes, I can do this or No, I can't do this".

Having a successful attitude include having a thought process of knowing that you will succeed and that you will overcome challenges, whatever you may be faced with.

As someone new to pig farming, you must have an optimistic attitude about your project and your future in pig farming. An optimistic person sees the glass as half full but also accepts that it's half empty, whereas a pessimist only sees it as half empty. However, the successful farmer sees the *glass* completely *full*, *half* in liquid state and *half* in gaseous."

"The pessimist complains about the wind; the optimist expects it to change; the realist adjusts the sails."

The optimist has a positive attitude, cultivates positive thinking, and expects a favourable outcome from any situation. The pessimist complains, worries and fusses about almost everything.

To develop optimism, you must develop a natural likeness for farming business because it will increase your willingness and patience to work and be painstaking, to be open-minded and to be as alert in detecting irregularities to adopt and apply new knowledge.

Yes, you will have some challenges and suffer some disappointments on your way to your success. Yes, some of your pigs might be sick, one or two might even die, your best staff may leave your farm abruptly without notice and the cost of feed might skyrocket for a season, etc.

Optimism is important in every business and endeavour but more especially as a farmer because you are investing today with the hope of reaping very much in the far future. And in-between this period, you are dealing with livestock that needed daily input just to remain alive, you also depend more on nature and on your staff to do the right thing. Having optimism is one of the ways to avoid getting stressed or depressed easily with events and situations that you are going through.

Being hopeful, confident and having positive expectancy about the future does not mean that you are living in denial. It actually is allowing the law of attraction and deliberate creation to work where you get what you are expecting and thinking about.

I like the quote from Daniel L. Reardon which states that, "*In the long run, the pessimist may be proved right, but the optimist has a better time on the trip.*

You need optimism to keep your sanity and your determination. Some people are natural optimists but if you are not; here are some steps that could help you to cultivate optimism from about your personal goal.

a. Make a positive decision about your ambition — articulate, write down and visualise why you want to go into pig farming, your initial goals, excitement and inspirations and also the goals that you desire to acquire.

Take a piece of paper and list your goals under this topic, I believe a winning farmer is a writing farmer:

• What do you want to do?

• Where do you want to be in 1,3 5 and 10 years?

- What do you want to have?

- Where do you want to go?

b. And explain why you want to achieve each of these goals, make sure you have strong convincing reasons for each of your goals.

c. Discipline your mind to think positively — consciously give instructions to your brain to think positively and to create constructive mental pictures. Monitor your innermost self-talk and use only internal words that will boost your confidence and self-esteem.

d. Recognise and interrupt your negative patterns of thinking that are ineffective, especially those thoughts about your past failure at school, at work, your family or in your past business. Apostle Paul emphasises this point very well, Philippian 4: 8 "Finally, brethren, whatsoever things are true, ... whatsoever things are of good report; if there be any virtue, and if there be any praise, think or meditate on these things".

e. Focus on what you can control — Unexpected things turn out in everyone's life and people are disappointed every now and then. You should accept responsibility of what you have caused and understand that you have within you the power to control your thoughts, actions and responses.

f. Get rid of the helplessness feeling — Put your focus on the things that you can control instead of the things that aren't working or on people who are uncooperative and energy drainers. Your personal growth and success depend on where you place your concentration most.

g. Expect the best from every situation and everyone that you meet — Whatever you expect becomes your reality.

Anticipate the best in situations and people and it will show up. You cannot go into any farming without having this attitude. It is important that you pay attention to only the good and believe in possibilities.

h. Accept what life throws at you confidently — Optimism doesn't put you on cloud nine all the time. At times, what you hope for does not show up fast enough. You will still face challenges and setbacks. But you will bounce back and will get up fast. If you have cultivated the positive outlook, you will accept that there are possible delays and that delay is not denial.

i. Stay away from pessimists — They have nothing good to say. They want to influence you to think like them. Look for people who believe and expect possibilities like you. Stick around them instead.

8.4 BE DURABLE

A farmer's day is an active one from sunrise to sunset, you need to be physically fit to be a farmer. You need to be able to handle a day's worth of physical labour. You should be able to lift 20kg of feed if you are female and up to 30kg bag of feed at a time if you are a man and generally be able to move about without any serious discomfort or difficulty. You must also be emotionally sound, you must be willing to do anything and everything, be ready to clean faeces and urine, kill pests like rats, cockroaches and spiders, be ready to castrate or slaughter your pigs, etc.

As a farmer, you must be able to answer 'yes' to these questions:

• Can you stand the isolation that is usually a characteristic of farm life?

- Can you survive without the hustle and bustle of city life and the nightlife, probably there may be no electricity on your farm, you might only have an irregular telephone network?

- Are you prepared to forego salary or income for months at a stretch?

- Do you know from experience the meaning of hard, manual work from dawn to dark — and then by lantern light?

I don't mean to frighten you but merely to indicate that though the farm life has its joy and satisfaction. It also has its drawbacks and as a farm owner, you must be prepared to face this.

8.5 YOU NEED TO HAVE A CLEAR AND A DESIRABLE PRIZE

To be successful, you must have an exceptionally desirable prize that you are aspiring to achieve through pig farming. Prize is a reward that you receive from winning a competition or achieve your goal. The bigger the goals, the bigger the prize and sometimes, it has to be something that is greater than just you. It might be because of your family, or for generations to come but it has to be more than just you.

What do you see as your desirable prize in pig farming?

Let me illustrate with this story. During the 2nd World War, out of desperation and shortage of soldiers due to the blitz inflicted by German superior air power early on the British army. The British military were compelled to recruit young boys from the age of 17 to go to the battlefront and fight for the Queen and the country. But before these boys were sent to the battlefront, they were all encouraged to fall in love with a sweetheart back home. The UK military realised that since these boys were young and have no war experience, they might want to give up too easily if the battle gets too tough, instead of fighting. By making them fall in love before going to battle, it meant that their sweetheart at home becomes their reasons not to want to give up or die in battle. In other words, their sweetheart became their prize, it gave them solid hope and reasons to fight on beyond themselves and not to die. To keep the love of the sweetheart burning in the young men's hearts at the battlefront, the military encouraged the girls (sweetheart) to regularly write letters to the boys in the battle. During the tough time at the battlefront, when they could have given up, the boys will read their love letter and they received strength to fight on so that they can come back home alive to meet and marry their sweetheart.

One of the British General commented, "You will be amazed what a motivated and purpose driven young man can do in battle when he has something to look forward to".

The military has discovered that prize does make the difference between those who will fight hard to survive and those who will give up and be defeated in battle.

As a farmer, you need to have a compelling reason for going into pig farming, the bigger the risk you are taking, the greater your prize should be.

Your prize should be truly valuable and should be strong enough to excite and motivate you enough to do whatever is required to be successful. And finally, your prize should make your sacrifice bearable.

I will round up this desirable prize with a quote from Steve Jobs at Stanford Commencement Speech 2005, it summarises what we are trying to communicate as per having a desirable prize for your pig farming business.

"Sometimes, life hits you in the head with a brick. Don't lose faith. I'm convinced that the only thing that kept me going (after being fired from Apple) was that I loved what I did. You've got to find what you love. And that is as true for your work as it is for your lovers. Your work is going to fill a large part of your life, and the only way to be truly satisfied is to do what you believe is great work. And the only way to do great work is to love what you do. If you haven't found it yet, keep looking. Don't settle. As with all matters of the heart, you'll know when you find it. And, like any great relationship, it just gets better and better as the years roll on. So keep looking until you find it. Don't settle."

8.6 LEARN FROM BAD EXPERIENCE DON'T KILL YOURSELF FOR IT

I am sure you are not surprised that Murphy's law also applies in farming business. It says, *"Anything that can go wrong will go wrong"*. In your farming business, one thing is certain something will go wrong, the question should be what do you do or tell yourself when things go wrong and how to make sure you don't do something that you will later regret?

When things go wrong, it is important that you bring yourself to order as quickly as possible. Listen and accepts your mistake, "Yes, I did that,".

Talk — to friends, family, and others who know and understand the good faith and positive intention behind your action -- and let them help you to remember it.

However, there comes a key moment when you have to stop blaming yourself and face the music. Blame if not properly managed can prevent change. When you stop blaming yourself, you can begin to learn.

You can console yourself with the fact that "behind every cloud there's a silver lining". And in every mistake, there is a gift.

8.7 THINK LIKE AN EXECUTIVE (LEADER), HAVE AN EAGLE VISION AND VISUALIZE THE BIG PICTURE

As the proprietor of a pig farming venture, you need to be very clear on the goals and the mission of your farm. You must believe it enough to be able to convince others to see it, understand it and believe it. In addition, you should be able to lead all your stakeholders, partners and staff towards transforming the goals and vision into reality.

Executive thinking is "the human and organizational manifestation of the executive's dreams, goals, and vision."

Solomon the wisest king in the Bible put it this way, Proverbs 23:7

> *"For as a man think in his heart, so is he:*

According to Myles Munroe, there are only two animals on the planet that the creator identified Himself with in the Bible. The first one is the EAGLE and the second animal is the LION. They are both leaders of their kingdom.

But let us look a bit about eagles. The eagle the spirit of Leadership.

a. **Eagles have an accurate Vision**. Eagles have the ability to focus on something as far as 5km away. No matter the obstacles or distractions, eagle will not move his focus from the prey until he grabs it.

Lesson: As a leader of your business, once you have established the long-term goals for your farm, you should remain focused on your vision no matter what the obstacles and you will succeed.

A winner's mentality is the ability to focus on your long-term goals even though your short-term results are not on track. This is more difficult than it seems. Too many people take their eyes off their long-term goal when they experience a slow month or two and end up focusing on their lack of results.

You should resist the temptation to blame the economy, competition, or current market conditions when things are not going to plan. Focus on what you can control, do not be a mediocre farm proprietor who redirects all the blame towards staff to take the heat off himself.

Finally, you should resist the temptation to jump after every business opportunity. Most of Sub Sahara countries are under developed countries, which means, there will always be new opportunities springing up (greener grasses), people who knows that you have some capital invest in Africa will kept on bringing different business opportunities to you, most of which have not been properly thought through and if you are not disciplined enough, you will be jumping from one business to another without achieving much. I have seen many diasporas getting lost in maze of businesses without success in any.

b. **Eagles fly Alone and at High Altitudes** — Eagles don't fly with sparrows, ravens, and other small birds. Naturally, birds of the same feather usually flock together. No other bird goes to the height of the eagle. Eagles fly alone. Never in a flock.

    Lesson: Despite the fact that farming is becoming popular in Africa, not everybody will buy your vision to in-

vest in farming. You should avoid narrow-minded people as they will bring you down. Ultimately, man's future
is determined by the company of friends that he keeps.
Always sit with the winners or those who are going to
where you are going, the conversation will altogether
be more like iron sharpening iron. Remember, Eagles fly
with other Eagles.

c. c. **Eagles do not eat dead things but fresh prey.** Do
not rely too much on your past success, keep looking for
new frontiers to conquer.

Lesson: Do not allow your past to determine your future, let go of your past both successes and failures.
They should be behind you and do not rely too much
on the past success. Keep exploring new horizons, new
avenues to conquer.

Never stop exploring different options and approaches
to producing and marketing your pigs. There is an old
IQ test that has nine dots, and you had to draw five lines
with a pencil within these nine dots, without lifting the
pencil, the only way to do this was to go outside the
box, so don't be afraid to go outside the box. The best
businesspeople constantly hone their skills. You will
definitely learn some new approaches from this book.
Winners know that business gets more competitive every day and they take action to improve their knowledge
and skill. While average pig farmers will aim only to offer animals at a cheaper price just to move the animal
off their farm, winners will concentrate on improving
the quality of their livestock and the environment they
are raised in and also motivate the staff to produce the
best pigs and show customers how their product is different and better than their competitors.

d. **Eagles Love the Storm**. When clouds gather, all other birds hide and do not fly, whereas the eagle gets excited, the eagle uses the storm's wind to lift itself higher. Once a certain height is achieved, Eagles then glide and rest on their wings.

Lesson: Face your challenges, believe that challenge will not break you but only make you stronger. Be determined to use the life storms to rise to the greater heights. Champions should never be afraid of challenges.

Yes, you will not win all the time, there will be series of 'disappointments" that brings you much closer to your success. Successful farmers learn from every production cycle, every challenge and sales interaction to improve future results. Winners take every opportunity to learn.

e. **Eagles Prepare for Change**: Eagles remove the feathers and soft grass that is in the nest so that the young ones can get uncomfortable in preparation for flying.

Lesson: Be prepared to leave your comfort zone, there is no growth there.

"You can't change the direction of the wind, but you can adjust the sails to always reach your destination". Jimmy Dean.

Change is everywhere today. Major change is occurring in almost every aspect of people's personal and work life. When major change occurs, everyone has similar types of feelings of fear, anxiety, and loss of control. However, what differentiates people is how they react to the change. One can act in a reactive or proactive manner.

Being **reactive** means, you let change happen and then they respond by fighting it and later adapt to it. They see change as loss or a threat in this situation. Being **pro-**

active means you plan for change and are open to new or multiple ways of doing things. You see change as an opportunity or, you are at least open to reframing how you view the change.

In the long-term, how one interacts with change is the difference between surviving and thriving and it also influences how that person will communicate, make decisions, and solve problems around that change.

f. **When the Eagle grows old and his feathers becomes weak.** He retires and plucks out the weak feathers on his body until he is completely bare. Then he stays in this hiding place until he has grown new feathers.

Lesson: You will occasionally need to shed off old habits no matter how difficult, things that burden us or add no value to our lives should be let go of. Try as much as possible not to take yourself too seriously, the best of us get tired, make mistakes and sometimes fail.

Generally, African culture frowns and is terrified with the concept of failure. This starts from when most of us are in school. You are regarded as a smart student if you can memorise the answer as written by your teacher, those that could not memorise teacher's notes word for word are regarded as dull, though they may understand and be able to apply the knowledge learned better and practically. As a result, many of us spend our days as students avoiding the humiliation of failure at all costs. Some of us fear failure so much; we never try to accomplish anything that we are not 100% sure will succeed. The thought of failure paralyzes most of us.

If the fear of failure is a major concern to you, then farming might not be for you, in farming, there is no 100% chance that you will succeed. Like Eagle you might fail and have to shed your ego for some time. You are only human. Don't take yourself too seriously.

According to Benjamin Franklin, *"failure on a farm is every bit as reliable as death, taxes..."*

While failure is painful at first, it helps us learn our personal limits of time and energy. It's an instrumental timesaver in the long run, letting us know what works well, and what will not work well. Failure provides us perspective for future enterprises, making us intellectually stronger, more emotionally resilient.

Many of the inventions that we enjoyed now are result of failure, this includes electricity, microwaves, etc.

Thomas A. Edison, the man that perfected the idea of the light bulb, was said to have answered the reporter, when he asked why he failed 9,999 times before he became successful, he replied *"I have not failed. I've just found 9,999 ways that won't work."* This is a man that does not take himself too seriously but understands the need to discover new things.

As a farmer, be ready to try new things, but while you're failing, fail well. Fail gracefully and thoughtfully. It's the only sure way to recognize success when it finally arrives.

8.8 NO TO ABSENTEE FARMING

The best advice that I can give to middle-class farms is that as much as possible the owner(s) should personally direct all operations. You cannot be an absentee farmer, neither can you entrust your interests entirely into the hand of hirelings. The greatest mistake a proprietor can make is to allow the staff to think that they know more about your farm than you, you will be running your farm at their mercies and you will not get their utmost respect or get the best from them.

As the owner, you must be experienced and competent to direct the operations (not necessarily getting overly involved in the daily chores) and any part of the necessary work. You must learn to do every kind of work yourself and be a keen observer and logical thinker. You should make yourself proficient and thinking while performing each operation, be prepared to first teach yourself the how, why and when. By thinking as you work, you can discover quick ways, shortcuts and timesavers; and you will thus make yourself competent to teach your staff how to do the work in the ways you have proved to be good.

In farming, more than any other business, you must teach yourself, for every day will bring its problems and lessons. Reading and listening to lectures, radio talks, etc., though important and often helpful, they are poor substitutes for observation and translation of the observations into terms of understanding, decision and action.

This will also guarantee that you earned your staff respect as a director and you will get the work done efficiently and economically.

9. How much capital do you need to start your pig farm?

"The small amount of capital required to begin farming operations creates great misconception of what is necessary for commercial farming; for, judging from the small number of acres wanted for commencing a garden, many suppose that a few hundreds of dollars are all sufficient for a market gardener. For want of information of this subject, hundreds have failed, after years of toil and privation."
— Peter Henderson, In The Gardening for Profit

The misconception mentioned by Peter Henderson is also relevant in commercial pig production, many new farmers assumed that the small capital require to raise few weaners to market size, means that you will only need few hundreds of US dollars to set up a commercial pig farm.

The amount of capital that you require to build your pig farm will depend on many factors such as the location, the size, the topography, the vegetation, the shape or features of the land and the area where you choose to build your farm in your country.

However, our experience from helping many farmers to set up farms across Africa has taught us that the most important factor when estimating the cost of a farm is the owner himself, his experience, preferences, ability and capacity, all of this will go a long was in determining the final cost of setting up the farm.

In this chapter, our goal is not to provide one answer that fits all situation but rather to answer this question based on our real life experience and at the same time supply you with relevant key cost (but based on Nigeria prices) that you need to consider (or extrapolate from) to calculate your own construction and running cost wherever you farm is located in Africa.

Assumptions

Below are the assumptions that I use throughout the chapter to calculate the cost of setting up a medium size pig farm:

- The pig farm is located in the Southwest of Nigeria

- The quotes were based on the cost of items in Nigeria.

- The calculation was done in both Naira and converted to US Dollar.

- The current exchange rate was N350 to 1 US Dollar

- The farmland is a virgin land (there are no existing structure on the land)

- The cost of the farmland was not included

- The housing was built with locally available building material blocks, cement, sand, gravel and wood planks and corrugated roof for the roof

- Pigs were sourced from reputable farms

- The farm uses a combination of concentrate along with locally available and affordable feed ingredients such as

PKC, Soya meal, brewery waste, rice bran, maize, grains, etc.

- A mature breeding pig will consume an average of 2.5kg of feed a day

- Cost of feed used is N70 per kg 0.20 US Dollar.

- The sows give birth to an average of 9 piglets every 4 months

- Each sow gives birth twice in a calendar year.

- The piglets reached market weight of 85kg @ 6 to 7 months

- The current market price is N500 per kg

The construction material, livestock and feed price figures stated in this section were carefully verified and are based on the current price of products and materials in the Southwest of Nigeria as of the time of writing the plan.

9.1 BUSINESS SUMMARY

The proposed pig farm will engage primarily in the breeding and fattening of pigs, that is, the parent stock will be sourced at the beginning of the project from a reputable farm, the breeder pigs will be bred on the farm to produce piglets, and the piglets produced will be fattened to a marketable size and sold to the market (few of the female pigs will be selected for future breeding on the farm).

The farm will sell different kinds of pigs initially at the farm gate, this will include the piglets, weaners, growers, breeders and fattened pigs to private individuals, middle men, open markets, butcher, retail outlets and institutional buyers and will eventually expand to slaughtering and processing pork after 2 years.

(NB: slaughtering and processing is beyond the scope of this business plan).

9.2 OPERATIONAL STRATEGY

This plan detailed how your farm will achieve 400 pigs within the first years of operation (and over 1,000 in the year 2) , this will automatically turn the farm into a medium size commercial pig farm from an African perspective.

This plan covers the construction cost for farmhouse, different pig pens and all other necessary infrastructure. It also detailed the cost of acquiring new livestock, recruiting, training and retaining staff, operational cost of producing and managing a large volume of pigs and the profitable marketing of the pigs produced.

Our key strategy is to start the farm with the minimal number of pigs required to achieve this goal. We want the enterprise to move into livestock farming with caution, so as to minimize the initial risk that is expected of a new start up business while also allowing the proprietor, the management and the staff to acquaint themselves with all the different aspects of running a successful commercial pig farm as the farm grew organically into a medium size farm.

The farm will start with 20 breeder gilts and 2 boars with the aim of raising 400 pigs on the farm in the first year of operation.

In addition to the 22 breeders, the farm will also buy additional 20 weaners. These weaners will be fattened and sold at market weight of 85kg within the first 5 to 6 months of operation. This is important from a marketing perspective, since most pig marketing in Africa is through word of mouth, it is important that the farm begins to attract the pig buyers to the farm as early as possible.

Warning Note: Livestock farming is a business that has to do with living animals, once you started you cannot easily switch off and restart like other businesses.

9.3 SUMMARY COST OF CONSTRUCTING A PIG FARM

Costs of Production — Farmer does have some control over the costs of production on the farm but he tends to have little or no total control over the prices paid for the final product i.e. pig or pork. We will see later in the marketing section how the price of pigs and pork in Africa are determined by both middlemen. Therefore, if a farmer wishes to increase the farm income, he will have to reduce the cost per unit of output.

Production costs are usually classified into two categories:

1. Variable cost
2. Fixed cost

Variable costs are short-term costs (usually incurred within one year or a single cycle)

A variable cost is a farm's cost that is associated with the amount of pig that a farm produce. A farm's variable cost are costs that increase and decrease with the production volume.

For example, the feeding cost of a pig from weaners to 85kg is N21,000 suppose the farm produces 10 units, its variable cost will be N210,000. However, if the company does not produce any pigs, it will not have any variable cost for producing the pigs.

The typical pig farm variable costs include:

1. Feed cost — this includes feed bought from outside and also home-grown grains or tuber, this would be calculated at its potential sales value, or growing cost, whichever is greater.

2. Wages and salaries — this include staff and labourers salaries

3. Fuel and Lubricants: These include the costs of fuel for farm equipment and especially the generator that is used to power the water pump machine and for lightning.

4. Veterinary Fees and Medicines: This covers all expenditures for animal health, mainly veterinary practitioners' fees, medicines. Prophylactic doses of mineral or vitamins and dewormers for pig).

5. Transport cost — the cost of moving feed to the farm and the cost of moving pigs to and from the farm, don't forget your cost of travelling to the farm.

6. Telecommunication cost — all business-related cost

7. Marketing cost

8. Losses due to mortalities

Fixed Costs

On the other hand, fixed costs are related to general farm costs, with a proportion being attributed to the farm, and may not vary with livestock numbers.

Generally, fixed costs are incurred before any production takes place and remain the same irrespective of any production increases. Fixed cost does not vary with the volume of production. A fixed cost will not change with the amount of pigs produced. It remains the same even if no goods or services are produced.

Using the same example above, suppose the farm build a pig pen at a fixed cost of N2,000,000 to house 100 weaners and the farm is paying N100,000 a month to the bank over 2 years, however, the cost still remains the same even if the farm does not produce any pigs. The farm would still have to pay N100,000 a month to service the loan used to build the pen. On the other hand, if the pen is used to house 110 pigs, its fixed cost remains the same.

The typical fixed cost for a pig farm includes:

1. Land —
2. Pig pen — grower, breeder and weaner pens
3. Fencing (e.g. wire mesh & pole)
4. Purchase of breeding stock
5. Farm equipment — water nipples, feeding trough, Feed scale, Self-feeders
6. Roads clearing
7. Farm fencing and gate
8. Farmhouse for the farmer and workers
9. Warehouse for storing feed — A room where the feed can be mixed and stored
10. Borehole or well
11. 10KVA generator and electric wiring
12. Water facilities which include: pumps, pipes, taps, drinking nipples, reservoirs and boreholes if this is needed.
13. Trucks for transportation of pigs and feed
14. Repairs and maintenance of fences, buildings and vehicles

Typical fixed cost on a typical pig farm

Item	Cost in Naira	Cost in USD
Building 1: Breeder Pen	1,675,550	4,787
Building 2: Grower Pen	1,293,800	3,697
Building 3: Farmhouse	3,097,500	8,850
For your pig farm Bulldoze 3 acres*	400,000	1,143
Fencing (wire mesh & pole) about 500 metres	850,000	2,429
Farm gate	350,000	1,000
1 Borehole and water reticulation	800,000	2,286
KVA generator with installation	250,000	714
Insurance	150,000	429
Provision of Protective (Overall, Boots etc.)	100,000	286
Training, Supervision and Mentoring fee	250,000	714
Prepare feasibility report	150,000	429
Miscellaneous (including all permit and necessary legal documents).	1,200,000	1,429
Total Cost	10,566,850	28,193

* You will only need to bulldoze land for your pig farm

9.4 BREEDER PEN

Breeder pen is where the mature breeder pigs are kept from the time they are brought to the farm. By breeder pigs, we mean the mature male pigs (boar) and mature female pigs (gilts), they are usually 7 to 8 months in age and are brought to the farm primarily for the purpose of mating and to give birth to piglets that will populate the farm. These are like the production machine of the farm and they remain on the farm for as long as they are producing (this is usually between 4 to 5 years).

They are usually housed as one animal per cell of 9 feet x 8 feet.

Breeder Pen

The design below is spacious breeder pen with 24 cells of 9 x 8 feet facing each other. It has a corridor in the middle of the pen that allows staff to move through the pen, it also allows staff to enter each cell without passing through another cell. This design is most suitable for boar, gilts and pregnant and nursing sows basically your maternity pen

This is an open design that ensures the free air movement, good natural ventilation and also provides adequate space for each pig. This design also allows enough light throughout the day for the attendant to carry out their daily routines properly.

NB: You will start with 24 of these cells to house 22 breeder pigs and additional 2 cells for sick and quarantine pigs.

The walls must be of solid concrete or cement plastered brick. Cell doors should be made of round iron bar. A feed and water trough should be carefully placed in the cell, the water trough for each cell should be 500mm long, 150 to 200 mm high and 250 mm wide to cool the animal.

Cool, clean water must be available at all times in each pen through water nipples. The nipple must be placed at a 90° angle with the vertical and between 550 and 650 mm from the floor.

Unit Breeder Pen (9 x 8 feet per per cell)

Cost of 24 Unit Breeder Pen (9 x 8 feet per cell)

S/N Building	Quantity	Unit Cost	Cost in Naira	Cost in Dollar
Gravels	2	10,000	20,000	57
Sand	2	10,000	20,000	57
Cement	115	2,550	293,250	838
Laterite	1	20,000	20,000	57
No of blocks	1,700	200	340,000	971
Labour (bricklayer)			180,000	514
Timber				—
Plank 2 x 3	190	350	66,500	190
Plank 2 x 4	170	500	85,000	243
Plank 3 x 4	35	700	24,500	70
4 inch Nail (bag)	1	8500	8,500	24
3 inch Nail (bag)	1	8500	8,500	24
Roof Nail (packet)	5	8500	42,500	121
Flirt (yard)	2	400	800	2
Iron sheet	14	20000	280,000	800
Labour (carpenter)			60,000	171
Plumbing			100,000	286
Iron door	24	4,000	96,000	274
Miscellaneous			30,000	86
Sub total			**1,675,550**	**4,787**

9.5   WEANING /GROWER PEN

Weaner pen is where piglets are kept after they are removed from their mother (sow). Each cell will house 20 weaners each until they reach the market weight, (the pig are referred to as grower from 4 months onward and the pen becomes a grower pen). For those that will be sold as finishers, they will stay in this pen until they reach the market weight and are sold.

For this project, we recommend that you build a minimum of 5 cells of 20 x 16 feet to house 20 weaners per cell (total 100 weaners) so as to take advantage of the economy of scale when building.

As mentioned earlier, the project will start with 20 weaners bought from a reputable farm at the beginning of operations. The rest of the cell will be populated by the piglets farrowed by the sows that are on the farm.

Weaning /Grower pen 20 x 16 feet

Cost of 100 Capacity Grower Pen 5 cells x 20ft x 16feet

Building S/N	Quantity	Unit Cost	Cost in Naira	Cost in Dollar
Gravels	2	10,000	20,000	57
Sand	2	10,000	20,000	57
Cement	100	2,550	255,000	729
Laterite	1	20,000	20,000	57
No of blocks	1,300	200	260,000	743
Labour (bricklayer)			140,000	400
Timber				—
Plank 2 x 3	170	350	59,500	170
Plank 2 x 4	160	500	80,000	229
Plank 3 x 4	30	700	21,000	60
4-inch Nail (bag)	1	8500	8,500	24

Building	Quantity	Unit Cost	Cost in Naira	Cost in Dollar
3-inch Nail (bag)	1	8500	8,500	24
Roof Nail	5	8500	42,500	121
Flirt (yard)	2	400	800	2
Iron sheet	12	20000	240,000	686
Labour (carpenter)		60000	60,000	171
Iron door	5	4,000	20,000	57
Plumbing			8,000	23
Miscellaneous			30,000	86
Sub total			1,293,800	3,697

9.6 COST OF A 3-BEDROOM FARMHOUSE WITH 2 BATHROOMS AND TOILETS AND KITCHEN

Typical pig farm house

Farm Office and Workers' Quarters

To improve the welfare and retention of staff, you might need to build a farm office and a farmhouse for staff, this house will have bathroom, a kitchen, a canteen, and a recreation room as well as bedrooms. This will not only reduce your staff absenteeism or turnover of staff and but also increase the security of your farm.

In addition, your farm should have offices where management stays while on the farm and where clerks kept production and financial records, received visitors, dispensed medicines and therapeutic drugs, and operated their computers.

The design below is an ideal standard, you can reduce the size and the number of rooms to make it more affordable.

Cost of a 3-bedroom farmhouse with 2 bathrooms and toilets and kitchen

Building	Quantity	Unit Cost	Farm House cost Naira	Farm House cost USD
S/N				
Gravels	2	10,000	20,000	57
Sand	2	10,000	20,000	57
Cement	150	2,550	382,500	1093
Laterite	1	20,000	20,000	57
No of blocks	3,000	200	600,000	1714
Labour (bricklayer)			350,000	1000
Timber			180,000	514
Iron sheet	15	20,000	300,000	857
Nails			20,000	57
Labour (carpenter)			150,000	429
Plumbing			250,000	714
Iron door	5	30,000	150,000	429
Timber			180,000	514
4 inch Nail (bag)		17000	17000	49
Roof Nail (packet)	4	2000	8,000	23
Labour (carpenter)			150000	429
Miscellaneous			300,000	857
TOTAL			3,097,500	8,850

9.7 SELECTION OF QUALITY PIGS FOR YOUR FARM

One of the greatest effects on profitability on a pig farm is the number of piglets reared per sow per year. Your boars and gilts should come from a good parent breed that possess the genetic potential that will improve the production characteristics of her offspring. In summary, the gilt or sow selected for your farm must have the ability to rear large and healthy litters. They should be selected on performance, namely growth rate and lean and fat composition. We will look later at the various selection indices that are available which should be taken into consideration later in the book under gilts selection.

In most African countries, there are 4 categories of pigs that a farmer can start his or her farm with, they include:

1. The indigenous breed
2. The Popular Breed
3. First generation Hybrid
4. Enhanced Imported Breed

We will look at each of these categories in details under gilts selection. However, the decision on which category of pigs to start your farm will ultimately be determined by the market that you are targeting, the categories of breeder pigs that are available in your locality, your budget for the pigs, and the cost of feeding the pigs.

For our plan, we prefer the first-generation hybrid parent stock. These are the offspring of the crossbreed between the imported Large White boars that is mated with the female of the local popular breed to produce first-generation hybrid (crossbreed) sets of pigs.

The advantages of the first-generation hybrid are that they grow faster in lean meat than muscle, which means they are weightier (as muscle is heavier than fat) than the popular breed, they also produce larger litter an average of 9 piglets compared to the average of 6 litters produced by popular breeds and because of the genetics of the popular breed of their mother, the pig produced are more resistant to diseases and they can part survive better on locally available feed than the exotic breed.

9.8 THE ECONOMICS OF PIG PRODUCTION

For this plan, we are starting the farm with 20 Hybrid Gilts and 2 boars.

Expenditure	Cost /sow (N)	No of pigs	N	$
Cost of Boars	60,000	2	120,000	343
Cost of Sows	60,000	20	1,200,000	3429
Sow & Boar Feeding/year	63,875	22	1,405,250	4015
Medication	500	382	191,000	546
No. of piglet produced/year	18	360		0
Cost of feeding piglets/cycle	14,380	360	5,176,800	14791
Others	500	360	180,000	514
Total Expenditure in Yr. 1			8,273,050	23,637

We will now look at how the figures on the table are calculated

- The current cost of ready to breed first generation hybrid gilt or boar in Nigeria is N60,000 or $171

- The average cost of breeder pig's feed is N70 per kg and a breeder pig will consume an average of 2.5kg a day @ 365 days a year. That means that the cost of maintaining a breeder pig on your farm for a year = N70 x 2.5kg x 365 days = N63,875.

- This figure is very significant as it shows that the cost of maintaining a breeder pig on the farm is high, and as a consequence, the farm should do all it can to productively utilise all the gilts or sow that are brought to the farm effectively. This involve making sure that each female breeder pig gives birth twice a year to a minimum of 18 piglets per annum, this will ensure that the farm recuperates the total cost of maintaining the breeder on the farm and also makes a profit.

- The hybrid pig should give birth to an average of 9 piglets twice a year = 18 piglets

- To achieve this production rate, your staff will be prompt at detecting the heat and mating the female pigs. Mated gilts and sow should also not be exposed to stress after mating

The table below shows the amount and value of feed that a piglet will consume from birth until they reach market weight.

Cost of fattening piglets to market size

Month	1	2	3	4	5	6	7	
feed /day	—	0.3	0.5	1.1	1.3	1.5	2.2	
N/kg	70	70	70	70	70	70	70	
No of days	30	30	30	30	30	30	30	
	—	630	1050	2310	2730	3150	4620	14,380

Cost of fattening piglets to market size of 85kg from birth is N70 per kg and the pig will eat N14,380 ($41)

Revenue	Revenue/sow	N	$
Total no. of piglets produced	360		—
Mortality (5%)	18		—
No of market size pigs for sale	342		—
Live weight (kg)	85		—

Revenue	Revenue/sow	N	$
Selling price	500		—
Revenue from piglet born on the farm		14,535,000	41,529
Gross profit		6,261,950	17,892
Gross profit %		44%	44%

Analysis

- Total number of pigs produced by 20 gilts x 18 piglets per annum = 360

- Maximum mortality expected is 5% = 18 piglets

- With good management practices the piglets should reach the market weight of 85kg within 6 to 7 months and be sold at N500 per kg,

- The expected revenue is N500 per kg x 85kg live weight pig x 342 pigs = N14,535,000 ($41,529)

- Expected gross profit is (Revenue 14,535,050 ($41,529) — (the operational cost) 8,273,059 ($23,637) = Gross Profit 6,261,950 ($17,892)

The operational cost of raising 20 weaners to market weight within 6 months.

	Cost	Unit	N	USD
Cost of weaners	12,000	20	240,000	685.7142857
Cost of feeding	13,350	20	267,000	762.8571429
Medications	100	20	2,000	6
Total cost of raining weaners			509,000	1454

- Weaner are bought from a reputable farm @ 14,000 each

- The weaner will consume N13,350 over 5 months to achieve 85kg.

- The total cost of buying and raising the weaner is N509,000 ($1,454)

Revenue

	N	USD
Total no. of weaner	20	
Live weight	85	
Selling price	500	
Revenue from 20 fattened weaners	850,000	2,429
Gross Profit	341,000.00	974
Gross profit %	40%	40%

- The expected revenue is N500 per kg x 85kg live weight pig x 20 pigs = N850,000 ($2,428)

- Expected gross profit is (Revenue) $2,428 – (the OPEX cost) N509,000 ($1,454) = Gross Profit N341,000.00 ($974)

9.9 BUDGETED CASH FLOW FOR THE PROPOSED PRODUCTION

Month Num.	1	2	3	4	5	6	7	8	9	10	11	12	YTD
NUMBER OF PIGS ON THE FARM													
No of Boars	2												
No of breeder Sows	20												
No of Weaners	20												
No of pigs birth/mnth					90	90					90	90	
No of pigs sold/mnth						20					90	90	
Cumulative no of pigs on the farm	42	42	42	42	42	132	202	202	202	202	292	382	
REVENUE FROM SALES OF PIGS													
Revenue						2,429					10,929	10,929	$ 24,286
Actual No of pigson the farm	42	42	42	42	42	112	202	202	202	202	202	292	
OPERATIONAL COST (OPEX)													
Cost of Boar Stock	343												$ 343
Cost of Sow Stock	3,429												$ 3,429
Cost of Weaner Stock	686												$ 686
Cost of feeding breeder	335	335	335	335	335	335	335	335	335	335	335	335	$ 4,015
Cost of feeding piglets							1,233	1,233	1,233	1,479	1,479	1,479	$ 8,135
Cost of feeding weaners	127	127	127	127	127	127							$ 763
Medication cost	18	18	18	18	18	18	18	18	18	18	18	18	$ 218
Fuel cost	47	47	47	47	47	47	47	47	47	47	47	47	$ 566
Staff and other cost	143	143	143	143	143	214	214	214	214	214	214	214	$ 2,214
Total OPEX cost	5,127	670	670	670	670	741	1,847	1,847	1,847	2,093	2,093	2,093	$ 20,368
PROFIT													
Gross Profit	(5,127)	(670)	(670)	(670)	(670)	1,687	(1,847)	(1,847)	(1,847)	(2,093)	8,835	8,835	$ 3,917
Profit before Tax	(5,127)	(670)	(670)	(670)	(670)	1,687	(1,847)	(1,847)	(1,847)	(2,093)	8,835	8,835	$ 3,917
*Provision for Tax												196	$ 196
Profit After Tax	(5,127)	(670)	(670)	(670)	(670)	1,687	(1,847)	(1,847)	(1,847)	(2,093)	8,835	8,639	$ 3,722

9.10 NOTES:

The spreadsheet is divided into 4 sections

1. No. of pigs in the farm
2. Revenue from sales
3. Operational Cost (Opex)
4. Profit

NUMBER OF PIGS ON THE FARM

The cumulative no. of pigs on the farm

- The cumulative no. of pigs on the farm row shows the total number of pigs that have gone through the farm i.e. either bought or birthed and sold since the commencement of the farm.

- This row starts with the number of pigs that were brought to the farm at the beginning of the operation. You will notice that from the 6th month, this number will continue to increase by the number of piglets either birthed on or brought to the farm.

- For example, you will notice that the farm starts with 20 gilts, 2 boar and 20 weaners, making a total of 42 pigs at the start of the farm. However, by the 5th and 6th month, additional 180 pigs were added. These were from the piglets birthed by the mated gilts in 1st and 2nd month of operation and the 20 pigs were sold, i.e. the weaners that were brought in, in the 1st month, have reached market weight.

- The table also shows that the piglets born in the 5th month will reach market weight and sold in the 11th and 12th month.

No of pigs birthed/month

- The assumption is based on the fact that with good management, a sow should farrow twice a year

- A sow gives birth to an average of 9 piglets at a time

- The production cycles take into consideration the mating of a sow, the 4 months of pregnancy duration and the fact that piglets are nursed by the sow for 2 months before they are weaned

- For example, it is assumed that the gilts brought to the farm in the 1st month were mated during the 1st and 2nd month. As a result, half of the gilts gave birth on the 5th month and the rest gave birth in the 6th month.

No of pigs sold/month

- It takes an average of 6 to 7 months for newly birthed piglets to reach a market weight

- The 2-month-old weaners purchased with the breeders in the 1st month will reach market weight in and sold on the 6th month

- The table also shows that the piglets born in the 5th month will also reach market weight and sold in the 11th and 12th month.

Actual No of pigs on the farm

- This takes into account the actual number of pigs on the farm at the end of each month. This is useful for farmers to determine the number of new pig pens that are required and when he should start constructing.

- The variation in the number of pigs each month is the number of pigs birthed minus the number of pigs sold.

REVENUE FROM SALES is calculated using the average market weight of pigs on the 6th month.

85kg multiply by N500

The current sales price of live pigs multiplied by the number of pigs sold that month.

OPERATIONAL COST (OPEX)

- This is the most important section of the spreadsheet as this is the day to day cost of running the farm and until the farm breaks even, the farm management will need to make sure that the required fund is available at the beginning of every month for the farm to survive

- Unlike other businesses, failure to have sufficient operating funds to buy feed or fuel to pump water, etc. can jeopardise the whole pig business

- We strongly recommend that this section be seriously considered when determining the number of pigs that the farm should start with

- The cost of breeder is calculated by multiplying the number of breeder pigs that the farm starts with by the current market price

- Cost of weaner is the number of weaners bought multiplied by the current market price

- Cost of feeding — breeder pig consumes 2.5kg of feed daily multiplied by N70 per kg cost of feed multiplied by 365 days a year

- Cost of feeding piglets to market weight multiplied by the number of weaners within 6 months

- Other operational costs such as medication, fuel cost for generator, staff cost of staff and supervisor, was calculated using our experience of running a pig farm for the last 10 years

9.11 CASH FLOW MANAGEMENT ON A PIG FARM

Cash flow management is a key aspect of the financial management of a profitable pig farm. It involves planning for future cash requirements to avoid a crisis of having no cash at a time when it is needed.

As the proprietor of the farm, you and your manager need to know how much cash is required every month throughout the entire financial period so that appropriate plans can be made to ensure the necessary cash is available when needed.

As a pig farmer, you are dealing with live animals that need to be fed daily. For example, if you starve a grower pig for one day, it will take the pig one week to recover and it will delay your reaching the market weight by two weeks. If you starve your weaners or piglets for a day, the animal would probably die and the pregnant sow may lose a few piglets if she is starved.

All these examples are to let you know that as a pig farmer, you need to have at least sufficient funds for 2 months of feed on hand at all times.

If the finances of the farm are stable, your cash-flow adjustments can be done on a monthly basis. However, if you suspected that your financial circumstances might change and the farm will soon be struggling, you should revise your cash flow daily and start planning well ahead of the time on how to find an alternative capital that you will need for the farm.

Here are some of the ways to manage cash flow:

- If you are just getting into pig farming, make sure that you have a business plan that is prepared by someone who is experienced in pig farming

- The business plan should have a dedicated section for your cash flow projection

- Take time to study and understand your business plan and especially your cash flow

- Study the cash flows section carefully to understand the expenditure for each month, how you plan to source the fund and also when you will start earning revenue from the farm to cover some of these costs.

- If you are an existing pig farmer and you keep good records, look at the cash flows (or other financial records) of previous years to know when the highest expenditures occur (for example when you spend additional funds to buy breeder pigs) and when the revenue starts coming in (i.e when pigs will be sold on your farm). For example, based on our plan above, you will not earn any revenue from the farm until the 6th and 7th month when you sell your first sets of growers and later when you start selling weaners that are farrowed earlier on your farm.

- Identify periods when cash is likely to be insufficient and rearrange your expenditures accordingly.

- Where possible, ensure that payments to regular suppliers of inputs (e.g. feed suppliers) are staggered in such a way that cash obtained from your sales (revenue) is sufficient to make those payments.

- Purchases of non-urgent items should be made when cash inflow is stable or high.

- Always save some revenue to cover periods when sales are low or payment delayed.

- Ensure that you properly manage credit offered to customers (or buyers of your products) in order not to deplete your cash.

10. How to finance your pig farm

Now that you have gone through the finances in the previous chapter, you now have some ideas on how much you will need to set up and to run your commercial pig farm. You next course of action is to source for the capital that you need to achieve your dream.

The type of finance that you choose for your business will depend on the size of your farm and what kind of pig farming business you desire to do, e.g. production of weaners, growers, finisher, slaughtering and processing, etc. This will ultimately determine how much money you need when you need it and what you will use it for.

For most farmers, your first point of call will be using your own personal savings to kick start the business and later proceed to approach friends and family or the bank.

In this chapter, we will look at the benefits of each source of fund and the challenges it may have on your pig farm.

10.1 SELF-FINANCE

Naturally, if you're starting your pig farm in sub-Sahara Africa, there is a high chance that you will have to put down the first set of money yourself to initiate your project. It will be difficult if not impossible, to borrow from a bank or attract other investors unless you are seen to have committed some of your own money into the project.

Using your savings is the easiest and most cost-effective way to provide the initial financing required to build and operate your farm.

Advantages of self-financing your business:

1. With self-financing, you will know exactly how much money is available to start and run your farm and you will not have to spend valuable time trying to secure other forms of funding from investors or banks.

2. Self-financing your farm gives you much more control than other finance options.

3. You do not need to pay back or rely on outside investors or lenders, who could decide to withdraw their support at any time or threatened to take control of your farm.

4. You will retain full ownership of your farm, which in turn means that you will receive 100 per cent of future profits.

5. Funding the farm by yourself will instil the discipline in you to be smart with your fund and only invest in equipment and marketing when you need to. This can also help you to master how to prioritise your business expenditure and avoid excessive spending.

Disadvantages of self-financing your pig farm

1. Using your own money to finance your farm may limit your goals and aspirations as you may not have enough

to cover the entire cost that you need to construct and operate a commercial pig farm.

2. It may put a strain on your family and personal life.

3. Pig farming can be overwhelmingly demanding, and you may not have enough money left over to cover your living costs. I have seen farmers who have to forfeit someof their own meals to feed their pigs on the farm.

4. You will need to have a sufficient contingency fund; in case you need extra money to see you through a difficult period.

5. If your business were to fail, you could lose your home and other personal possessions.

6. By going alone, you might have to forfeit the contacts, the mentoring and the networking opportunities that investors and venture capitalists can provide for you and bring to your business.

10.2 HOW TO KEEP YOUR EXPENSES LOW AND HAVE A BUFFER OF SAVINGS

- If you are self-financing your project and want your farm to succeed before you ran out of money, then you must learn to embrace frugality and downsize your lifestyle. This means keeping your personal expenses low so that you have sufficient funds for your farm, especially for the first few years of raising your pigs.

- I like the quote of Joel Salatin, "*In the beginning you take care of business and later business takes care of you, If you start another way, taking care for you first then your business will suffer.*"

- Avoid starting too big, start small and build your farm organically.

- Don't spend more than necessary on your fixed assets e.g. don't buy lots of expensive new equipment or build overly constructed pens. Focus more on your "must-have" and "need to have" features and structure of your farm (refer to what your pig needs chapter"). At the beginning avoids spending too much on "nice to have" features.

- If there is a poultry pen or space at the back of your house, feel free to convert it into a pig pen instead of building a new one, you can expand later as you progress.

- From our many years of working with farmers, we noticed that farmers who have made it in pig farming all started frugally in cheap housing while investing the money they saved in operation of their farm.

- Finally, if you are going to self-finance your farm, have a buffer of savings. The bigger the savings, the more time you have to build your farm to the size you desire without having to make short-term decisions at the expense of long-term ones. No matter how good your business plan is, there is a chance that it might take longer before you start making the amount of income you desire. If this happens, your ability to go through this will be determined by the size of your buffer of savings. Having some extra cash will also give you security and the confidence to try new things.

- Please note not having a stable source of income to support your pig farm can be a very unnerving and stressful experience, but you can mitigate this factor by accumulating cash before starting out and make sure it is available before you need it.

10.3 FINANCING FROM FRIENDS AND FAMILY

It's common in Africa for owners of the medium-size farm to look to relatives and friends for support when they needed additional business funding for their farm. In a communal culture like African, this can work very well, and in most cases, these arrangements are informal and based purely on trust and verbal assurances. The risk of such an arrangement is that any misunderstanding about the agreement could damage personal and long-term relationships.

To prevent unnecessary conflict from happening, it is important to make sure that before you approach a friend or relative for funds to support your farm business, you should be clear about your requirements and what any investment will involve. For example, you need to be clear if you are looking for a loan or an investment.

Loan

If your farm needs immediate and relatively short-term funds e.g. funds for feed to fatten your pig to market weight within a few months, a loan may be most appropriate. Then you and the borrower should both discuss and decide whether it is going to be with interest, or whether it is going to be an interest-free loan.

Investment

However, if the business requires a longer-term or permanent funding for example to construct pig pens or buy large equipment like feed mixer, you may want to consider giving your investor a share in the business. But before you opt for this option, think about whether you need an active partner or shareholder. If you are just looking for a passive partner who will have no involvement in the business, make this very clear at the beginning.

As a rule of thumb and personal experience, you should always retain at least 70 per cent of the shares that are issued out, this should ensure you keep control of your business. I will also advise that you keep a close eye on the number of investors joining your farm business. There is a saying that "too many cooks always spoilt the broth".

Explain to your investors that the money they invest is risk capital — they may not get it back. However, if your business goes well, they might look for returns that reflect the risk, i.e. greater than they would receive if they placed their money in a bank.

Advantages of raising finance from friends and family

There are clear advantages to approaching family or friends, rather than conventional sources of funding, for a loan or investment.

Family or friends:

1. The term of the funding is often more flexible than banks.
2. On a practical level, they may offer loans without security or accept less security than banks.
3. May lend funds interest-free or at a low rate.
4. May agree to a longer repayment period or lower return on their investment than formal lenders.

5. They may also seek a lower rate of initial return than commercial backers.

6. Your investors probably know your character and circumstances and so are less likely to need a detailed business plan.

Disadvantages

1. As mentioned earlier, transactions of this nature can be complex, and expectation may also be different.

2. Any misunderstandings about the arrangement can damage relationships.

3. There is a risk your investors may expect faster returns than you are offering or they may also have invested more money into your farm than they can afford to lose, or they will demand their money back when it suits them but not your business.

4. They may also want to get more involved in the business, which may not be appropriate because their perspective about how the farm should be run versus your original goal for setting up the farm may not be consistent. Always remember, all your investors will always have their own plan and agenda which may not be in line with your original plan of setting the farm. The more the number of your shareholders in your business the more difficult they are to manage.

Managing your shareholders expectations

I cannot emphasise enough the importance of managing investor expectations. There's one golden rule that you should always reiterate to all your investors whether they are offering a loan or taking a share in your farm, they should "never invest money that they can't afford to lose".

If possible, educate your investors on the significant difference between saving and investing "Investing is not the same as saving". Saving is putting money aside in a safe place where it stays until you want to access it in a few days, a few months, or even several years. It might earn a little interest depending on where you put it, and it will be there for you in case of an emergency or to achieve the goal you're saving for.

Whereas investing is the process of putting your money to work for you. When done properly, it can typically make more money for you than the interest you might earn in a nice, safe savings account or certificate of deposit. But with reward comes risk. If the business makes poor choices or even if things beyond the farm control go wrong, you could lose that money. It might not be there for you in case of an emergency.

Ask the friend or relative to set out their expectations clearly and plan how you will manage those expectations. This can help create a win-win situation for you and for your investor.

Remember many of your investors would not have invested in farming before, so you need to discuss the concept of early profit versus building a large farm. Building a large profitable farm takes a longer time. You can use an example of building a bungalow and skyscraper. With bungalow the foundation is shallower so you see the house rising quickly, however, for skyscraper you could spend up to 2 or 3 years working on just the foundation day and night before you start laying the blocks that people can see.

10.4 HOW BEST TO APPROACH FRIENDS AND FAMILY FOR FUNDING?

It's a good idea to approach friends and family in the same way you would a formal lender:

1. Be crystal clear about your own expectations — specify your short and long-term goal for the farm and how long you need the money for.

2. Don't be too eager or desperate to take funds from people that have different plans or agenda about your farm.

3. If you opt for a loan (which is sometimes preferable when you are just getting acquainted with your investors) make sure you detail the repayment level that you can afford. (Later in this chapter we will look at the rules of borrowing money).

4. If you opt for shares option, make sure you spell out how many shares or what profit the investor will receive — and when any returns will be paid.

5. Clarify whether an investor will have any financial liabilities for your business activity.

6. Draw up a formal written agreement.

7. A word of warning: think twice about approaching a friend or family member, especially if other sources of finance have turned you down. Try and analyse the reasons for this and review your business proposition. Remember that if your business fails you, lenders and investors may lose their money.

10.5 BANK FINANCE

A loan is an amount of money borrowed for a set period within an agreed repayment schedule. The repayment amount will depend on the size and duration of the loan and the rate of interest.

Loans are generally most suitable for:

- paying for assets — e.g. building a pen, feed grinding machine, feed mixer, vehicles and land

- running capital e.g. feed, staff salary, fuel

Banks and financial institutions do offer short- and long-term debt finance via loans and overdrafts as well as other types of finance to agricultural projects. These are available by application to any commercial or Agricultural bank; it usually involves a decision process by the finance institution. Most governments of countries in Africa are putting pressure on commercial banks to give more loans to farmers.

There are several types of bank finance that are available for businesses, with different packages available, but you need to make sure that the loan you apply for suits your needs as well as your farm requirements.

Banks will loan money to businesses on the basis of an adequate return for their investment and they will factor the risks of defaulting and also cover administrative costs. If you already have an established relationship with your bank, they will have developed a good understanding of your business. This will help them to advise you about the best product for your financial needs.

Typically, your loan application would ultimately be based on your farm's cash repayment ability; other criteria that the bank will be looking at are your farm's financial history or business plan to establish whether the projections in terms of the predicted revenue and expenses are realistic, your farm experience, training, knowledge and skills in pig production techniques, staff management and marketing of produce and finally, the value of the collateral in case you default on credit repayments.

As you prepare to apply for a loan, you need to ensure that you have a well-prepared loan application taking on board these factors to optimise your chance of obtaining agricultural credit.

Bank Facilities

Short-term finance

Overdrafts are used in conjunction with business bank accounts and are a flexible source of working capital for short-term needs. For example, if you need money to fatten your pig in a few months so as to get additional weight for few months before selling it to a buyer, you can use this facility.

Medium-term finance

Medium-term loans have a fixed or variable interest rate and mature over a one- to seven-year period. They are typically used to buy fixed assets such as feed grinder and mixer machine, pig pen or other purchases of a capital nature.

Long-term finance

Commercial farm mortgages, these are loans provided by banks to finance long-term projects of about 10 to 15 years, e.g. the purchase of a big farm or to erect a modern abattoir and processing plant. Types of mortgage available include repayment, commercial endowment or pension. The mortgage will usually be repayable over a 15-year period.

Advantages of term loans

1. The loan is not repayable on demand and so is available for the term of the loan generally from 6 months to ten years — unless you breach the loan conditions.

2. Loans can be tied to the lifetime of the equipment (e.g. feed hammer mill and feed mixer) or other assets you're borrowing the money to pay for.

3. At the beginning of the term of the loan you may be able to negotiate a moratorium, meaning that you only pay interest for a certain amount of time while repayments on the capital are frozen.

4. While you must pay interest on your loan, you do not have to give the lender a percentage of your profits or a share in your company.

5. Interest rates may be fixed for the term so you will know the level of repayments throughout the life of the loan.

6. There may be an arrangement fee that is paid at the start of the loan but not throughout its life.

Disadvantages of loans

1. Larger loans will have certain terms and conditions that you must adhere to, such as the provision of quarterly management information or regular inspection and monitoring of your farm.

2. Loans are not very flexible — you could be paying interest on funds you're yet to use on your farm.

3. You could have trouble making monthly repayments if your customers don't pay you promptly, causing cash-flow problems.

4. In some cases, loans are secured against the assets of the business or your personal possessions, e.g. your home.

5. The interest rates for secured loans may be lower than for unsecured ones, but your assets or home could be at risk if you cannot make the repayments.

6. There may be a charge if you want to repay the loan before the end of the loan term, particularly if the interest rate on the loan is fixed.

10.6 SHOULD I TAKE OUT A LOAN OR NOT?

Contrary to our cultural belief in sub-Sahara Africa, borrowing money for production is no more dishonourable than borrowing tools for the same purpose. What is bad is borrowing to pay the cost of living the high life, and for "living high".

Loans are a powerful agency for good for those who know how to use it, however, it can be dangerous for those who do not know how to use it.

You can start a small backyard farm with your money but as you expand to a moderate medium-size commercial pig farm, you will need lots of capital to buy good land, build pig pen, farmhouse, sink a borehole and other infrastructures required to run a commercial pig farm. Agriculture is a volume-based business, so the more efficient you are, the less your cost becomes and the more the profit.

The main source of additional capital once you start running your farm will originate from the profit that you get from the difference between your selling price and your cost of production. As soon as this additional capital start coming back into your farm, you will need to exercise discipline not to prematurely spend this additional income on amusement to satisfy your desires e.g. "buy a Jeep vehicle to celebrate", instead, you should use the additional income to buy more weaners or feed or build additional pens to accommodate more weaners on your farm. If you do this you are investing the additional capital back to your business; you are using the extra capital to create more monies.

However, if you do not have sufficient money coming from your farm and you need to expand, your only chance to expand your farm might be to borrow money from the bank.

In summary, the capital to build additional pens for the weaners on your farm can be secured in only two ways; accumulation of funds generated from sales overtime, or from borrow it.

The disadvantage of waiting and accumulating funds from sales is that you are delayed until the necessary money for the project is accumulated; while the advantage of borrowing is that this delay can be eliminated and the additional pen can be built and used to pay for itself. This is the only advantage that loan has in any business. For those who know how to use it wisely, it is a powerful aid.

However, loans should not to be invoked without due diligence and calculation. Equipment may wear out, disease and mortality may affect your pigs , volatility of feed ingredient price and fluctuation in the price of pig and pork may impact your cash projections, other unforeseen events could occur but you still have to pay your loan, it is inescapable and it comes with fatal certainty. Debts, unless paid, will lead to bankruptcy of the borrower.

In reality, borrowing money from the bank to expand your pig production can be perceived as a forward-moving business enterprise.

According to Maurice Kains, in his book 5 Acres and independence, here are some fundamental rules that farmers should observe when taking out a loan.

1. The borrower must be sure that the project for which the money is sought will produce more money than will be needed to pay both principal and interest, it is bad policy to borrow for anything that will not pay for itself.

2. Ensure that the repayment date of principal fall when most convenient to the borrower; i.e., when the borrower is most likely to have cash to meet the obligation; for instance, repayment for loan for fatteners should be when the weaners will be marketed.

3. The duration of the loan, how long it is to run. The loan should follow your production cycle. It should not run for longer. For example, if the loan is to raise weaners, it should be paid back immediately the weaners are marketed.

4. In long-time loans, provision should be made to reduce the principal in installments. The borrower should aim to repay part of the principal on any interest date. In such cases, the amount of interest is also reduced with each payment until the whole debt is canceled.

5. As much as possible, a low interest rate should be secured; It is important for farmer to avoid loans with exorbitant interest rates. Let's look at this scenario: If you borrow N1million at 20% for a year, the debt that you will pay when payment due is N1.20m; however, if you borrow from a cheaper source at 7% the debt is N1.07m, that is a difference of N130,000 saved for later use instead of being wasted.

Let us put these rules to test on a typical pig farm.

For example, a farmer wanted to borrow to raise weaners for 6 months to market weight of 85kg, however, out of desperation to get the loan he agrees to 4 months moratorium with the bank (instead of 6 months when the pigs will be sold). That means he has to start payment from (Month 4) into the project about 2 months before the weaner reaches market weight. It is obvious that there will be difficulty making this payment that he agreed to from the sales.

Under such circumstances, the farmer will have to use the following options to satisfy the debt:

Option 1 — Use money from some other source apart from the business;

Option 2 — Renegotiate and ask for the loan to be extended;

Option 3 — The creditor may sell out the borrower.

This is not a farfetched example; it did happen to a pig farmer who entered this predicament because he wanted to get an Agric loan from the bank at all cost. Let's look at each of the options that the farmer has:

Option 1, violates rule 1, the good business precept that each part of a business should pay its own expenses and a profit;

Option 2 is asking for a favour of the creditor and thus disrupts business arrangements;

Option 3 can easily result in a more or less heavy loss for the borrower.

This scenario also violated Rule 2 as the period is shorter than the production cycle and it also violates rule 3, duration of the loan should follow pig production cycle. It should not run for longer.

10.7 WHY ARE BANKS AND FINANCIAL INSTITUTIONS IN AFRICA RELUCTANT TO GIVE LOANS TO FARMERS?

1. Moral hazard — there is an historic lack of trust among many lenders and farmers, this was based on the historical fear among lenders that when a farmer receives their loans, the first thing he does is marry more wives. While what people uses loan for nowadays might have changed from many wives to buying a jeep vehicle. There is still a fear that some farmers would not use the fund for the original purpose and to complicate the matter some farmers actually believe that bank loan is free money from the government and they do not need to pay it back.

2. Lack of credit history information — there is a general absence of customer credit history information in most African countries especially among farmers, and information about applicants can be difficult to obtain. This means that the lender knows very little about their potential borrower and are therefore unable to make an informed decision.

3. Lack of farm records — most are small scale pig farmer. Usually they have a low level of formal education and are not used to keeping documents or filling in record books. Consequently, the loan appraisal is often based on information obtained by interviewing the potential borrower.

4. Farming is a risky business — Livestock may be sick and sometimes die and crops may fail and, weather influences the productivity and sale prices fluctuate and are sometimes difficult to predict. If productivity is lower than expected, farmers may not be able to repay loans.

5. Production and yield risk — agricultural yields are some-times uncertain, as natural hazards such as the pests and diseases like African Swine Fever and other production calamities impact on farm output.

6. Seasonality of agricultural production provides an additional risk. Farmers invest and work in the present for a return several months in the future. The relatively long period of time between starting livestock activities and the realisation of farm output implies that market prices may change from what has been projected.

7. Invalid collateral — If a borrower does not repay on time, collateral is sometimes used to compensate for the potential loan loss. Traditional collateral, however, is rarely available from small farmers.

11. Are you running a backyard farm or a business?

Now that you know how much you need and where you are going to get the money to set up and run your farm, the next question you need to answer is how you are going to run the farm.

Is your farm a hobby or a business?

Only you, the owner, can ultimately decide whether you want your farm to be a business or not, but for your farm to be regarded as a business it needs to meet certain criteria.

Your farm is a not a business if all the goods produced on your pig farm are used and consumed for the sustenance of you and your family and those who work the land. Then you are but a hobby or smallholder farmer.

Smallholder farmers usually farm for one of three reasons:

- Exclusively for home consumption with rarely any surpluses produced

- Mostly for home consumption, but with the intention of selling surpluses on the market

- Majority for home consumption and partly for the market

Your pig farm is a business only if the majority of the goods produced (e.g. weaners, growers, sow and boar) are (intended to be) exchanged or sold, to the market. This could be to a middleman, to an organisation (such as a slaughter house or supermarket chain) or to another farmer for other agricultural goods.

However, if your pig farm activity meets these criteria then your pig farm is a business and if it is a business it should be run and managed as such and all the rules of business and economy should be applied to your farm as much as they do to any other business for it to be a successful business.

Pork Joint in Ghana

What is entrepreneurship?

Entrepreneurship is a key factor for the survival of commercial farming in an ever-changing and increasingly complex global economy.

An entrepreneur is someone who produces for the market. An entrepreneur is a determined and creative leader, always looking for opportunities to improve and expand his business.

As an entrepreneurial pig farmer, you should see your farm as a business and as a means of earning profits. You should be passionate about your farm business and be willing to take calculated risks to make your farm profitable and your business grow and assume responsibility for both profits and losses.

As a farmer, you operate in a complex and dynamic environment and you are part of a larger collection of people including other farmers, suppliers, traders, transporters, processors and many others that supply the much-needed food to the African populace. Each of you has a role to play in producing pigs and moving them through to the market — through the market chain.

To be successful as an entrepreneur, you need to be technically competent, innovative and be able to plan ahead and have an organisation structure that could steer your farm business through the stages of enterprise development — from establishment and survival to rapid growth and maturity.

11.1 ORGANISATIONAL STRUCTURE

Organisational structures exist primarily to handle legal and accounting obligations. You will need a clean, carefully organized account book to present to banks, potential investors and inland revenue. A business structure is the foundation of your business plan.

Before you consider the business structure to select for your farming business, you need to consider the following:

1. Will your farm be for-profit or not for profit?

2. Will you have partners?

3. How many, and how will the responsibility and profit be split?

4. How many employees will your farm require to run the farm?

Sole proprietorship

You can operate your pig farm business as a Sole Proprietorship.

A sole proprietorship is a person trading on their own. That means that you control, manage, and own the business and as a result you are personally entitled to all profits and liable for all business taxes and debts. Sole proprietorship allows you to start the business without following many formal or legal processes to establish it. You can also employ other people to help run the business.

The advantages of operating your business as a sole proprietorship are:

1. The owner has full control over the business for daily operations as well as how large they wish to grow the farm.

2. Fewer reporting requirements — sole proprietors do not need to complete many of the forms and accounting information that limited companies need to produce.

3. As there are fewer paid staff on hand, the owner also takes all of the profits made by the business.

4. All financial information is kept private.

5. Decision making is also fast as it's just the owner who decides where the business is heading and whether or not to expand the farm or not. You retain complete control of your assets and business decisions.

6. It is a simple setup as you only need to declare to yourself that you are going to be a business and it is also relatively easy to expand the legal structure if the business grows, or if you wish to wind things up.

The disadvantages of sole proprietorships are:

1. Unlimited liability which means all your personal assets are at risk if things go wrong, any losses incurred and may have to offset such losses against other income earned (such as your investment income or wages).

2. The negative aspects of operating on your own are that everyone else perceives you as "small" which may make it difficult to bid and accept larger supplier contract from the government.

3. Fewer staff to delegate to if you have an accident or fall ill.

4. It's usually difficult to scale a business to a large commercial size on your own.

5. it is also harder to raise capital when you are alone.

6. You have to buy-in knowledge and expertise if you don't have it yourself.

Partnerships

In a partnership, two or more people run a business together. Each partner shares responsibility for running the business, shares in any profit or loss equally, unless the partnership agreement states otherwise, and is liable for any debt within the partnership. A partnership is relatively inexpensive to set up and operate but it is highly recommended that you establish your partnership with a formal written partnership agreement.

The advantage of a partnership:

- It is easier to raise the start-up capital, as all the partners will contribute towards the start-up capital.

- If 2 or more of the partners are actively involved in the business, there will be an advantage of skills diversification, whereby one might have experience in the pig business, and the other experience with marketing issues, etc.

- The combined skills, experience and knowledge can provide better products and service in the business.

- You can also consider a partnership for example if you are based outside of your home country — a diaspora or you are in permanent employment and you find someone in your home country or who is fully available who has the expertise to run the farm on your behalf.

- There is an increased ability to raise funds when there is more than one owner

The disadvantages of a partnership include:

- Potential for disputes over the future direction of the business, maximising opportunities, administrative control and over profit-sharing.

- There is a high chance of conflict of interest, especially if the business grew from sole proprietor to partnership, especially with the goal of the founder of the company and the partners who brought in capital to the business.

- Another disadvantage is joint and several liability of partners, which means that each partner is fully responsible for debts and liabilities incurred by other partners — with or without their knowledge.

- Changes of ownership can be difficult and generally require a new partnership to be established.

- Partnerships can potentially be unstable because of the danger of dissolution or too many cooks spoiling the broth.

Company

A company exists as a formal and legal entity in its own right. It is separate from its shareholder(s) or owner(s). It's responsible in its own right for everything it does and its finances are separate to your personal finances. Any profit it makes is owned by the company, after it pays Corporation Tax. The company can then share its profits. It will have to be registered at the Registrar of Companies. A company is a complex business structure, with higher set-up costs and administrative costs because of additional reporting requirements.

The advantages of registering your business as a company include:

- Shareholders are not personally liable for the debts of the corporation. If the corporation fails, shareholders may lose their investments in the corporation, but are not personally responsible for the corporation's debts.

- There is a pooling of capital from many investors and it is therefore easier to get the business up and running.

- It is also easy to sell and pass on ownership.

- A company will require you to open a bank account, and as a registered company you will then have access to loans and credit facilities for your business.

- Operating as a company increases trading confidence and credibility.

- Customers and suppliers will feel more confident and comfortable doing business with you.

The disadvantages include:

- Shareholders that control and own a significant amount, or majority, of the corporation's voting stock have a dominant voice in the management of the business in comparison to shareholders that do not own as much stock.

- Too many shareholders might also dilute the original goal of the business.

- Significant set-up costs and maintenance costs.

- Complex reporting requirements and company can't distribute losses to its shareholders.

We will recommend that you start your pig farm business simple, as a Sole Proprietorship.

A sole proprietorship is the most straightforward option for starting a farm business as quickly as possible. After forming the legal documentation for the proprietorship, you can then seek a registration, the second big step toward being recognized as a business. After you have those two steps covered, you can then approach a bank and open your first business account.

Even if you are concerned that a sole proprietorship won't offer enough options, you can always expand your business structure to a more complex option down the line with only a little additional work.

11.2 YOUR FARM ORGANISATION STRUCTURE

Organizational structure is important for any business that intends to grow and expand into a commercial business. Your farm organisation structure will provide guidance and clarity on the chain of command. Even though your pig farm is just starting, you must begin to think about a formal structure early in the growth stage of your business.

Your organizational structure will also provide guidance to all your staff employees by laying out the official reporting relationships that govern the workflow of the organisation. A formal outline of an organisational structure will make it easier for you to add a new post in the organisation, as well, providing a flexible and ready means for growth.

The structure you choose will depend on the size of your business, along with your personal circumstances and how much you want to grow the business.

We will recommend that at the beginning of your pig farm, you start with a simple organisation structure. This structure centralizes decision-making with the owner.

From our experience, this is how we saw many organisation structure evolved within many small farms that we have helped establish.

At the first stage, the farm might be a one-man operation, where the owner does all the activity especially the initial planning e.g. preparing or commissioning a business plan, source the farmland and sourcing the initial fund for the project.

Owner – Manager - Worker

Then the farm proceeds into the second stage where there is separation of management and non-management functions. Subordinates are hired to do some of the manual and/or mental activities while the owner manages the strategic aspect of the business.

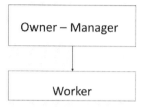

The farm then progresses into the third stage, which is the separation of ownership and management functions; The owner begins to relinquish the responsibilities for the day to day running of the business activities to a professional manager

The manager reports to you and delegates tasks to individual employees. By delegating managerial responsibilities to the manager, the owner can focus on larger goals. Meanwhile, as employees grow more skilled and knowledgeable in performing specific functions, you might decide to give some staff more responsibility to manage the farm's marketing, production, accounting, sales, etc.

A simple organizational structure enables a business owner to have tight control over his organisation's operation. No decisions are made without his approval, and he is aware of every important decision made. There is no hesitation on the part of employees in a simple structure because their orders come directly from the top.

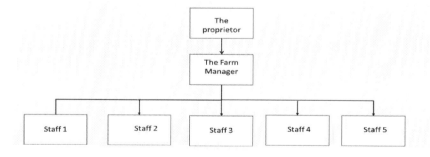

11.3 MAIN ROLE OF THE PROPRIETOR

Your role as the proprietor is to direct, fund and control the farm's operations and to give strategic guidance and ensure that the farm achieves its mission and objectives.

Main responsibilities

- Prepare or commission a business plan and monitor progress of the farm against these plans to ensure that the farm attains its objectives as cost-effectively and efficiently as possible.

- Source, direct and control the work and resources of the company.

- Ensure the recruitment and retention of the right staff numbers

- Motivate, train and develop staff to ensure that they achieve the farm's mission and objectives.

- Establish and maintain effective formal and informal links with major customers.

- Develop and maintain research and development programmes to ensure that the farm remains at the forefront in the industry.

- Prepare and monitor the implementation of the annual budget to ensure that budget targets are met, that revenue flows are maximised and that fixed costs are minimised.

- Develop and maintain an effective marketing and public relations strategy to promote the products and image of the company in the wider community.

- Prepare, examine, and analyse accounting records, financial statements, and other financial reports to assess accuracy, completeness, and conformance to reporting and procedural standards.

- Represent the company in the media and in negotiations with customers, suppliers, government departments and other key contacts to secure for it the most effective contract terms.

11.4 MANAGER

At least one person will act as the manger to run the day to day of the business. The duties will include:

- Supervises and coordinates activities of all the staff, assigns workers to duties

- Directs maintenance and repair of facilities and equipment at the farm

- Trains new workers

- Make day-to-day operational decisions

- Source of feed ingredients and transporting them to the farm

- Ensure the proper hygiene of the farm and the health of their animals through medication protocols

- Responsible for marketing animals and transporting stock to farms or processing plants

- Checking for proper ventilation and temperature conditions of the pens

- Analyse business operations, trends, costs, revenues, financial commitments, and obligations, to project future revenues and expenses or to provide advice

- Develop, maintain, and analyse budgets, preparing periodic reports that compare budgeted costs to actual costs

11.5 PIG TECHNICIAN

The number of pig keepers needed will depend on the scale of the operation. These workers will be responsible for taking good care of the pigs and their environment.

The duties will include:

- Compound and distribute feed to the pigs

- Wash, clean and disinfect the pig pen, footdip and surroundings

- Monitoring the health of the pigs

- Detect sow's heat and arrange the mating of pigs

- Assist in administering medication

- Observe animals for signs of illness

- Assist with problem births

- Perform facility maintenance

- Coordinate waste removal

- Miscellaneous chores which include medicating, repairing equipment, mowing grass, removing caked litter

Picture of participants learning basic pig farm routine

11.6 DOES YOUR STAFF ATTITUDE AFFECT YOUR PIG PRODUCTION?

Lots of work was done by Paul Hemsworth and Temple Grandin in the pig behavioural field. Both researchers have spent much of their lives studying staff/pig interrelationships and have tried to measure scientifically the effect of good staff on pig performance.

Paul Hemsworth has scientifically quantified the impact of pleasant treatment of pigs by staff e.g. (gentle manner, soothing voice, slow approach) and he compared it to adverse` handling of pigs by another group of staff e.g. (noisy, rapid approach, abrupt movements, use of sticks or electric goads) and how this effects performance of both growing pigs and breeding females.

According to his research, growers can experience daily gain of up to an additional 8% and breeding gilts can increase their conception rate by as much as 50% due to good staff handling.

Hemsworth's "approach test" measurements of Tender Loving Care were made from how long it takes a pig to approach staff standing still in a pen with whom they are familiar, (or are fearful of), compared to a person who is new to them. Naturally, pigs should move quickly towards staff that treat them well e.g. give them feed and clean their pen than towards a complete stranger. The research shows that some staff behaviour to pigs is so bad that the pigs that they were supposedly in charge of daily took twice as long to 14 times to come to them compared to a stranger. Some were even fearful to approach the staff at all.

This approach response is particularly important in a one-on-one situation such as around mating time when staff need to take a sow or gilt to a boar or during farrowing when staff need to stay close to a farrowing sow and even pick up her piglets and position the piglets on the nipple.

The following conclusions were made from this pig behavioural work:

- Human behaviour does have a significant effect on the productivity of both growers and breeding stock.

- Staff who maximize the number of physical actions of a positive nature (pats, strokes, tone of voice, gentle movement among, and allowing the pigs to sniff them regularly) are likely to improve their productivity considerably.

- Managers should regularly monitor the level of fear in their animals to staff by the individual responses to the 'approach test'.

- In situations where the level of fear is high or is increasing, the attendant should re-assess his/her behaviour when near to the pigs.

- Good approach test results pay dividends to farms especially when handling pigs (i.e. attending to sows gently at breeding or attending to gilts around service — and also farrowing, is beneficial in terms of conception rate and latterly more piglets weaned.

- Sticking to a time routine. All animals habituate and follow their expectations as to when things ought to happen to lower stress, i.e. feed at the same time in the morning, afternoon and evening.

- Our experience shows that most staff are sympathetic and caring around farrowing and after, because they are well aware of the trauma involved during this farrowing, but they are sometimes less caring during the mating stage. By rushing the mating process, they unconsciously intimidate the boar and the unsympathetic handling of the sow or gilt.

- More patience is required from staff when the female starts to ovulate, accepts insemination and needs to implant the results. Any rush during this time can cause lots of stress to the pigs and interrupt all the delicate hormonal balances

- Staff need to be trained and regularly briefed on how critical and important this period is and their need to handle and look after the sow in a gentle, 'friendly' manner. Failure to do this well will impact on their overall work and the profitability of the farm.

11.7 THE IMPORTANCE OF THE ROLE OF GOOD STAFF

The success of your farm depends a lot upon the selection and motivation of the staff that are working on your farm.

For small farms of less than 50 pigs, the owner and his family can provide the labour. And because of their vested interests in the business, a farmer and his family will be highly motivated to ensure that work gets accomplished in a timely and effective manner. But for a commercial pig production where the staff are not the owners of the farm, your work as the owner or manager is not only about managing pigs but is as equally important about managing people. As your farm grows in size, you will have to depend on more and more outside labour.

Research has shown that farms that are highly successful do have a good management structure and rapport between pig people and pigs. People management in all aspects of pig farming is probably the most crucial part of successful pig farming. Most of the time, if there is a problem of production or disease, it usually arises from bad management decisions, bad attitude from staff and their implications.

This is why as the owner you should do whatever you can to keep your most experienced staff, especially those that have worked with you and your pigs over time.

Pig staff are usually one of two types: (1) non-experienced but thought to be motivated to do their job (e.g., new employees) or (2) experienced but unable to take on the responsibility of doing more technical jobs (established employees).

11.8 HOW MANY STAFF DO YOU NEED ON YOUR FARM?

The number of people that you need on your farm varies depending on these factors:

a. Farms that have more task automation will require fewer people than those with little automation. For examples, if you use a power washer to wash the pig cells as opposed to using pan and brush or if you have a feed mixer machine to compound and mix your feed ingredients, as opposed to using manual compounding of spade and broom.

b. The scope of the responsibilities of farm staff also influences the level of staff needed. For example, if you are buying concentrate and bringing it to the farm, then you will need fewer staff but if you are buying individual ingredients (about 10 different ingredients) and are having to measure each ingredient and mix it together to compound feed tonnes of feed for hundreds of pigs, you will require more staff

c. Work schedules of the farm often vary in the amount of staff they require. Schedules such as 5-day shift and 2 off will require a higher staffing rate than 11 day on / 3 off schedules.

d. If the farm employee turnover rates are high, that means the farm will have fewer trained and experienced staff and, subsequently, with less efficient staff, more staff is required.

e. How well the daily work is scheduled for the farm staff are planned and thought through, for example, if farm works starts at 7am, cleaning and feeding of pigs will have finished by 11am, allowing the staff to take a break when it is getting hot in the day. They can then jointly compound feed in the afternoon.

f. The more educated and skilful your staff is will determine the number of staff you require on your farm.

g. The more non-production work required of your staff (e.g., marketing, meetings, report preparation), the more service staff is also required.

11.9 HOW TO RECRUIT THE RIGHT PEOPLE

Hiring the wrong people on your farm will not only result in high employee turnover, but it also results in lower pig productivity, employee dissatisfaction, and higher labour costs.

Advertisements in a chat room or verbally asking your neighbour if they have anybody for farm work is not enough. I once challenged a farm owner when he casually employed two farm attendant to start his new farm. Someone he does not know and without going through the proper recruiting channel of interview, references and guarantor. I asked him how much he bought his vehicle jeep (which looks new) for, he said N5m ($15,000) I asked him that if he needs a driver for his vehicle will he just call any male passing by and hand him the vehicle key without asking for his driver's license, reference and guarantor, he said never. I then asked him why he was able to handover the farm that he built with over N12m ($35,000), to people that he has never met before and he only asked the new staff member two questions and recruited him.

As a proprietor of a farm, you need to take more proactive steps to recruit new employees e.g. by visiting colleges of agriculture or those that have at least gone for some agriculture training. Candidates that have just graduated from colleges of agriculture or finishing training are definitely keen on working on the farm and are also easier to hire without exceeding labour budgets.

However, there is a saying a that "a bird at hand, is better than a thousand in the wild". If you manage your existing staff very well, they can become your best recruiters for the farm. As much as possible, where possible, your staff should be given incentives to actively participate in the recruitment of new staff. Having a fully staffed farm with people who enjoy working together can sometimes be adequate incentive to attract new quality staff. You can also offer financial incentives to staff for the identification of candidates who are eventually hired and who remain an employee for six months.

11.10 RETENTION OF STAFF

Many pig farms experience annual employee turnover rates in excess of 90% per year. Several studies have shown that the first 90 days of employment are key, not only to the effectiveness of new staff but also to reduce employee turnover. The first 90 days is often the period in which employees set their work habits and expectations, whether good or bad.

New staff must be formally inducted to your farm and trained in the jobs that they will be doing and they should be retrained even if they have years of experience in other farms. Responsibilities and expectations should also be clearly defined at the onset of employment. Attempts should be made by the farm management to meet the personal needs of newly hired staff (e.g., initial feeding and transportation before the first salary and if they are living on your farm provide comfortable farmhouse and beddings, equipment, clothing).

Fundamental needs of the staff

According to Maslow, hierarchy of needs is based on the fact that individuals' most basic needs must be met before they become motivated to achieve higher level needs and strive for constant betterment. The basic four layers of the pyramid contain what Maslow called "deficiency needs" or "d-eeds": physical needs, security and friendship. If these "deficiency needs" are not met, the individual will feel tense and might not give the best on your farm. However, if these basic levels of needs are met the individual is then motivated to proceed to the secondary or higher-level needs.

To satisfy basic biological needs

Farm owner should endeavour to provide for their staff an acceptable standard of living at work, for example, a decent staff house, an adequate wage (national minimum wage is a good measurement) and fair distribution of work. Farm owner should also make sure that the staff feel safe in the environment from predators such as snakes and also protected from attack and armed robbery. Improve the sense of belonging, by providing work overalls and uniform with the farm logo for staff. If the farm is remote in Africa, a form of electricity (solar panel or generator) for your staff to charge their mobile phone and visit social media on their phone will go a long way in retaining youth to your farm. A sense of belonging is a motivating factor and worth the little extra it costs.

To be in a secure position

Satisfaction of the biological needs leads to the second requirement, that of security in the position of good employment. With the high level of youth unemployment in Africa, the qualification of most of our farm workers will range from secondary school certificate through to new university graduates. How you deal with these group of people is different, those that are lowly qualified will usually seek reassurance about their job, they will rarely take risks and if treated well their retention rate can be high. Those that are graduates will need to see that there are opportunities for them to grow within the organisation. Give such people more responsibility for a job and allow them to develop their own initiatives and thereby move into more challenging roles.

Have job descriptions and even an 'employee handbook' to cover aspects of farm routine, health and safety, emergency drill and general instruction and guidance outside the more personal aspects of a job description list.

To belong to the business

Through education, training and friendships teamwork develops, where people are free to make suggestions and are listened to by their manager or the proprietor, they become motivated in their job. I had a first-hand example of this on my farm. We used to clip piglets teeth on day 1 after farrowing according to the piggery textbook. However, one of my staff noticed that piglets that we clipped so early were not growing as well as those we clipped 3 days after birth. He brought this to my attention and after witnessing the process and analysing the effect of the early clipping on the piglets, I moved the clipping day to the 3rd day because suckling colostrum for the first 3 days after farrowing is more important than clipping. The staff was so motivated that I followed up his observation to make a complete change on the farm processes.

From friendship and sense of belonging comes achievement. A sense of achievement on the pig farm involves recognition by senior management and in the process builds self-esteem.

To become confident

It is through the development of a sense of achievement that your staff will develop confidence in their jobs and direct and help others. This is the point at which efficiency across the farm will improve considerably.

Make sure you have a planned training schedule. This can be carried out by a good pig farm consultant who knows your farm and its staff.

To develop new skills

The final and ultimate part of the process is where the confidence reaches a level such that through further education and application, new skills can take place. A typical example of this on my farm was when this guy that brought the teeth clipping issues that I mentioned earlier was promoted to supervisor. This is the ultimate goal of the education process throughout the farm, though of course, the pathways upwards will be limited by the capabilities of each individual and the size of the farm.

Supervision

If you want workers to do things your way, you must inspect their work. People need to know that they are important and that what they do is important to support the leadership and company in achieving desired results.

Let them know you are monitoring what they are doing. Remember, a blend of the "carrot" with the "stick" will be necessary for motivating employees. Too much of either is not effective.

Carrots include: financial remuneration (base pay and bonuses), benefits, days off, work schedule, public recognition and praise.

Sticks include: verbal and written warnings, disqualification for bonuses, salaried staff being forced to work additional time to get their work done, and not giving annual merit increases in base pay.

11.11 HOW TO IMPROVE YOUR STAFF MOTIVATION ON YOUR FARM

According to Herzberg's' Motivators and Hygiene theory, factors leading to job satisfaction in an organisation are "separate and distinct from those that lead to job dissatisfaction. Therefore, if you only set about eliminating dissatisfying job factors among your already demotivated employee, you may create peace but not necessarily enhance your staff performance at work.

To apply Herzberg's' Motivators and Hygiene Factors, you will need to adopt a two-stage process to motivate people. Firstly, you need to eliminate the dissatisfaction that your staff are experiencing, these are called the "hygiene factors." You can do this by creating and supporting a culture of respect and dignity for all team members, provide effective, supportive and non-intrusive supervision to your staff, ensure that wages are competitive and fair and where possible provide job security for your staff. All of these actions will help the farm to eliminate job dissatisfaction. However, you cannot stop at just eliminating the job dissatisfaction in a demotivated staff, the fact that someone is not dissatisfied, does not automatically translate to being satisfied.

As the employee, you need to take the second step by turning your attention to building job satisfaction. To achieve job satisfaction among your worker, Herzberg reckons that you need to address the motivating factors associated with work. He called this "job enrichment." This include, things like recognizing people's contributions to the farm, providing opportunities for achievement, creating work that is rewarding and that matches people's skills and abilities, offering training and development opportunities, so that people can pursue the positions they want within the company and providing opportunities to advance in the company through internal promotions.

11.12 TOPICS THAT SHOULD BE CONSIDERED IN THE BASIC TRAINING PROGRAMME

As mentioned earlier, your farm should have a planned training schedule. A veterinarian or a good pig farm consultant who knows your farm and its staff can be called in to train your group of staff on best practices or be invited periodically to watch how your staff are carrying out their task and identify learning opportunities.

Basic training

- Technical pig production terminologies and their meaning.

- Aspects of health and safety on a pig farm.

- Management of:

  ▪ Boars and Dry sows.

  ▪ Farrowing houses.

  ▪ Weaner production.

  ▪ Feeder pig production.

  ▪ The sick bay.

  ▪ Understanding reproduction.

- Recording and the use of records.

- Recognising the healthy and diseased pig.

- The disposal of dead stock.

- The storing of medicines on the farm.

- The administration of medicines on the farm.

- Nutrition and the application of feed.

- Slurry disposal.

- Cleaning, washing of pen with soap and disinfectant.

- Managing the gilt.

- Understanding simple pig production economics.

And also, within each section of your farm, there might be a need for specific and targeted training to improve the performance. For example, in the farrowing house, here is a list of all the various tasks that need to be executed well to get better results:

- Preparing the house for sow or gilt occupancy.

- Recording farrowing details.

- Preparing the sow for farrowing.

- The signs of farrowing.

- How to assist at farrowing.

- Removing teeth and tails.

- Injecting with iron.

- Managing the litter.

- Recognising disease.

- Recognising piglet diseases.

- Assessing the healthy and diseased udder.

- Castration.

- Feeding the sow.

- Moving the sow.

- Catching the litter in preparation for tasks.

Intermediate training

Training on a pig farm should be ongoing to improve staff performance.

Here is some intermediate training aimed at the supervisor or a trainee manager.

This can be carried out either on the farm or alternatively by the development of seminars at the veterinary practice or at the agriculture schools. The following topics should form part of the senior staff training programme:

- Understanding infectious agents.
- Anatomy of the pig.
- The use and misuse of medicines.
- How diseases are spread.
- The healthy and the diseased pig.
- The collection, understanding and use of records.
- The relevance of disease control to profitable pig farming.
- Understanding reproduction in the male.
- Understanding reproduction in the female.
- Non- infectious infertility.
- Infectious infertility.
- The process of farrowing.
- Approaching farm problems.
- Aspects of vaccination.
- Welfare of the pig.
- Notifiable diseases.

- Respiratory diseases.

- Problems of the dry sow.

- Nutrition, production and disease.

- Controlling parasites.

12. Where to locate your pig Farm

A farm is a piece of land on which a farmer undertakes agricultural activities as part of its livelihood. And as in any Land or Real Estate enterprise, location is important.

"It is Location! Location!! Location!!!".

Acquiring your farm is one of the most critical farming steps that you will need to take as a farmer and one of those that is very difficult to correct once you have invested in construction and infrastructures on the land, so you must think very carefully before you buy your farmland and start investing on it. A common mistake that many new farmers make is to buy a farmland and then ask, "What can I produce on it?".

This can be described as "putting the cart before the horse", i.e. starting your farm in a way that is contrary to a conventional expected order.

Ultimately where you choose to locate your farm is a very personal question. However, there are many factors that you need to consider when choosing a farm or farmland. This section should give you enough information on factors that you need to take into consideration when locating your farm.

12.1 PROXIMITY AND FAMILIARITY

In general, you will want your pig farm to be located in a place that is easily accessible to either your work or your house. It should not be too far so that you can visit the farm regularly. We have talked earlier about the challenges of absentee farmers. A good pig farmer should visit his pig farm regularly, even if you have a manager or veterinarian running the day to day of the farm. You must be able to visit your pig farm at least 3 to 4 times a week announced and unannounced.

The more you visit your farm, the more you will know about what is going on in your farm, and the quicker you can detect problems on the farm. Don't forget as the proprietor, you have more to lose than anybody else for any mistakes made on your farm. From my farming experience, I will recommend that the farm should not be more than 45 minutes to an hour drive to the location where the owner either works or resides.

Secondly, it is also wise to choose a place that you are familiar at least a bit with the culture and language. Using an interpreter at all times is costly and may lead to confusion and misunderstanding. You will also avoid costly mistakes due to ignorance of the peculiarities and nuances of the different culture or language.

Thirdly, chose the land in the climatic region with which you are already familiar with and is most suitable for your pig farming, for example you cannot do pig farm on swampy or water-logged soil land.

12.2 ACCESSIBILITY AND GOOD NEIGHBOURLINESS

Your farm should have access to an approachable good road and it should be accessible to both the pig market or the feed suppliers. I will recommend that your site be no farther than 1km from the main or tarred road. Actually, the closer your farm is to a good road, the better it is. In sub-Sahara Africa, most of the roads leading to the village and rural roads are not tarred and some of them are also poorly constructed.

It is advisable for you to look out for the streams and the rivers that cross the road on the way to your farm. During the dry season they may look small or dry but during the rainy season it is easy for a simple flowing stream in the dry season to suddenly overflow its bank and break bridges during heavy rain, thereby making your farm inaccessible for days. Most of the bridges built across the streams or rivers on the rural road are usually not strong enough to withstand the weight of the trucks that will be bringing feed regularly to the farm and loading the fattened pigs to the market.

Generally, farms that are farther from the main road are cheaper than those that are closer to the main road. If you have to buy a farm that is farther than 1km to the main road, we would advise that you should check this route during the rainy season to make sure it is accessible all year round.

Try and avoid been a loner. You are more likely to succeed where the land that you prefer has few pig farms in the neighbourhood and an already well-established market because such a locality has already been proved favourable in terms of access to either market or raw material. You will also have neighbours who could help and advise you, and you will also find experienced labour easily.

However, your pig farm must be at least 250 meters away from another pig farm site to prevent the spread of airborne diseases to your farm.

A friendly neighbourhood is very important, especially in sub-Sahara Africa where there is a high Muslim population, your neighbours do not have to like or eat pigs but they must not be against pig farming.

In summary, proximity to the market and access to good roads, good neighbours, roads, electric power and telephone connection are important. If possible, choose a property in town where pig farming or market is already well established than elsewhere because such locality has already been proved favourable for feed, labour and expertise like a veterinarian.

Too much caution cannot be used in selecting farm location, as mistakes in this matter are often the sole cause of the want of success for some farmers, even when other conditions are favourable.

12.3 SIZE OF LAND

Just one acre of land would be enough for an intensive piggery of 1000 or more pigs but if you are just starting small you can use the space at your backyard for 20 weaners and be ready to move to a bigger farm as your volume of pigs increases.

Farming visions, goals and preferences do change over time, so you need to make sure that the land that you select offers an appropriate degree of flexibility. Having 1 to 2 acres or more for a commercial pig farm will give you enough space to accommodate your waste without becoming a public health risk and will also allow future expansion.

Try and have your pig farm in one location; managing farms from two different locations is not for the faint hearted, it will stretch your time energy, wear and tear and resources.

While talking about size, it is important to point out that buying too many acres of land that you are not planning to use for a long time, even when it looks cheap may also not be commercially wise, it is literally tying your much-needed capital for your pig farm down. Any additional land that you bought without a clear plan of usages may become a liability instead of an asset. Like lots of new farmers, I made this mistake of buying 105 acres of land thinking that I can find a use or sell the excess land later, only to discover that the excess land was just growing bushes and woods and luring wild animal and predators like snakes and wild cat closer to my pig farm. There is also the issue of land encroachment, especially in Africa where most lands are owned by a landowner with many children.

In terms of how much to spend on buying your farm, this depends on the area you are, however, good location is very important. An acre of land in a good location may cost you between $1,500 to $2,000 per acre in Nigeria depending on the location, proximity to road, to good road network, market and feed supplier. Such land may be much better than another farm of equal size purchasable at $1,000 per acre, of which large areas are practically useless owing to streams, rocky swamps which cannot be drained, or rough stony areas not suitable for raising pigs.

In conclusion, when choosing the size of a pig farm, it is essential that you buy not the total area of the land that the owner wanted to sell or that is available but the area that you need for profitable use. This may range from just having a pig farm to having an integrated pig farm with arable farming and plantation, etc.

12.4 AVOID MEDIUM OR HIGH-DENSITY AREAS

With the speed of growth and urbanisation in most African towns, it is important that you avoid buying farmland that is situated within medium to high density areas, i.e. too close to a residential area. Such land has the potential of becoming urbanised within a short time. With my experience as a consultant, who has helped lots of new farmers to set up pig farms across Africa, I have seen many farmlands in supposedly medium density area that were rapidly surrounded by real estate and residential properties, within one year of opening up the road, construction and starting commercial pig farm operation. The price of land in the area also skyrocketed as a consequence.

A well-managed pig farm has the potential of expanding very quickly in pig volume and with this comes more pig waste. Pigs produce lots of waste, about 3 litres of waste a day from faeces, excreta and from the washing of the pen, not only that your farm of 86 pigs can easily expand to over 800 pigs within a year and along with this is a tenfold increase in volume of waste produced daily. If the waste is not properly managed and disposed of, you may soon start receiving lots of complaints from public health officials and protests from your neighbours because of the smell and noise that your piggery is producing.

We recommend that you buy 1 to 2 acres of farmland. Such a landmass will give you the opportunity to deal with your waste within your farm. You will also be able to compost and divert some of the waste to your arable farm that supports the farm.

12.5 HOUSING

The shelter that you build for your pigs is known as a pig pen; the individual rooms within the pen are called a pig cell. Your pen should keep your pigs safe from the elements such as weather and other diseases or contamination. You may build your pen with wood, iron or concrete depending on which one you prefer and the most affordable in your locality. When constructing your pig pen, you should build a proper drainage system for your pigs where all the waste will pass through.

A typical pig pen

Selection of housing locations

While the size of your farm may be big, it is important that you carefully select the location and the space where you are going to build your pig pen on your farmland. Pig houses do cost lots of money, and once constructed, it is difficult to move.

a. The site that you choose for your pig farm should be at least 500 meters away from the residential house to avoid creating a nuisance from odour and flies.

b. Your pig pen should well-connected to good roads throughout the year; this will improve marketing as a buyer will find your farm accessible and easy to find.

c. Your pig pen should be away from areas where there are lots of noise and where traffic is high, so as not to cause stress for your pigs.

d. The site should be at an elevated place that cannot be flooded by rainwater.

e. The site should be dry and well-drained; the building should be on a slight slope to facilitate drainage and disposal of effluent.

f. The slope also makes it easier to design a pig flow with the farrowing house at the top of the slope and the fattening pens at the lower end. This prevents cross-infection from effluent between piglets and the adult pigs.

g. The house should be well ventilated, easy to clean and allow plenty of sunshine.

h. The area must have access to a source of clean water — pigs consume 2 gallons of water a day and you will require three times of that volume to clean their pen daily.

i. The site should be protected from the extreme sun rays, rains, and wind draught.

j. Large evergreen trees like Plantain, Banana and Papaya should be planted around the house to serve as shade and as a wind breaker.

k. You might want to select an area in the middle of the land so that you can divert any waste as manure to the rest of the land that you are not using for pig farming.

l. Construction of pig houses should be with open sides, which may be screened or protected with iron protectors and should provide ample ventilation.

m. The house should be constructed in an area where it is easy to load outgoing pigs

n. The place must be accessible for the people working on the farm and must be in an area where it is easy to deliver incoming feed and other farm inputs.

o. The entrance to your pig farm must be fenced and gated, no animals or materials should be allowed to enter the pig farm unless absolutely necessary: this includes humans, especially the pig buyers. They might be infected with pathogens and diseases from other farms.

p. The pen area must have a foot dip at the entrance.

q. Siting should be done to avoid obstruction of air movement by other buildings.

12.6 ORIENTATION OF THE HOUSE

Ensure that the longest side of the building from the north to south allows sunlight in the pen evenly in the morning as well as in the afternoon. Sunlight helps to keep the floor dry; this also lowers the chance of disease build up on the farm.

12.7 SPACE

As we mentioned earlier, pigs need plenty of room to move, eat, sleep and defecate. Whilst it sometimes looks like pigs are only sleeping and eating, pigs do spend time wandering around their cell throughout the day. Pigs that are restricted to too small an area will tend to put on too much fat rather than meat and may express their confinement stress or boredom through their destructive to aggressive behaviour to your farm structure e.g. biting the blocks or digging the floor of the pen and to other pigs e.g. tail or ear biting.

Your pig cell should be big enough to let the pigs run for at least a few paces. This will help both in their exercise muscle (remember meat is muscle and muscles are heavier than fat) and space also give the pigs the ability to get away from each other during the fighting. Having space in the cells also allows pigs to wander around. You should also allow enough space for a bed area, a feeding area and a dunging area.

The recommended dimension for each cell below is calculated so as to allow each cell to accommodate the pig's growth up to the target weight. Inadequate floor space may lead to higher disease incidence and lower productivity.

Type of pig	Pen size	No. of pig per pen
Breeding boar	8ft by 10ft (72sq ft)	Single
Breeding sow/gilt	8ft by 9ft (72sq ft)	1 or 2
Pregnant sow (farrowing pen)	8ft by 9ft (72sq ft)	1
Weaners (1-3 months)	20ft by 15ft (300 sq ft)	In group 20 piglets
Growers (3-7 months)	20ft by 15ft (300 sq ft)	In group 20
Finishers (1-3 months)	20ft by 15ft (300 sq ft)	In group 20-15

12.8 CONSTRUCTION MATERIALS

Ideally, brick and concrete material should be used for the construction of a commercial pig pen. If you are starting small in your backyard, you can use a wooden wall for a temporary enclosure for piglets and weaners if it is cheaper in your locality but your adult pigs will test the strength of wooden walls as well as try to eat the wood, so we recommend that for adult pigs you should use something more substantial like brick or concrete material.

Floor and wall should be constructed with concrete. When making concrete for pig house, it is important that you use the correct concrete mixing ratios to produce a strong, durable concrete mix. To make concrete, there are four basic materials you will need, cement, sand, aggregate (stone), and water. The ratio of aggregate to sand to cement is an essential factor in determining the compressive strength of the concrete mixture. A concrete mixture ratio of one-part cement, three parts sand, and three parts gravel will produce a suitable concrete mix for the floor of your pen.

However, to reduce the overall cost of your construction, the roof should be made of locally available housing material like bamboo, jungle wood post, thatch, tree leaves (e.g. palm trees) tin plastic, etc.

Where available, thatch tree leaves are preferred for construction of the roof to maintain lower room temperature in the tropics, compared to an aluminium roof.

Make sure you manage your budget and do not overspend on construction, not at the expense of your operational cost such as piglets, feeds, medication, etc. These are more important components for running a productive farm.

12.9 **VENTILATION**

The building needs to be airy with plenty of ventilation. Pigs kept indoor in poor ventilation will become prone to disaster. Ventilation helps in keeping the cell dry. Ammonia is the most common poison in the pig's environment. Farmers should aim to improve the quality of air in pig pen to prevent the accumulation of ammonia by increasing the ventilation cell and the removal of urine and faeces daily. Your goal is to keep out drafts at the lower level of the cell (up to 3 feet in height or row of 4 coaches of standard blocks) but let air freely enter and leave the building above this height. Leave the top half of the pen open and use a perforated iron door that will allow wind to go circulate the cell. As long as the pigs can find a dry draft-free area away from the entrance, they will be happy. Also use wood shaving or straw as bedding to keep the pigs warm in the cold period.

Light

The construction of pig houses should be with open sides, which may be screened or protected with iron protectors. This should provide enough natural light. It has been proven that pigs raised in darker enclosures tend to suffer more from disease. Electric light should be considered to assist in feeding, monitoring, and keeping the pigs warm.

Water

Water can be provided through the borehole, well and municipal water. This should be stored in a tank that is taller than the pen to allow water to flow using gravitational force to get the water through the pipe to the water nipples. However, if you opt for the water trough, you need to consider the drainage, where the water will flow towards in relation to their bed area. The water trough also needs to be emptied and cleaned daily. As per nipple, adult pigs also tend to pull nipples and pipework off the wall; you need to consider an alternative source of water when this happens.

Feeding

Feeding provides the ideal opportunity to let the pig exhibit their foraging behaviour. You can actually train your pigs to eat and defecate at different sections within the cell. Naturally, when pigs want to defecate, they sniff around the cell for the area with the most stench and that is where they will defecate. That means that you can determine the defecating spot in the cell by making sure that on the first day of bringing the pig to their cell, you place their faeces on the spot where you want them to defecate and the feeding space should be adjacent to where they defecate.

Drainage system

A drain of about 1 foot wide and 0.5 feet depth should be constructed on the slope side of the floor. Two manure pits should be constructed for disposal of farm wastes and to convert them into farm manure. Drain should be gradually sloped towards the manure pit

If the pig farm is integrated with crops, the drain should be constructed in such a way that the farm waste flows to the crop field. Adequate care should be taken to drain the required quantity of farm waste to the crop field in an appropriate time.

The building should be built on a slight slope to allow drainage and disposal of effluent

12.10 THINGS TO CONSIDER FOR THE LAYOUT OF A PIG HOUSE

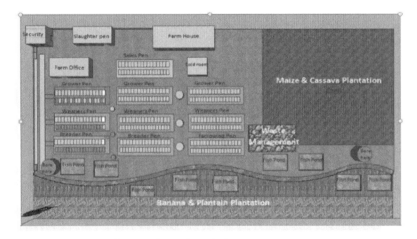

Picture of a typical pig farm design layout

- **Feeding arrangement:** the feed troughs and water containers must be positioned within each cell so that the attendant is able to place feed and water in each cell without needing to enter the pig cell.

- **Feed store**: the feed store should be located close to the pig pens as this will enable the attendant to supply the feed to the pigs without having to lift 25kg of feed over long distances. There must also be enough room to enable weighing of the feed.

- **Observation of animals:** The pen must be constructed in such a way that the farmer is able to observe all the pigs without entering the pen.

- **Access to pens**: Where many cells are constructed, each cell must have a door to the corridor so that the farmer can enter each pen without passing through another cell. The corridor in each pen should not be less than 3 feet so as to allow staff to push a wheelbarrow through the pen to each cell.

The roof

The most practical approach to roofing your pen is to use the same material that is commonly used for the local roofing in your area. Corrugated iron or aluminium sheets would last longer but might be more expensive. If possible, the roof should be constructed with its longest slope against the prevailing wind and rain.

If an opening has been left between the walls and the roof there should be sufficient outside overhang to prevent the rain entering. The roof should be tall to allow air to cool the pig pen.

The floors and bedding

The floor of the pen should be slightly raised above its sur-roundings to avoid flooding in wet weather. It is also advisable to slope the floor slightly. This will allow the liquid manure to run off more easily. If a drain is fixed at the lowest part of the run, the floor should slope slightly at least 5% for easy drain-age of urine and dung.

Concrete floor is preferred but it should not be too smooth to cause slip and fall of the pigs, and it should not be so rough that the animals can scratch themselves, especially the female breast while lying down.

The disadvantage with concrete is that it is a bad insulator, it is always colder than the ambient temperature. During hot weather, the adult animals can take advantage of this by ly-ing on the cold concrete to cool themselves down, but in cold weather too much body heat will be lost and the younger ani-mals will get too cold. In young animals, this increases the risk of diseases like pneumonia. The coldness of the concrete can be reduced by ensuring that the animals have bedding material in the pen like wood shavings on the cell floor.

Walls

In humid areas in the tropics, the height of the cell must be lowered a little for free circulation of air. The construction of the walls should take the regional climate into consideration. For pig farms in West Africa, the wall should be left as open as possible for good ventilation. A low wall approximately 1 metre in height will suffice, with an opening between the wall and the roof. The part above 1 meter may be covered with wire / bamboo netting to prevent crows and other predators.

In windy areas, the roof (or ceiling) should not be too high, otherwise the pen will cool down too quickly in the strong winds. Cement walls will be the most expensive, but they are stronger and last longer. If the supply of cement is limited, it should be used in priority for the floor.

Netted pig pen

In thick jungle or forest where there are lots of insects like Tsetse flies, netting of the pen might be necessary.

Feeding and water trough

In commercial pig farming, feeding and water trough are part of the floor plan. These are constructed on the floor adjacent to a wall. The feeding and water trough should be 1ft deep and 1.5 feet wide. The feeding trough should be longer and narrower than the water trough.

You may also use aluminium bowls for feed and water. As a low-cost measure, tyre, wooden block, concrete bowl, etc. can also be used as a feeding trough.

As a farmer, your planning must be based not only on the present but on the future of your farm. Below is other infrastructure that you may require for smooth running of your pig operation.

Office and Workers' Quarters

If the farm is in a remote place you will need to build a farmhouse for staff with showers, a kitchen, a canteen, and a recreation room as well as bedrooms. This will reduce your staff turnover and also increase the security of your farm.

Office — A commercial farm should have offices where clerks keep production and financial records, received visitors, dispensed medicines and therapeutic drugs, and operated their computers.

As a proprietor, you should have a comfortable office on your farm, where you can relax and be encouraged to stay for a longer time on your farm. In some parts of Africa, it might not be expedient for the proprietor to stay overnight on the farm because of poor security, but you should at least be able to spend more quality time on your farm during the day to observe the animal and to also go through the farm books so as to fully understand what is happening on your farm

The feedstore or mill — should be located within sight of the office and should be accessible for vehicles to get close enough and deliver feed. Most labour on a pig farm involves handling feed, and most of this feed is consumed by pigs. Therefore, the feed store should be located as close to the pig's pens and there should be a route for the wheelbarrow to take feed to and from the pen.

Source & storage of clean water– A sunk borehole is preferred or a drilled well that is capable of yielding good quality and quantity of water all year round. A pig consumes 2 gallons of water a day and about three gallons of water is required for the daily cleaning of the pig cell and the farm environment. Your farm must have at least a 2,000-litre water storage tank to guarantee regular supply of water.

13. Pig Production System

According to Adam Smith, in his text The Wealth of Nations (1776):

"Consumption is the sole end purpose of all production: and the interest of the producer ought to be for promoting that of the consumer."

Before you decide which pig breed or which pig type you are going to buy for your farm, you need to be very clear about the final products that you intend to produce on your farm, who is your target market and how will this produce meet the market needs.

As a farmer, marketing is not an activity that you should turn your attention to after you have produced pigs. Rather, it is important for you to start thinking about the customer and market demand from the time that you start thinking about your pig farm and set up your farm in accordance to the clear signals that is coming from the marketplace. This will increase your chances of succeeding in pig farming.

Marketing is an ongoing process of understanding your customer's/buyer's needs and striving to fulfil those needs better than your competition. Marketing is everything that happens before and after the sale that facilitates both current and future sales transactions with your customer/buyer.

One of the biggest mistakes that many new pig farmers made is to establish a farm and produce lots of pigs without researching if there is an actual market for them.

All the factors we mentioned so far in the book such as accessibility of your farm, i.e. good road system, proximity to the material does not only impact the production cost but also your speed of selling and the final price that you will sell your output.

In this chapter, we will look at how your final output to the customer will influence your production system.

13.1 PIG PRODUCTION CYCLE

Pigs breed at all times of the year so pig production is a continuous cycle.

1. The life cycle begins at birth event (farrowing), 8 to 12 piglets are born with each piglet weighing 1-4 kg.

2. The piglets remain with their mother for 6 to 8 weeks and are weaned by removing the sow from the pen.

3. The weaned piglets are fed formulated creep feed and are kept in weaner pens for an additional 30 to 60 days until their weight reaches 20 kg.

4. They are then moved into grower pens where they remain until they reach their market weight of 75-100 kg.

5. The life span of a finisher is anywhere from 6 to 8 months from birth to the abattoir. When slaughtered, the dress weight of a finisher weight is approximately 80% of live weight.

The main inputs in pig production are:

- Breeding stock (gilts, sows, and boars);

- Water for drinking and cleaning;

- Feed (grains, protein supplements, minerals, and vitamins);

- Preventive medicines and therapeutic drugs;

- Housing and material handling;

- Management and husbandry; and sanitation, disinfection, and waste removal.

- Waste removal.

Pig Production System

Ultimately, the pig production system that you decide to practice will determine the product that will be produced on your farm and the consequence marketing activities.

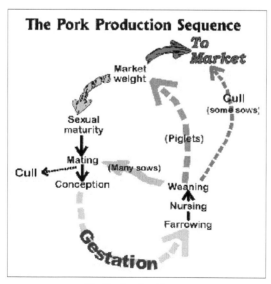

Pig Production System
Source: https://binged.it/31lLkPT

A farmer has 3 options:

1. **Farrow to Wean system** — i.e. Weaner production — this production system involves maintaining sets of breeder pigs, (boar, gilt and sow) that will be bred to produce piglets that will be sold at around eight weeks of age (see the light blue line in the above diagram).

2. **Fattener system** — i.e. finisher production — this involves purchasing pigs at a weaner stage from a reputable producer and then raised the weaners for 6 months to market weight (the pink line in the above diagram).

3. **Farrow to Finish system** — This is a comprehensive pig raising system in which piglets are born, weaned, grown and fattened in the one unit. Unlike other systems where piglets move to other operators at each major stage of their development, here they are grown until marketable slaughter weight at the same farm. The system involves marketing of pork or live pigs for slaughter to abattoirs (slaughtering houses).

As a pig farmer, you need to decide at the early stage of your planning which aspect of pig production system you want to focus on.

Let us look at the benefits, the challenges faced by each production system and the potential market. This is a very important decision as you will see later. Each production system has different requirements in terms of how much to invest in the construction of the farm, the expected operational cost and the kind of skills and expertise you need to operate each system effectively.

13.2 FARROW TO WEAN SYSTEM

If a farmer opts for this system, he will need to keep a set of good breeding stock of gilts, sow and boar that will regularly produce weaners to the market.

The farm that focusses on this type of pig rearing system alone are very few in Nigeria. On such farms, the gilts and sows are promptly mated by the boar or through artificial insemination and they are pregnant for four months after which they farrow piglets. These piglets are reared up to 6 to 8 weeks until they are weaned.

The final output of this type of farm are weaners and they are marketed to other farms. The output will attract formal markets such as non-government, commercial and government organisations working on poverty alleviation and agricultural development programs. And informal markets include new farmers who are stocking for the first time and those replacing their old/sold stock or poorly performing pigs on their farms. Such weaners are then raised into breeder pigs or fatteners.

This system is the best for experienced pig farmers with lots of expertise in pig breeding e.g. heat detection, mating and managing pig pregnancy but has limited finance and limited space to raise the weaner (or at least all the weaners) pigs to adulthood.

The farm will need to consistently follow good breeding practices in order to meet market requirements and keep good farm records, biosecurity and vaccination to gain market confidence. This is important because other farmers buying the weaner stocks are depending on them for good quality weaner stock.

Advantages:

- Requires relatively small capital inputs on construction in terms of space for keeping a large number of weaners and growers

- Requires relatively small capital inputs on feeding, piglets are sold long before they start consuming large quantity of feed

- Shorter production cycle — farmer can finish a cycle of production within 6 months (4 months pregnant and 2 months to weaning)

- Possible to generate a relatively consistent income — farmers do not need to wait for 11 months before selling (4 months of pregnancy and 7 months of fattening).

Disadvantages

- Requires greater technical and management skills and labour to handle potential problems — detecting heat, mating, managing pregnancy and farrowing is not for the faint hearted. Farmers operating this system need to be sound in boar, gilts and sow management.

- 40% of the mortality on pig farm happens in the first 8 weeks after farrowing.

- Disease & management problems such as the conception rate, embryonic survival, pre- and post-weaning survival rates, sow's feed intake, milk production, etc.

- Variations in the price of weaners, i.e. season to season — the demands are usually high after major festivities, for example, in January when most farms have sold their existing stocks and want to restock and replace the pig sold or slaughtered.

For your farm to be successful with this production system you will need the following:

a. A good reputation of consistently following good breeding practices in the market

b. Carry out research about the characteristics of your buyer and the attributes of pigs they seek after;

c. Consistently produce quality weaners that meet the demand of the locality

d. Please note, market for piglets is seasonal, so you will need to have plan B for raising the weaners that are not sold i.e. raise the weaners leftover to marketable slaughter weights;

e. Good marketing skills and enough knowledge about different pig breeds and their potential in terms of meat quality/quantity and litter size to meet buyer need;

f. It is important to note that every farmer buying from your farm for breeding is a potential future competitor.

g. Advertise your production plan to make buyers aware of when piglets will be available for bookings;

h. Register your farm and make available documents necessary, for example, good farm records that can trace the lineage of the breeder, receipts, invoices, quotations, etc.;

13.3 FATTENING

Fattening farms buy weaners from a reputable supplier for fattening and the farm do not keep any breeding stock.

This production system is also not popular in many African countries, but it might be the most appropriate if you are new to the pig production industry or you are a young person with limited fund. It involves purchasing weaners from a reputable breeder farm. You then house and feed them on your farm to the market weight and sell them off. And after the sales of that particular batch, you start another cycle of production by ordering another set of weaners to continue with your farming activities.

It does not involve keeping sows or boars for reproduction and totally avoids the need for greater technical and management skills and labour required to handle potential breeding challenges mentioned earlier.

However, fattening of pigs requires larger space on the farm to accommodate the growth of the weaners and growers, it also requires large sums of operating capital to feed the pigs to market weight. From weaner to grower each pig will consume approximately 250kg over 5 months costing $40 to $50 per pig.

The fattener's primary market is the live pig traders — the buyer usually come to the farm and buys live pigs. On most farm pigs are weighed and sold, payment is made at the farm gate for the whole pig and from the farmgate all risks are taken by the trader

Fatteners are also sold to abattoirs (slaughtering houses), in this case, pigs are usually transported by the farmer to the abattoirs, where pigs are weighed, slaughtered, and paid for against kilograms recorded. All risks (e.g., rejected carcasses due to health issues, death during transportation, etc.) are taken by the farmer.

Fattening production system is best suitable on farms where:

- There is shortage of skilful labour to manage the complexity of sow-herd management

- There is abundant space to accommodate weaners

- Pig feed ingredients are readily available and affordable for farmer e.g. close to food factory or the farm has large expanse of arable crop

- The operator has good connection with abattoir or slaughtering houses

- Have an adequate capital to prevent such losses and even sell on credit

- The operator is able to withstand periods of financial losses and ability to use various marketing techniques

- Operator is up to date with the meat industry and keeps up with the market.

Advantages:

- Rate of capital turn-over is relatively fast with fattening compared to farrow-finish operations. For example, with the breeder stock, the period from start-up to first sales is approximately 1 year, whereas fattening is only 4 to 6 months.

- Specialised labour not required e.g. detecting heat and farrowing and other demanding management needed by breeding herds and new-born pigs are not required with fattening.

- Requires less labour and management — two staff can handle 100 grower pigs

- Produces lots of pig waste that can be processed or used as a fertiliser.

- Has a flexibility to shut-down business at the end of each cycle — the cost for stopping a fattening operation is relatively smaller and the loss associated with shutting down is the cost of idle buildings and equipment. Unlike a sow-litter operation, which is more complicated.

Disadvantages:

- Significant expenses of regularly buying large quantity of pig's feed which accounts for over 80% of total production costs.

- Likely to stock poor quality pigs if pigs are purchased from different farms, which may lead to unknown health status, variations in growth performance and increase medication costs, biosecurity threat and high mortality rate.

- Lack of uniformity when you amass young pigs from various sources.

- The volatility in pig feed means that the profit is determined and highly influenced by current market prices. It may be at a loss if the feed prices go up and the selling price of pig remains stagnant.

- Supplier may become competitor, combine farrow to wean and to finish as a system type of choice due to the lack of market for their piglets.

13.4 FARROW TO FINISH

This is an encompassing pig raising system in which piglets are born, weaned, raised and fattened on your farm. Unlike other pig production systems, where piglets are moved from one operator to other operators during the different stage of their development. With farrow to finish system, pigs are grown on the same farm until they reach marketable slaughter weight.

The final output of the farm depends on the market, it could be marketed live pigs for slaughter to middle men, live pig traders and abattoirs (slaughtering houses) or weaners, gilts or boar to breeder farms.

Furthermore, a farmer can decide to operate a pork joint alongside the operation in order to sell their pork directly to consumers.

This system fits best for farms:

- In areas where market for pigs is not robust enough to specialise

- Where pig production is the sole enterprise of the farm and the owner is in the business for the long-term

- The farm has an adequate number of skilful labourers who can manage both the breeder pigs and the fatteners

- The farm has sufficient capital to manage both the breeder pigs and the fatteners

Advantages

- More pigs can be produced/unit of labour

- The profit potential per staff equivalent is greater

- It is also the most profitable sector

- Can target different pig markets throughout the year

- More independent of adverse weather

- A uniform labour requirement

This is currently the most suitable pig production system for sub-Sahara Africa where there are underdeveloped pig markets. This system positioned the farm to take full advantage of all the different sectors of the pig market — weaners, finishers, breeders etc. For example, at the festive season, lots of orders for market size weight pigs and at post festive seasons, there are orders for weaners to replenish the pigs sold.

Disadvantages

- The operation is capital intensive

- High-investment cost on buildings, equipment, breeding stocks, and others

- Requires knowledge and lots of in-depth skills in modern pig husbandry, e.g. genetics, nutrition, breeding

- It also requires lots of time to perfect the process and it can easily become a serious business, i.e., can be exposed to financial problems just like any other businesses

- Must be willing and able to adhere to a relatively tight production schedule.

- Have good links to market

14. Selecting pigs for your farm

To start your piggery farm, you need to select the healthy pigs. The type of pig selected will be determined by your targeted market and your expected farm output.

Starting a pig farm with a poor set of breeds is the wrong thing to do and would severely impact the profitability of your farm. The quality of your breed, feed and housing all play a vital role in determining the ability of your farm to meet your farm goal.

At this stage, it is important to go through some terminologies that will help you to clarify the type of pigs that you need on your farm.

- Boar — is a breeder male pig, a mature uncastrated male bought with the purpose of mating your female breeder

- Gilt — is a young breeder female swine that has just reach puberty, but has not farrowed, these are the new batch of female that will populate your farm with piglets after mating

- Sow — is a mature breeder female swine that has farrowed

- Piglets — are new sets of baby pig born and are still with their nursing mother going through suckling

- Weaners — are piglets that have finished the suckling period and are removed from their mother to live independently

- Growers — are weaners that have matured to over 25kg live weight. At this stage they are called growers

14.1 WHICH IS THE BEST BREED?

As a farmer and a trainer, people always ask me what breed of pig is the best for their farm?

My answer is that it depends on the goal of your farm, this is not always the answer that people expected from me. They expected me to recommend a particular type of pig breed usually one of the exotic breeds that was imported to Africa.

However, as a pig farmer and a trainer, I always stress the word 'profitable' during my training because I realised that just ad-vising farmer and their staff on how to increase their physical performance of the pigs on the farm was not enough for two main reasons.

First, I have seen many farmers, who started their farm with superb performing exotic breed of pigs recently imported into Africa without taking time to fully understand the fundamentals of pig farming. The price of this newly imported pigs and the cost of feeding them were so expensive (concentrate) that with the current pig market situation and the price of pig especially in Nigeria, there is no way such farmer can break even despite all the praiseworthy effort, skill and courageous capitalisation that they have invested on their farms.

Secondly, I also discovered from experience that an hybrid pigs (a cross breed between an exotic breed and a local popular breed) which is cheaper in price to the exotic breed and which

also require less capital to feed (because they can partly utilise locally available feed ingredients) though this hybrid performed below the superb performing exotic breed but they are
more profitable when you look at it from return on investment
in fixed and working capital.

The right breed for your farm should be the breed that helps
you to achieve the following:

- Makes up for and corrects the deficiencies in the pigs
  you already have

- Most suitable for your market outlet

- Should improve the profit margin of your cost of production

- Should have a track record of performance

- Should be able to perform better in your climate and
  your farm environment

There are over 90 recognized breeds and an estimated 230 va-
rieties of pigs in the world. However, the pigs that are reared in
sub-Sahara Africa can be broadly classified into 4 types of pigs

1. Indigenous or local types
2. Popular breed
3. Modern exotic types developed for specific commercial
   purposes
4. Cross Breed (or Hybrids)

Indigenous or local breed

Indigenous or local breeds are characterized by stunted growth,
poor reproductive performance, with three to six piglets per litter. They are very hardy. They have a pointed snout and sharp

feet. Skin colouration could be black, black with white or grey patches or can be pure brown. They are very well adapted to local feed ingredients and water shortage and they are trypano tolerant. They are becoming more and more extinct as most of them have either been killed as wild boar and some of them were cautiously eradicated during the last outbreak of African Swine Fever (ASF) as they were seen as the vector for ASF.

A recent blood sample taken from 410 litters of both pure and crossbred progenies of the Nigerian pigs showed that traits of indigenous pigs were found in 83% of the pig tested.

Popular Breed

Popular breed accounts for majority of the pigs in Nigeria and most African countries. They are neither indigenous nor exotic. They are 4th of 6th generation of crossbreed pigs that resulted from indiscriminate crossbreeding of local breeds with imported breeds particularly those of the Large White, the Landrace and Hampshire in the 70s and 80s, with the aim of improving the production potential of the local breed. And as a result, the majority of the initial characteristics and traits of both the exotic and the indigenous breed have faded to an extent that they cannot be categorised as either indigenous breed or exotic breed from which they were crossed.

However, this category of breed is very popular and preferred by many small-scale farms because they are perceived by farmers to be fast growing, prolific, and give better returns on investment when compared to the indigenous breeds. They are also cheaper and readily available to buy locally, for example, a weaner of popular breed is N8,000 compare to N40,000 for exotic weaner and they can survive entirely on locally available ingredients of less than N70 per KG compare to exotic feed which costs N120 per kg.

Some of the reasons for the poor state of pig breed in Nigeria include:

1. Government lackadaisical attitude and policies towards pig production

2. Unending red tape and obstacles on the importation of exotic breed to Nigeria

3. Poor funding on Research and Development on pigs especially when compared to other livestock like poultry and fish

4. Nonchalant attitude of research institutions towards pig production

5. The devastating impact of African Swine Fever on pig production in the 70s and 80s which devastated pig industry throughout west Africa

6. Not to mention the pervasive external influence of culture and religion on both the buyer's and consumer's behaviour towards pig consumption.

Exotic breeds

The most popular exotic breeds that are used for breeding in Nigeria include the following:

- Duroc: Golden brown to black in colour, thick auburn coat and hard skin and It is very docile

- Landrace: It is a very versatile breed performing well under good management. They are white in colour, Large dropping ears and a straight snout. They have the longest body size

- Hampshire: It is black, easily recognized by white belt around the shoulder, including the front feet. Highly prolific and good survival rate of piglets. Has more meat than the large white and landrace

- Yorkshire: It has erected ears and is white in colour and females are prolific. It is renowned for its strength of leg. The breed can be used for both pork and bacon production

- Tamworth: This hardy animal is reddish in colour with erect ears. The breed is relatively slow-maturing

- The Camborough® is an outstanding mother. Bred to maximise the pounds of weaned pigs per year with excellent feed efficiency.

Over the years, there has been a preference for high yielding breeds of animals that are good litter size, birth and weaning weight, faster growth rate, good mothering ability and give better returns on investment. However, exotic breeds are very expensive to buy and the feed required to sustain them are also very costly and sometimes do not justify the price of pork meat in most African countries but they are good as breeder pigs. In addition, exotic pigs do not perform to their full potential under tropical and sub-optimal conditions.

Cross Breed (or Hybrids)

The mating of two animals of different breeds is called crossbreeding. Hybrids are the crossbreed offspring of a cross between the Exotic breed and popular breed.

Crossbreeding produces improvements in the offspring due to a large number of fresh genetic combinations coming into existence. This condition is called hybrid vigour. It is the easiest and the affordable way to improve pig performance in sub-Sahara Africa. It allows the farms to get the benefit of the quality and characteristic of the exotic breed while also making the new generation more adaptable to tropical and sub-optimal conditions.

The goal of each African farmer should be to procure animals that meet market demand, perform well in the environment where the pigs will be raised and make good profit.

Importance of hybrid

Some of the benefits of crossbreeding popular breeds with exotic breeds, include:

1. earlier age at puberty
2. low cost of rearing from the ability to survive on low quality dietsgood mothering ability
3. reduced mortality through resistance to local diseases
4. ability to reproduce

The advantages of crossbreeding is:

- The crossbred offspring combines the best qualities from both parents. Especially if the parents are from different breeds and have been selected for good economic traits, these can be brought together in the crossbred.

- The effects of hybrid vigour can improve the commercial performance of the crossbred animal. Hybrid vigour has most effect on those traits such as litter numbers and birth weights.

- A crossbred sow usually produces larger litters and more milk than a purebred sow.

The disadvantage of crossbreeding is that the crossbred animal will not pass on its improved performance to any offspring.

- Hybrid vigour is strongest in the first cross (F1 generation) and it has much less effect in the second and subsequent generations of crossbreds.

- As an example, if a Large White boar is mated to a Nigerian popular breed, the offspring will show the effects of hybrid vigour. However, if two of these new crossbreeds are then mated, the crossbreeds produced by this mating (the F2 generation) might not have the performance of either of their parents.

The implication of this is that to improve the current popular breed pigs, the African government needs to allow the importation of exotic male breed or via Artificial insemination, the goal is not to replace the current popular breed but to improve them over time. For example, as long as a crossbred sow from the F1 generation is continually mated with another exotic boar from a different pure breed, the offspring of that cross will continue to produce hybrid vigour and perform well.

I would like to use this medium to appeal to the livestock research institute in Africa to work harder to find the most suitable breeds designed with sub-Sahara African environment in mind.

I will end this section with a word of advice to farmers. It is a quote from Francis of Assisi, *"Start by doing what's necessary; then do what's possible; and suddenly you are doing the impossible."*

While waiting for government and research institutions to invest and do more on pig breed and pig production in sub-Sahara Africa, we should keep on doing what we can locally to improve our breed.

14.2 HOW TO CHOOSE YOUR HERD OF PIGS

As a new start-up, your primary objectives of selecting pigs should be to achieve the following:

1. To improve litter size — litter size is the number of piglets born. i.e. the number of fully-formed individual piglets birthed during farrowing. You want to watch out for low litter size. Farmers should be concerned when less than 6 pigs are littered and weaned on your farm.

2. To improve growth rate — Growth rate is the rate of increase in body weight for a unit in time, e.g. grams per day (g/day).

3. Good mothering ability

4. Good meat quality that meets the market demand

5. To improve your farm resistance to diseases and the viability of the farm

As a pig farmer, there are many factors that you need to consider when choosing the pigs for your farm. Ultimately, you want to select pigs with correct health status that is appropriate for your farm goals and your farm environment (e.g. housing, feed, staff).

But along with this are other factors such as the availability of such breed of pigs, in the quantities that you want and at a price that you can afford and to ensure that the breed is what the market desires.

Your foundational stock is very crucial to the success of your farm, so you should investigate the farm where you want to buy your pigs from. If possible, speak to or visit the farm of those who have bought pig from the supplier farm in the past. While at the farm, check the biosecurity of the supplier farm and the state of the flock.

I am a strong believer that "a good pig farmer is a writing farmer (i.e. a farmer that writes)", there are so many things going on the farm that it is impossible to carry everything in your head or in your mind's eye. Always write what you want down e.g.

- Your overall pig farming objective

- The number of pigs you want to start your farm

- Be specific with how many boars, gilts, weaners, grower male and female that you want to start your farm with and stick to it

- The quality of stock that you want

It is very important that you determine this before you approach the farm where you want to buy your pigs. It is very easy for non-experienced pig farmers to be overwhelmed or get carried away by the volume and the sheer size of pigs in the seller's farm. Don't forget the interest of the seller is to sell as many pigs to you. So, write the details down as you are thinking about it. Write down what you desire from each category of pigs — weaners, gilts, boar.

General shape and conformation

Remember to examine each animal front, left, rear, right and dorsal (top) surface before selecting the animal.

Examine each animal front, left, rear, right and dorsal

1. Check your prospective seller; you should always buy your stock from a reliable and reputable farm. Always ask for names of other farms who have bought this stock and if possible, telephone them.

2. Nothing beats good friendliness. Where possible get to know the staff and talk to them.

3. As someone new to pig farming, when you are inspecting the pigs, where possible use visual aids like diagram charts that will guide your eyes as they travel around the body of each pig, noting in detail what you desire on each part of the animal's body as you go along, make notes of what you do not like, for example, mark down pigs with narrow chest, poor shoulder, legs and movement, crossed toe, hernias etc..

4. Relying on your brain might not be enough, human eyes and brain tends to look for and pick up what you are looking for– but miss others.

5. Don't rush, examine the animals one at a time. Do not jump from one to another. It is a great temptation and you will get confused if you do this.

6. Try and choose an animal that is quiet and amiable and quite unconcerned by your presence, a total stranger.

7. Always get the animal to walk briskly or move around. Gilt that can move her legs with ease stand a better chance of being able to stand and carry a boar during mating.

The number of pigs you need to purchase would depend on the size of your pen and your goal, for example, you might want to start with 20 gilts and 2 boar because you have 24 pens but you need to also bear in mind that you will need accommodation for an additional 140 pigs within the next 6 months when your gilt begins to give birth. You should always bear in mind that pigs can multiply very quickly.

No matter which pig you are buying, you should look out for signs of a healthy pig:

- A pair of bright eyes.

- Has a glossy coat.

- It must be alert and responsive to its surrounding environment.

- Avoid aggressive pigs. Instead opt for pigs with good temperament.

- Good appeal to food.

- Easy and normal movement.

- Free from lameness or any other unnatural signs.

- Ask the seller about their parents and their health information, production history and other records.

- Ask the seller if the pig has been dewormed or not. If not, ask him to do it urgently.

14.3 SELECTING YOUR GILTS

Careful and rigorous gilt selection is critical for the long-term success and productivity of your farm. Gilts are the future of a sow herd and that is regardless of whether they are home-raised from birth to puberty or purchased as a weaner. Poor gilt selection is more difficult to overcome with later management actions in the breeding herd.

Your goal is to select gilts that will set the standard that you expect on your farm. By this I mean, your gilt must produce between 30 to 50 offspring in their lifetime and the first 16 to 20 of these piglets should be produced in the first two farrows or the first twelve calendar months of production.

Achieving this goal with your gilts makes them the second most important animal in your herd after the boar. She is your future production machine as a breeder and the bedrock for a long productive life.

You should therefore aim to select a breeding female that will give a good litter with minimum intervals between and go on to produce at least three to four years thereafter.

You should consider the following points when selecting gilts for breeding:

- Health and longevity — this means that you select your gilts from farms that have history of raising pigs for at least 2 to 3 years in longevity.

- Prolificacy — by this we mean pigs with parent that have history of producing a good number of healthy and strong piglets

- Mothering qualities — by this we mean pigs with good temperament and milking qualities in the sow.

- Milking capacity — by this we mean the mother must produce rich and sufficient milk to nourish the piglets

- Good food converters — this refers to the Food Conversion Ratio or FCR. A good FCR in Nigeria is usually 4kg of feed to yield 1kg of meat because the majority of the feed ingredients are waste or industrial feed by-products.

- Good carcass qualities or good conformation- your gilt should have at least twelve well-spaced teats.

- No abnormalities on the body.

Selecting breeder pigs for your farm

Below are the general characteristics of a good female pig (gilt) to be selected for breeding:

- Gilts should be selected preferably at 4 –5 months of age, just before they reach puberty

- They should come from a parent that gave good litter size of at least 9 piglets, birth and weaning weight, faster growth rate, good mothering ability.

- They should be in good health, looking physically fit and free from diseases

- Gilts should have at least 12 to 14 prominent, evenly spaced functional nipples.

- Teat rows should be fairly close to the midline of the abdomen so that piglets can nurse easily.

- The nipples should be spaced out and well developed and start far forward on the underline.

- Teat troubles – Avoid blind, inverted and immature teats (button teats). avoid poor and asymmetrical teat placement

- Reproductive problems can often be predicted by evaluating the external genitalia.

- Vulva size — A small vulva coupled to a small pelvic spread should be avoided as they tend to cause problems during mating or farrowing.

- Avoid animals that have injuries to the vulva. Even if they heal, they may impair mating or cause farrowing difficulty.

- Breeding gilts should have a large skeleton, a long, thick, deep, rectangular body and a square rump, with good depth in the rib and flank area.

- Feet and leg problems — The ideal pig to be selected should be one that has strong leg. Strong legs are particularly important for the gilts.

- Good feet are important for a good distribution of weight and avoid a lot of problems for the whole life cycle of the sow.

- Sound feet and legs i.e. strong hind and fore limbs to be able to withstand the weight of the mounting boar and should have good springing to cushion the effect of hard floors.

- Poor feet are the second largest reason for sows leaving the breeding herd. Gilts should be able to move freely and get up and down easily.

- Animals that get up and down easily are less likely to suffer from leg injuries

- The toes of your selected pig should face forward. It should be big, even and well-spaced to take the weight of the animal. The toes should have no visible cracks, swellings or injuries. Avoid those with toes that are different e.g. point inwards — "Bow legged" or outwards or splayed

- The position and angle of the dew claws indicates the strength of the pasterns. Ideally the dew claws should only just contact the floor. Avoid pigs with weak or dropped pastern position or bucked knees.

- Avoid gilts with swollen joints or inflamed tendons, inverse toes, splay footed or pigeon toed

- The gilt must not have abnormalities like lameness, hernia and the posture must be normal

14.4 PROMPTLY REMOVE ALL UNPRODUCTIVE SOWS FROM YOUR HERD

Apart from the fact that gilts or sows are the second most important in your farm, they are also the most expensive to keep on the farm. A smart farmer will keep a close eye on the performance of the sows and always check the record to see how many sows are redundant or have not been successfully crossed within the last 3 months.

Sows that farrow regularly and weaned litters of 8 or more piglets and are free of other problems and diseases should be reared for up to 5 years before they are culled from the herd. You should remove a sow from breeding herd when her litters start dwindling to 6 on two consecutive farrows or when she does not readily come on heat 5 days after weaning or every 21 days.

Not doing this can affect your farm profitability

A sow will consume 2.5kg of feed daily on your farm for 365 days a year. Assuming a kg is N70 or 20 cents (USD). 20 cents x 2.5kg x 365 days = $182.5 per annum.

So if your sow is not producing a minimum of 14 to 20 pigs every year, she is not productive and needs to be culled.

I once went to a farm that has 60 sows and only 65% of the sows farrowed twice a year. And the owner was not aware of the cost implication of the sows that are redundant on his farm for a year until I told him that 18 of his sows have consumed 2.5kg over 365 days at 20 cents = $3,285 of food for 12 months without producing enough piglets.

As a pig farmer, it is important that you regularly review your sows and cull those that are not productive from the farm and sold them as soon as possible. Replacement gilt can then be brought into the herd immediately.

Some of the major reasons for culling sows in many pig farms in the UK are:

Reasons for culling	% of sows to be culled
Not pregnant	17
Failure to conceive at service	12
Do not come on heat	5
Abortions	6
Lameness	12
Poor performance (small litters, etc)	14
Old age	25
Disease	45

Source: Farmer's Handbook on Pig Production

14.5 SELECTION OF PIGLET OR WEANERS FOR YOUR FARM

Instead of starting your farm with mature gilts and boars, you can decide to buy a weaner breeder of about 10 to 20kg live weight. Starting with weaners has the advantage of allowing the pigs a long period of acclimatisation on your farm prior to using them for breeding. In addition, pig raised by yourself on the farm will also be cheaper than those bought as adult from another farm and it also allows you to rear them in the way that you think is best for your farm.

Selecting piglets

You should look for the following features when you are procuring weaners:

- Minimum weight of piglets should be about 10kg

- Must come from a litter of more than 9 piglets, don't take the farmer's word for it, inspect the farm especially the other nursing mothers on the farm and observe the size of their litter.

- Make sure the piglets have been weaned for at least a week and have started taking solid feed during the time of procurement

- They should be healthy, active and free from any skin or other diseases.

- Piglets should have fine shiny hair coat (should not be too hairy).

- Healthy piglets have clear bright eyes and moist noses.

- Pigs should breathe clearly. They should not be coughing, sneezing, bleeding at the nose or have crooked noses.

- Pigs should have long thighs and shoulders and thick muscling.

- Their thigh and shoulders should be thicker than their well-rounded loin according to their age

- Piglets should have faecal material that is normal in colour and consistency

- Look out for the parent. The boar and sow should have high reproductive performance, be docile, have good feed conversion ratio, and good mothering ability.

- In case of female and male piglets, there should be a minimum of 6 pairs of teats equally distributed on both sides.

- In case of male piglets, testicles should be uniformly developed.

14.6 SELECTION OF BREEDING MALE BOAR

The boar is the single most important animal in the piggery farm because half of his genes will be carried by all his offspring. You should exercise great care in choosing a boar because of the large number of offspring to which he may transmit his characteristics.

The productivity and profitability of farms can be increased by giving sufficient attention to boar selection.

The following parameter for selection of boar should be kept in mind:

- Good body constitution.

- Boar should be active and alert.

- Conformation (the boar must have good conformation and particular attention should be paid to his feet and legs).

- The boar should show true breeding character

- Boar should be healthy and masculine

- Particular attention should be given to the boar's legs and feet as they are subjected to considerable strain during mating. Boar should have sound feet i.e. strong hind and fore limbs to withstand its weight and to aid while mounting.

- The body should be long and deep strong back and neck with smooth shoulders.

- Nipples (the boar must show at least twelve even and well-spaced nipples to pass on this trait to his female offspring).

- Good looking, non-inverted, and well-placed teats

- Age of the boar should not be below 7 months at the time of breeding

- It should have both the testicles well positioned and size should match with its body size and age.

- There should not have any injury on the body or physical deformity

- The boar should be free from any parasite, infectious or contagious disease

- The boar should be free from any stress during the time of breeding

- Boar should have good sex libido.

- Scrotum and testicles — Select boars with good sized testes. There is a correlation between testicular size and semen output. Avoid any abnormalities including difference in size between testes and avoid loose testicles

Recent research has shown that at 30 weeks of age, young boars need physical contact with other pigs in order to develop high serving performance. After puberty, it is important to house boars near female pigs to maintain courting and serving behaviour. Boar is also the most expensive to keep, so you should keep a close eye on the performance of your boar.

Boars must be replaced when they become too large to serve most of the gilts or sows on the farm. Boars usually have a maximum working life of between 18 and 24 months. This means they should be replaced when they are 30 to 36 months old.

It is very important to keep a record of the boars' use so that infertile ones can be detected and replaced as soon as possible.

Please note: It is advisable not to buy boar from the same farm where the gilts come from to remove any chance of inbreeding.

15. Transporting your pigs to the farm

Pause and remember — Slow and steady will get you where you want to go. If you put too much pressure on yourself for results too quickly, you will quickly give up. — Jennifer Young

Now that your farm construction is now complete and the entire infrastructure that you need to house and raise your pigs are now in place. You are now ready to transport the animal that you selected from a reputable pig supplier's farm to your farm.

You would need to transport your pig when you are bringing you first batch of pigs to your farm, as well as when you are re-stocking your farm with replacement gilt (and boar) and when you are ready for sales from your farm to the market or to the slaughterhouse.

Transporting livestock is undoubtedly one of the most stressful and injurious stage for pigs in the chain of operations between farm and the market and if this is poorly managed, it can contribute significantly to poor animal welfare and can also lead to significant loss of quality and production. It is therefore important that transporting of pigs be conducted in a manner that minimises stress, pain and suffering. Pig selected for transport should be fit and healthy, be in good condition and be able to stand for extended periods of time.

15.1 THE EFFECT OF POOR TRANSPORTATION AND MOVEMENT ON PIGS

Stress — Stress during transportation causes loss of quality and production in pigs. It is not advisable to buy and transport pregnant pigs. Moving such pigs on poor roads for a long time might lead to losing some of the unborn piglets in transit.

In finisher, meat of pigs exposed to poor transportation stress is always of inferior quality with poor taste and has a shorter shelf life. This is due to the abnormally high pH-value of the meat produced under stress.

Bruising — Bruising is the escape of blood from damaged blood vessels into the surrounding muscle tissue. This can be caused by a physical blow by a stick, beating or continual prodding of animals, poor handling and transport loading technique or by a metal projection from the vehicle or animal fall. Bruising and injuries such as torn muscles and broken bones can delay sow and gilt breeding significantly or even make breeding impossible, especially if the limb of the animal is affected.

In finisher, bruising can considerably reduce the carcass value of an animal to be slaughtered and if secondary bacterial infection occurs in those wounds, this can cause abscess formation and septicaemia and the entire carcass may have to be condemned.

Trampling- this occurs when pigs fall down during transportation due to slippery floors or overcrowding, suffocation usually follows on trampling and eventual loss of the animal.

Heart failure — occurs a lot in pigs during transportation, when pigs are overfed prior to loading and transportation;

Heat stroke — High environmental temperatures increase the risk of heat stress and mortality in pigs during transportation. It is important to transport pigs in vehicles during the cooler mornings and evenings or even at night.

Sunburn — exposure to sun affects pigs seriously especially the white pigs.

15.2 HOW TO TRANSPORT YOUR PIG SUCCESSFULLY

During the process of transportation of pigs, the following precautions should be taken:

1. Transporting of pigs should be conducted in a manner that minimises stress, pain and suffering.

2. Animals that are diseased, injured, emaciated or heavily pregnant should not be transported, and unfit, heavy animals should not travel far as they cannot stand up to the rigours of transport.

3. Stock selected for transport should be fit and healthy, be in good condition and able to stand for extended periods of time.

4. Pigs should be fed not later than 4 hours before loading pigs because the feed ferments and the gas builds up causing pressure on the heart in the thoracic cavity, leading to heart failure and death. And again, overfed pigs will defecate and urinate excessively. This will make the floor dirty and slippery and uncomfortable.

5. Transporter should never lose temper and should never hurry, the truck should be driven carefully, slowed down on sharp turns and sudden stops are to be avoided.

6. Pigs should be handled quietly and patiently, especially in new environments and always with a stock board.

7. For transportation of pigs or piglets by road, truck or mini truck should be used (not the boot of a car) depending on the distance and the number of pigs to be transported.

8. Transport vehicle should be cleaned and disinfected.

9. Pigs should be transported with bedding materials about 1inch wood shaving or straw, etc. to minimise slipping and trampling.

10. Pigs showing signs of stress such as sudden lying down, panting, trembling and with a splotchy skin appearance should be allowed to rest and relax before being transported or moved.

11. Pigs are unable to sweat to regulate their body temperature so travelling during hot and humid conditions can be dangerous to the health of the pig.

12. Spraying pigs with water to calm them down is a good practice.

13. Transportation should occur early in the morning or late in the afternoon and stocking densities should be lowered by 10% if the temperature is above 25oC.

14. The surfaces of the sides should be smooth and there should be no protrusions or sharp edges.

15. Non-slip floors are necessary in the vehicles to reduce the risk of animals falling causing broken legs and other injuries.

16. Where possible vehicle floors should be level with off-loading platforms. If this is not possible staff should carefully load the animal onto the vehicle without being rough handed.

17. Trucks should be covered to protect the pigs from sun to prevent heat stroke and sunburn.

18. The transport vehicles should never be totally enclosed, as lack of ventilation will cause undue stress and even suffocation, particularly if the weather is hot.

19. Poor ventilation may cause accumulation of exhaust fumes in road vehicles with subsequent poisoning.

20. Pigs are particularly susceptible to excessive heat, poor air circulation, high humidity and respiratory stress. The free flow of air at floor level is important to facilitate removal of ammonia from the urine.

21. For long distance travel, it is advisable to transport pigs in vehicles during the cooler mornings and evenings or even at night to minimise the heat stress.

22. Pigs require sufficient floor space during transportation so that they can stand comfortably without being overcrowded.

23. Overloading results in injuries or even death of livestock but farmers should note that below capacity loading of a truck with pigs can be just as dangerous as over loading.

24. Efforts should be made to keep the pig quiet and the animals should not be beaten.

25. Hot and excited animals are more prone to injury or death.

26. Unloading of pigs should be done slowly and carefully. Pigs must not be dropped on the ground.

27. Quarantine does not apply for the first stock and subsequent new stock that are brought into an existing herd should be quarantined for at least a fortnight.

16. Managing gilt in your farm

At the start of your farm, a large percentage of the pigs transported to your farm will be gilts and a few boars and probably some weaners.

One of your primary goals is to get your gilts to production as soon as possible.

16.1 HOW TO QUARANTINE YOUR PIGS

Do you need to Quarantine your pigs?

Every farm (including your farms) has a different pattern of inherent challenges; these include viruses, bacteria and moulds. The problems that is in your own herd is different to that of the new set of pigs that you are bringing to your farm.

This means that before the new sets of gilts reach your farm not only are they bringing new challenges from the farm of their origin to your farm which they might have acquire certain degree of immunity against (but which the pigs on your farm may not have immunity against) and they are also going to face diseases that are on your farm which they do not have immunity from. You quarantine by holding the new sets of pigs separately away from the rest of flocks for a while.

As a new farmer, because you do not have any pigs already on your farm, your problem is not as complex and so you do not need to quarantine your new set of pigs, but you will definitely need to quarantine subsequent animals that you bring to your farm from another farm.

But if you already have pigs on your farm and you are bringing new sets of gilts from a reliable breeder farm source, the new gilts will have developed immunity to the microbes that they are exposed to on their farm of origin but not necessarily to those present on your farm.

This difference may be sufficient to cause trouble once they arrive on your farm, hence you need to provide strict quarantine for the new sets of pigs, at least three days in case a hidden problem should appear caused by the stress of transportation and this few days will enable your staff to check physical factors like leg movement, etc.

Please note: When certain diseases and their severity are present in a locality, a strict isolation period may require at least 2 weeks.

Why do you need to quarantine?

- To prevent transmission of disease from a new pig to a resident pig.

- To allow the new pig to build immunity for their new location

- To allow for better observation of new pigs.

- To identify disease, behavioural issues, nutritional issues in new pigs.

You should quarantine the following pigs?

- Any pig that looks unhealthy.

- Any pig that comes from a pig farm (pigs that have fallen off trucks, for example).

- Any pig that comes from a questionable home or a herd situation.

- Any pig that comes from a feed store (because you do not know where the pig originally came from and what its care might have been).

- Any pig that will be part of a breeding program.

- Piglets that are too young because of their poor immune systems. These piglets are less of a danger to your own pig — but your pig may infect them.

How does disease spread from a new pig to your herd?

- Direct contact between pigs.

- Insects, rodents, birds — they do carry organic waste from sick pigs to resident pigs, acting as a source of the disease.

- People (staff), clothes, shoes, hands. Most disease organisms survive in organic material and soil for a long time (in some cases, years). The most common way that disease is transmitted, other than from direct contact with a sick individual, is from contact with this organic material. Faecal material, contaminated soil, pus, and other discharges cling to clothing, hair, and skin. Failure to change clothes, wash boots, and wash hands and other exposed skin, is a common way that disease is spread from quarantine to resident pigs.

- Water, food, soil, wind — When contaminated with fae-ces, urine, nasal discharge, and pus from a sick animal, it can easily transmit the illness to resident pigs.

- Open fencing can lead to direct contact between pigs, drainage of contaminated water into residential areas and other foodstuffs falling into residential areas, and direct deposits of stool or discharge on the resident side of the fence.

How to quarantine?

- Ensure that there is no contact between new pigs and old pigs — no common fencing, a closed area where wind and water cannot carry waste into your herd

- At least 10 feet between quarantine area and your herd

- Disinfect — Bleach is an excellent and cheap disinfec-tant, 1 tablespoonful of bleach in a gallon of water will kill most viruses and bacteria.

- During your pen cleaning, take care of resident pigs first. After they are fed and cared for, you can go and take care of your quarantined pigs. But ensure that you do not go back to resident pigs without changing clothes, washing boots and hands.

- No common water source or food source between new and old pigs

- Leftover food from quarantine pig is never fed to resi-dent pigs.

- Buckets, utensils, troughs are not used with quarantined pigs, then used for residents without washing and thor-ough disinfecting.

224 □   PRISTINE INTEGRATED RESOURCES LTD: **PROFITABLE PIG FARMING**

- Easy to clean surfaces — Solid floors, such as concrete, tile or linoleum that can easily be washed. A drain in the floor makes cleaning much easier.

- Waste disposal in a safe area — make sure that drainage from the waste dump is kept from resident pigs.

- Disposing of waste from quarantine pigs in an area where your farm pigs cannot get it.

- Foot bath for disinfecting/washing boots.

- Changing area to put on coveralls, boots, head cover if appropriate.

Most infectious diseases cause symptoms to develop within 7-10 days. Quarantine for a minimum of 14 days is recommended. This gives sufficient time for symptoms to develop and be recognized.

If rescue pigs are sick, then quarantine should continue for at least 1 week after the last symptom resolves.

If rescue pigs have non-infectious problems (such as nutritional problems), then quarantine should last for a minimum of 14 days, but for as long as needed so that the affected pig will not be infected by your resident pigs and for as long as it makes it easier to treat, feed a special diet, wash wounds, etc.

Suggested injections on arrival — Two injections of ivermectin 0.3mg/kg should be given to each animal on arrival and 7 days later. This is to remove the risk of mange and other internal parasites (not tapeworms).

Consult with your local veterinarian regarding any specific pathogens that might be present in the area and take necessary precautions.

16.2 HOW TO ORIENTATE YOUR NEW PIGS TO YOUR FARM?

The process of orientation

Once quarantine is over and the new stock has received the go ahead to join the old stock, they now need to be introduced gradually to the microbial and fungal populations that are on your farm. This is to allow your new set of pigs to reinforce their immune defences against the organisms that your own herd possesses, as well as to allow your existing pigs to also upgrade their own immune patterns to deal with those microbes that the new pigs are bringing with them to your farm. The period the new intake needs to re-adjust their immune shield is usually a 4 to 6 weeks fortification period

This period will also allow the gilt to recuperate from the challenges and stresses of transportation and relocation. The gilt will have the opportunity to eat, rest and quietly calm down to allow her body to strengthen into a sound immune shield.

The gilt's third heat is particularly important especially if you are not sure of the age of the gilts or you are dazzled by the size of genetically-superior exotic or hybrid gilt. While most of these exotic or hybrid pigs may look big and mature, they are still very young and need time for their reproductive hormones to catch up with physical growth.

It is important that the gilt has at least two real heat periods before mating. The number of ova produced during each cycle tend to increase. For gilts, the ovulation rate can be further increased by a high energy intake for 10–14 days prior to service (flushing). This should gradually be reduced for the first 3 days after mating. The feed should provide the gilt with the necessary elevated levels of protein, lysine, calcium, phosphorus, and micronutrients. This will minimize any risk of insufficient bone mineralization and fractures during later mating or pregnancies.

Flushing is only done for sows that have just finished nursing. Flushing works best when the sow's body condition has been allowed to greatly deteriorate during lactation. By increasing the normal (maintenance levels) feed intake, this can speed up ovulation and increase subsequent litter size.

16.3 PREPARING YOUR GILTS TOWARDS PRODUCTION?

Housing

You can house your gilt individually i.e. one in a cell (or maximum two), or you can house them in a herd of 8 to 10 pigs. If you are keeping gilts in a herd, make sure you did so from weaning so that the gilts are familiar with each other from weaners.

Also avoid housing gilts in continuous physical contact with a mature boar or else they will develop brotherly love; however, a short 20-minute period of daily boar exposure is essential.

The dimension of your gilt cells:

1. Raised in groups: your gilts can be raised in groups of 8 to 10 pigs on a concrete floor cell with a cell dimension of 20 feet x 16 feet. This cell should be swept, scraped and cleared out each day and washed with water, detergent and disinfectant. The cell should be a rectangular shape to allow bullied gilts to get out of the way more easily. Each cell should have sufficient feeders to avoid fighting and bullying at feeding time.

2. Raised in individual cell — a breeder cell with 9 feet x 8 feet dimension will provide sufficient accommodation for each sow:

Puberty

It is the period when the reproductive system of an animal starts functioning. In gilts, it is symbolised by the appearance of first oestrus (heat symptom).

Here are some of the factors that can influence puberty in pigs:

- Age at puberty varies among different breeds — local breed or hybrids tends to come on heat faster than the exotic breed.

- Poor nutrition can reduce growth rates especially if the feed is deficient in a particular nutrient.

- Poor body condition delays puberty.

- Puberty may be delayed by poor environmental conditions, cold, sunburn and poor light.

- Overcrowding and the associated bullying and stress may result in delayed puberty.

- Disease may affect the gilt by reducing body condition or by causing pain.

- Lameness reduces bodily condition and precludes behaviour associated with oestrus.

- Dirty housing and poor observation for signs of oestrus may result in real or apparent delays.

- Finally, puberty may be delayed by housing with young boars or by contact with old boars too early.

Female pigs usually attain puberty around 6 to 8 months when they attain about 50kg of body weight, male requires 7 to 8 months to attain sexual maturity.

Breed	Age at puberty
Exotic breed	6 to 8 months
Cross breed	7 to 8 months
Indigenous pig	5 to 6 months

The first clinical signs of delayed puberty are usually the failure of gilts to show oestrus (enlargement of the vulva, reddening of the vulva, remaining still for back pressure, clustering round a boar) by the time they would be expected to have reached puberty.

16.4 BOAR PRESENCE

Research has shown that regular boar contact provides the most potent natural stimulus for puberty attainment in young gilts.

While your goal as a farmer is to get your gilt to start cycling as soon as possible, you should not be in a hurry to serve the gilts until the third oestrus.

Your gilt should be approximately 5 to 6 months old before she starts her heat. This pre-service stimulation by boar will help prepare your gilt reproductive system but they should not be served until they are 7 to 8 months.

When the time for mating arrives, your staff can assume that the gilt has reached full heat on the basis of vulva colour and swelling and should bring the gilt to the boar for 30 minutes in the morning and the evening. While sometimes the gilt might not be ready when she is brought to the boar, waiting for another 24 hours before bringing the gilt back to the boar is reckoned to be the leading cause of fewer conception rate and fewer returns. To avoid this delay, once you notice the signs of heat on your gilts take her to a male and if mating does not take place in the morning bring her back to the boar after 12 hours in the evening.

The response of the boar to your gilt depends on how close together the sexes have been housed previously. Having the gilts in the same pen or next to boars continuously for too long during the rearing period could make the females become too accustomed to the male`s signals and can also lead to a reduction in the expression of oestrous behaviours. This phenomenon is referred to as **habituation**. This meant that the excitement and novelty of a boar's presence has worn off because he is always there.

Boar should be allowed with gilts for 10-30 minutes per day.

While the smell of the boar`s pheromones is sufficient enough to stimulate cycling heat in female pig, studies have shown that the boar pheromone(s) need to be picked up physically by the female from the 'snout in the mouth' behaviour, rather than being sensed in the air.

Points to be considered for successful breeding

- Flushing is recommended for a 10 to 14-day period before expected date of heat as this increases ovulation rate especially in first litter gilts.

- Only one boar should be allowed to serve one sow at a time.

- Though one service is enough to fertilise the ova in the female, it should be repeated 12 hours after the first service. The more the service the better as long as the female accepted the male.

- The service should be supervised, to ensure that it actually happened and the records, like service date, sow and boar name/number and the expected farrowing date should be recorded.

- Feeding broad spectrum antibiotics prior to mating has shown to have increased litter size.

- Feeding intake should be reduced immediately after mating, as high level of feeding tends to reduce implantation of embryos.

16.5 SYSTEM OF BREEDING

Your breeding objective is to produce superior quality piglets through combining good quality parents (gene). There are different methods of breeding, and they include:

1. Inbreeding
2. Crossbreeding
3. Artificial Insemination

1. Inbreeding

Why is Inbreeding not good for your farm

Inbreeding is the method of breeding between close relatives such as brother-sister, mother-son, father daughter, cousin brother sister, etc. Mating individuals within 4-6 generations is also termed as inbreeding. While many farms know that this is not the best for their farm, they still practise it because it is convenient using the same boar that has performed well with other gilts. It seems to make sense, limited availability of boar from another source, most farms do it due to poor record keeping or lack of knowledge.

Research has shown that inbreeding causes the following:

- Depression, thereby reducing the productive and re-production performances of the animals in subsequent generations

- The animals show generic abnormalities in the subsequent generations

- Due to inbreeding most of the animals die before weaning age

- There is loss of fertility and survivability in inbred animals

2. Crossbreeding

It is the method of mating sows of one breed by boars of another breed e.g. Large White and Duroc, exotic with local breed.

Advantages

- Crossbreeding commonly makes new generation piglets more productive and healthier than their parents

- Good superior qualities of the two breeds manifests in the crossbred progeny

Disadvantages

- Expensive to maintain the exotic breed

- The individual breed characteristics gradually disappear eventually

3. Artificial insemination

In this method the semen is collected hygienically from the boar having better breed characteristics and then the semen is scientifically processed in the laboratory.

16.6 HOW TO INDUCE OESTRUS (HEAT) IN GILT

Oestrus is defined as a period of sexual receptivity and ovulation during which gilt or sow will accept the boar and are capable of conceiving. As we mentioned earlier, the first oestrus usually occurs in gilt at about 5 to 7 months in indigenous breed and 7 to 8 months in exotic breed.

Inducing heat is a procedure used to advance oestrus by days, weeks or even months. This is particularly important for farmers because the ability to control and advance oestrus will allow farmers to better plan and coordinate the farm to meet the farm goal and also reduce the non-productive days.

Daily stimulation of gilts with a boar should begin a few days after the gilts are introduced into your farm as long as they are older than 6 months.

The best way to achieve contact with boar is to make sure your gilt's cells is linked to where the boars are kept and are exposed to the boar for 20 minutes.

Some farmers like to put a male among a pool of gilts so that they do not miss the gilt heat, but this guarantees too much closeness to allow habituation to take place as discussed above. Habituation usually leads to a decrease in oestrous detection rate and a decrease in the observed duration of oestrus.

The best method to give gilts sufficient boar stimulation is to move small groups of gilts into the boar's pen for at least 10 to 15 minutes of physical contact each day.

These are the methods you can use to induce heat in gilt and sows:

- 10 days before service, give the sow/gilt 3 — 4 kg of feed extra per day. This is called flushing and should be done for a maximum of 10 days or until the service takes place.

- Increase the energy content of the feed

- Feed the sow twice a day for 5-7 days.

- Continue the flushing for one week after service.

- Gently stroke the sow's vagina with a freshly cut papaya stalk every morning for 3-5 days.

- Spray the sow's (or gilt's) pen with boar's urine every morning for 3-5 days.

- Your sows should not be too fat or too thin when they are served. It is important to keep this in mind when determining the ration during the sow nursing period.

- Bring your sow to the boar or place the sow in a pen next to the boar for 15 minutes twice a day when the heat is expected. The physical touch (i.e., tactile cues) and smell (i.e. pheromones from their saliva and urine) that a boar produces would stimulate the onset and expression of oestrus in females.

- Each boar should be kept in its own pen to avoid fighting.

- Once you perceive that the female is on heat, always take the sow to the boar. This is less upsetting for the boar and will increase the chance of the boar mating the sow instead of marking the new territories in an unfamiliar pen.

16.7 SIGNS OF HEAT

Since accurate heat checks are so vital, it is essential that you know the typical signs of female pigs that are approaching oestrus display.

The ultimate sign that confirms a gilt or sow is in oestrus is immobilization or "standing" in response to back pressure from a boar or from a person. However, this sign is not very obvious in indigenous or the popular breed as most pigs in Africa tend to be more temperamental and they rarely wait for humans to come too close.

However, there are several other behavioural and physical changes that you can observe hours or even days before the onset of standing oestrus.

Swelling and Reddening – Two to three days before onset of oestrus, there is an increasing oestrogen levels from developing ovarian follicles which stimulate increased blood flow and fluid retention in the reproductive tract, and this causes the vulva and clitoris to swell and turn red. This is commonly observed in gilts.

Mucous Discharge – Clear sticky mucus may drip and hang from the vulva in response to the increasing levels of oestrogen (NEW PHOTO)

Riding – Gilts and sows coming into or going out of oestrus often mount and ride pen mates when group housed

It should be noted that most local breeds or hybrid females will not tolerate being mounted and will vocalize loudly and make moves to escape.

Seeking the Boar – Sow will move towards a passing boar

Groaning of sow – When a sow is on heat sometimes, she will emit a deep groaning sound. This usually occurs at a peak of the oestrous cycle.

Standing Reflex – Some females in oestrus will exhibit the "standing reflex" without any direct physical stimulation when a boar passes nearby. The ears may spring into an erect position and females often arch their back slightly.

Back-Pressure Test – Conversely, a few females in oestrus will stand in response to back pressure with or without the presence of a boar.

It is important that you or your staff take note of a gilt that is showing these physical signs and behavioural changes during your early morning inspection of the farm. Mark, identify and record such pigs using their ear tag.

If the gilt is not yet on the third heat, remind your staff to examine her again at the next heat check (in 21 days). If it is the third heat of a gilt or if a sow is on heat, your staff should take her to the boar as soon as possible.

When in doubt, take the sow or gilt to the boar. Most of the time, the two together will let you know if the female is in heat.

Apply all the principles of stockman ship

- Ears to detect a calling sow

- Eyes to detect the restless, nervous sow, which is off her food, has a swollen vulva, which is slightly red

- Touch to exhibit back pressure test in the presence of the boar

- The common sense to be quietly patient in observing animals

Many new farmers and their staff always complain that their gilts and sows do go through heat without exhibiting any of the preliminary signs of oestrus. They call it "silent heats" but the chances of this happening is very low. There is more chance that oestrus is missed due to human error or inadequate boar stimulation than incorrect assumption that your females have not come on heat.

The time of day that oestrus starts in most female pigs is the same time as their cousin in the wild usually during the late night and early morning hours and this is common also in the domesticated pigs. It is advisable that you carry out your heat check just before or after morning feeding and this seems to be the best time of the day given that it is the coolest part of the workday and the breeding herd is up and active

You should not overlook the crossed females on your farm, from our experience the greatest oversight that happens in farms is the failure to detect oestrus among females pigs that were crossed earlier but have failed to conceive or had false pregnancy, or lost their pregnancy due to severe prenatal mortality or abortion. There is nothing more frustrating than for a farmer to assume that 10 pigs were crossed but only to discover 4 months down the line that only 4 gave birth. This can be avoided by regularly checking those that have been crossed to make sure they did not come on oestrus and if they did, they should be promptly mated again.

Sows and gilts mated within the last 18 to 22 days and 40 to 44 days should be given special attention since this time period is approximately one or two oestrous cycles after the last mating and is the most likely time to detect sows that are not pregnant from the last mating and have returned to oestrus.

I will recommend that all mated females be checked for oestrus daily, even if they fail to return during this period, because they can lose their pregnancy at any time and begin to accumulate costly non-productive days.

You should not get discouraged when your staff takes the female to your boar and nothing happens. Sometimes, once females exhibit the standing reflex, they will often stand for 10 to 15 minutes and then become unwilling to be mounted even though they are in oestrus. This stubbornness state fades within a few hours and females will accept the boar and stand immobilized again.

As mentioned earlier, you should avoid putting your boar permanently into the sow cell, as such constant exposure to a boar can cause a reduction in the expression of oestrous behaviours.

Your boar should be sound, mature, and have a high level of libido. Bring the sow to the boar or place the sow in a cell next to the boar for 15 minutes twice a day when the heat is expected. The physical touch and pheromones from their saliva and urine that a boar produces would stimulate the onset and expression of oestrus in females. It is recommended that you put the sow and boar together just before feeding.

During her 24-hour peak heat period, allow the boar to serve twice, with an interval of about 12-14 hour between services. You can use 2 boars for the 2 mating but try and avoid mating animals during the hot time of the day.

16.8 HOW TO INDUCE HEAT IN YOUR SOWS THROUGH WEANING

Managing heat in your mature sows is easier than in gilts, especially if they are still nursing piglets. In mature sows, oestrus usually begins within three to seven days after weaning. This characteristic of the sow is very critical for you as a farmer as this behaviour can be used to your advantage to synchronise pregnancy naturally. A farmer can easily synchronise the heat in sows by weaning them at the same time.

While a sow is nursing piglets, the suckling action of the nursing piglets inhibits the development of the follicles on the ovaries of sows during lactation. However, during weaning though the sow's udder becomes more and more engorged with milk and since the piglets that could suckle the milk have been removed from the sow, the consequence is that the follicular growth is allowed to grow, which ultimately culminate into oestrus and ovulation within three to seven days after weaning. The significant of this to you as a farmer is that if groups of sows were weaned on the same day, this will happen to all of them at the same time. In a way this is a natural oestrus synchronization.

The implication of this for you as a farmer is that if you can determine when your sows come on heat, you can determine when they will be mated and when they will ultimately give birth. This becomes more important if you have a pig order to supply a certain number of pigs every month, you can work your sows to give birth at a specific time to meet your farm goal.

The ability to precisely control the onset of oestrus is referred to as synchronization.

As mentioned earlier, pigs in the wild wean their piglets at the 8th to 13th weeks. When weaning is done at eight weeks or more, the sow normally dries off quite easily, however, when weaning is done too early, as early as five weeks, the sow's milk yield is at its maximum. Your staff must step in to assist nature to ensure that the sow suffers no discomfort by adding one tablespoon of Epsom salts (magnesium sulphate) to her water to reduce milk production.

On the day of weaning, it is preferable that sow not piglets are moved to another cell. This is to reduce the weaning shock on the piglets. After removing the sow from the piglets, give her no food and only a little water for twenty-four hours. After this period, she could be allowed to have free access to water and 3.2 kg of feed until she comes on heat and is served.

Oestrus normally occurs spontaneously in gilts and mature females that are not pregnant or lactating. Once oestrous cycles have begun, they normally occur every 18 to 21 days, so your staff goal, once you have a new gilt on your farm, is to study her for 21 days to know her heat period.

16.9 THE BENEFITS OF SYNCHRONISING FARROWING ON YOUR FARM

As mentioned earlier, synchronisation is particularly important to farmers because the ability to control oestrus will allow farmers to better plan and coordinate the farm to meet the goal of the farm and reduce the sows non-productive days.

The profitability of sows in your pig farm is dependent not only on the size of litter your sows produced (i.e. number of piglets farrowed) but also on how frequently she farrows (short interval reduces non-productive time) in a year. As a farmer, you want your groups of sows to farrow in an organised way at a particular time; this is called batch farrowing.

The main benefits of having your groups of sows or gilt to farrow at the same time include:

1. It will allow you to have batches of larger groups and uniform animals to meet the market demand consistently, most buyers prefer to buy bulk (certain volume of pigs) to fill their truck than having to visit several farms buying or buying fewer pigs to load their truck.

2. Meeting the need of the buyer in turn gives the farmer the seller power to negotiate a better price.

3. Managing pigs in groups e.g. breeders, weaners and finishers results in more efficient use of time (e.g. selling in batches and cleaning the empty pen for another batch).

4. It also makes planning and scheduling work for staff, e.g. to know when you will need to recruit extra hands, especially during the busy weeks (e.g. during mating, farrowing, weaning).

5. It allows better coordination of farm activities such as medications and castrations (e.g. administering iron dextrose or implementing bulk castration).

6. Managing pigs of similar age makes it possible to source for particular feed ingredients in bulk and to compound food in bulk e.g. for the entire grower and finisher population.

7. Pig movements and management practices will also be easier to plan and predict e.g. scheduled transporter e.g. to pick and deliver 50 pigs to the abattoir.

8. Cross fostering is also easier. It gives you more foster mothers to choose from, when one of the sows cannot successfully nurse the piglets especially when colostrum is needed.

Detection of oestrus is relatively simple, but it is important that all your staff knows how to detect the signs of approaching oestrus in the female pigs and how to effectively utilize a boar to maximize the oestrus.

This is critical especially if you have a large number of sows in your farm that needed crossing, employee turnover, and unskilful staff with limited pig farm experience can increase the chance of errors. As the proprietor, you need to regularly train your staff on detection of oestrus. Staffs that are particularly observant, patient, and consistent are likely to excel at detecting oestrus if provided with some training.

You can also achieve sows' synchronisation through pharmacological means e.g. by giving P.G. 600 to induce heat in their gilts or sows.

P.G. 600 is a combination of serum gonadotropin (Pregnant Mare Serum Gonadotropin or PMSG) and chorionic Gonadotropin (Human Chorionic Gonadotropin or HCG). In gilts and sows, the action of P.G. 600 is similar to the action of Follicle-Stimulating Hormone (FSH), which is produced in the pig's brain. It stimulates the follicles of the ovaries to produce mature ova (eggs), and it promotes the outward signs of oestrus (heat).

But instead of using expensive medication, I will advise farmers to focus on how to achieve sow's heat through taking advantage of the natural characteristic of pigs and effective management of the farm.

As soon as your sow stops breast feeding, she should be moved into a cell that is near the boar to stimulate females to express oestrus.

Research has shown that 90 to 95% of sows come on heat within 5 to 10 days after weaning. The period of oestrus usually lasts for three days but the sow will only stand for the boar for only two of the three days.

The best time to mate your sow is 12 to 36 hours after onset of heat (standing heat). Second service at 12 hours after the first service is also advocated to guarantee higher conception rate and litter size.

Accurate and consistent detection of oestrus by your staff is necessary to ensure mating occurs near the time of ovulation. Errors in detection of oestrus will reduce reproductive performance and increase herd non-productive days.

The following poor management practices on the farm can reduce heat e.g.

1. Poor feed intake during lactation, several studies have shown that even short periods, 3 to 4 days of reduced feed intake during lactation can affect rebreeding success.

2. Too short lactation length — short lactation lengths are problematic because, often, the sows have not had sufficient time to recover after farrowing to elicit normal hormonal responses to weaning.

3. Too long lactation length — long lactation lengths, amount of demand put on the sow's body tissues during lactation exceed nutrient provided to the sow, which results in poor subsequent reproductive activity.

4. Number of litters the sow has farrowed — the higher the number of piglets the more the demand is placed upon the sow.

5. Boar exposure after weaning — adequate boar exposure in weaned sows is critical to stimulate post weaning oestrus.

6. Elevated ambient temperatures associated with the summer months do affect heat. Stress of heat makes the sow lose interest.

16.10 KEY POINTS TO A SUCCESSFUL MATING

- Always introduce the sow to the boar.

- Always observe every service to completion, have a staff on standby.

- Do not commence services too early, wait for 2 or more signs.

- Match the size of the boar to the size of sow.

- Make sure the sow is standing completely still and solid for the first mating.

- Serve in a pen that is dry, with no projections and a non-slip floor.

- The floor area for mating should be at least 8 feet by 10 feet

- Assist entry of the penis into the vagina if necessary, by cupping a clean or gloved hand.

- Ensure the penis is locked in and then observe between the testicles for the pulsation of the urethra to indicate that insemination is taking place.

- Observe that there is no leakage of semen from the vulva.

- Always use a fresh unused boar for the first service.

- Never use a boar that is stiff or lame, you will risk a small litter.

- Handle the boar and sow quietly and patiently.

- Kindness and good empathy mean good fertility.

- Only serve twice every 24 hours.

- Use two boars for one sow where possible and serve am and pm.

- Maintain the sow in dry warm housing for 21 days post-service.

- Do not mix sows after day 2 post-service.

- Feed sows 2.5kg maximum of feed for 2 days post-service then to body condition to day 21 (minimum of 3kg).

- Feed a balanced diet concentrate with 1% lysine from weaning to 21 days post-service.

16.11 **PREPARING YOUR BOAR FOR BREEDING**

At age three to four months, your boar will start producing immature sperm. The first mature sperm are produced at age five to six months old and the first ejaculation may also appear at this age, though this may start earlier with the indigenous breed. After puberty, the fertility of your boar continues to increase until he is twelve months old.

A year-old uncastrated male pig is at the peak of his reproductive potential. From eight to twelve months old, your boar will be able to cope with a maximum of four services per week. That is one service per day and a day of rest before the next service. During the peak of the mating season, this workload can be increased to six services per week. Two services will be done on every alternate day.

Selecting a boar

Your goal as a farmer is to teach the boar as quickly as possible that the reward for courting and mounting is mating. You must make sure that the first sexual experience of your boar is favourable and enjoyable. This will ensure that your boar get pleasure from his work. Naturally, it is best for young boar to serve a few smaller gilts alone in his own pen to gain mating experience before using him on larger or experienced sows.

The development and the building up of your young boar's confidence is vital. Do not allow a group of gilts or sows to intimidate a young boar. And do not let your staff tease your boar. Make sure the first set of gilts to be first mated by your boar is well on heat and standing firmly. Make sure your boar feels comfortable and at home in his own surroundings before you used him to serve the female pigs. This is why it is preferred to always take your sow to the male.

Like all male animals, boars are very territorial and will only mate in an environment that they are familiar with or feel in control of. Avoid using your newly bought-in boar for serving as soon as he arrives. To achieve the best results always bring your sow or gilt into the boar's own pen. If the floor seems wet cover it generously with sawdust, wood shavings or straw to provide a firm footing — this is very important for the boar's confidence.

Keep a close eye on the young boar and make sure that his sex drive is up to expectations. If the libido is low, give it another trial and if it continues cull the boar.

Make sure that the young boar is serving the sows correctly and that the boar does not enter the anus of the gilts and sows and ejaculate there. If this does happen, correct the boar by guiding the penis to the right orifice of the female pig with your hand. With age and experience, the boar will grow in confidence and expertise.

Mating should be done before the heat of the day and should not be done directly after a feed. Serving the boar before 10 am is the best as the sun is not yet out and the pig has a full stomach from the 8am feed.

Records must be kept of all mating so that the conception rate and litter sizes of the boar can be worked out. This will ensure that any infertile or sub-fertile boars can be identified and removed from the breeding herd as soon as possible. Both overworking and underworking can reduce the fertility of the boar. The best conception rates occur when a boar is used no more than six times a week limited to two services a day. The boar must rest for a full day before the next service.

16.12 RATIO OF BOARS TO SOWS

In practice, one boar should be able to handle up to 10 sows in a farm, while two boars can handle over 20 sow. An adult boar can deal with twenty sows a month if two are mated every alternate day. If farrowing is spread evenly throughout the year, one boar can be used for 30 to 40 sows as mating will be required about once a week.

While boars can be in active service for up to four years, they are often replaced earlier because of the following reasons:

1. the boar is too big and does not match the size of gilts

2. the boar is too fat and heavy to serve younger and smaller sows and gilts

3. the boar has gone off serving or is taking too long to serve his sows

4. the boar has become bad tempered and savage and is too dangerous to keep any longer

Time of mating

The best time to carry out mating is early morning before feeding or in the evening when the sun is setting but before it gets dark. Serving on a full stomach can impose unnecessary strain. Also, the boar is more active in the early morning and late evening, particularly during hot weather.

The actual number of services and their timing is dictated by whether oestrus detection is carried out once or twice daily. Two services 12–18 hours apart usually give better results than either a double service 24 hours apart, or a single service. Triple services can be used if litter size is considered to be low. Plan the third mating for about 12 hours after the second only if the sow allows the male.

Mating behaviour

As mentioned earlier, it is preferable to take the sow to the boar, as she normally assumes the major role in searching out the male. This initial contact is important in replacing the social contact behaviour with the sexual behaviour sequence.

When a sow is introduced to a boar, the boar will approach her, emitting characteristic grunts. She may run from him and he will follow, continuing to grunt, grinding his teeth and producing foaming saliva. He may urinate frequently. He attempts to make contact with her and if she stops, he may nose her flank quite forcefully, sniff the genital region and her head, and then attempt to mount.

If the sow responds by adopting the mating stance (standing immobile, back arched with ears cocked), it is a signal to the boar that she is receptive, and he will mount and copulation will occur. Ejaculation is signalled by tightening and relaxing of the anal sphincter and should last at least 3 minutes. If any less than that, the mating should be considered doubtful. The boar signals the end of copulation by dismounting.

Staff Assistance

Pigs rarely needs assistance during mating; however, it is important for your staff to be present during mating to ensure that a satisfactory service took place. Especially when the sow or gilt is introduced to your boar and she is reluctant for mating, she should be removed as quickly and quietly as possible. It is not advisable to leave a sow unattended with the boar. There is always the risk of the boar causing serious injury to the sow especially with a very aggressive boar.

16.13 WHAT HAPPENS WITHIN YOUR PIGS BEFORE, DURING AND AFTER MATING?

As we mentioned throughout this book, the more you know about the way pig bodies work, especially after mating, the better you can support and help your pigs to perform better and ultimately help you to achieve the farm's overall goal of large healthy litters. Not understanding, the way a pig's body works at all is worse than playing a lottery and this has been the bane of many pig farmers in Africa and some farmers have ended up doing contradictory things that have undermined the productivity of their pigs.

While we cannot all be a veterinarian, (this takes 6 to 7 years of intensive study and dedications). Understanding some basic anatomy and physiology of pigs that are relevant to your farm's productivity is important to every farmer. So, let's look at what happens inside your female pigs before and after your boar mate them.

Minus 3 days before heat

Three days prior to the manifestation of the early signs of heat in your female pigs, a hormone called FSH or follicle stimulating hormone will trigger the development of 8-10 eggs on each ovary. As the eggs matures, oestrogen, another hormone, which is responsible for the typical signs of oestrus is triggered. About 40 hours after the onset of oestrus, ovulation takes place which is the release of the egg.

Implication of this on your farm

If a pig produces 8 to 10 eggs in each ovary, that means there is the potential for a sow to farrow to 16 to 20 piglets. A farmer needs to know some of the factors that determine the number of eggs your female pigs will shed during ovulation, they include:

1. **Age.** The more mature a pig is the more eggs they produce, for example, sow may ovulate 18-20 ova while gilt may ovulate 12-14 ova.

2. **Nutrition.** The quality and the frequency of feed that you fed to your pig will also influence the number of eggs produced, for example, farmers that increase the energy levels of feed prior to oestrus (flushing) may increase the number of eggs.

3. **Breed**. The white or maternal breeds generally produce more eggs.

4. **Crossbred females** generally have a higher number of eggs than either of the parent breeds. While inbred pigs have fewer eggs.

Day 1

1. Your staff should be able to detect signs of heat in your gilt or sow at this stage and bring her to the boar's pen.

2. Oestrus may last only 12 hours in gilts or up to 60 hours in sow.

3. The boar climbs and deposits semen into the cervix of the gilt or sow during mating.

4. The muscular contractions of the cervix by the female stimulates ejaculation of the boar.

5. About 30 to 60 billion sperm were deposited by the boar during natural mating

6. Even though sperm are motile, sperm are transported through uterine contractions stimulated by oxytocin produced by the female pig — that is why it is important that your gilts and sows are treated with care and tenderness before, during and after mating.

7. Only a small fraction of these sperm reaches the vicinity of the egg.

8. Sperm must reside in the female for 6-10 hours before fertilization.

Implication of this on your farm

1. Since the actual time of the onset of oestrus is rarely known, it is recommended that a female receive at least two services during oestrus. This helps ensure that sperm are present at an optimum time relative to ovulation for fertilization to occur and it may increase conception rate and litter size by approximately 10%.

2. Uterine contractions are stimulated by the stimuli from mating behaviour and copulation. This is particularly important when a farmer is artificially inseminating a sow or gilt, more effort is needed to stimulate the sow.

3. It has been proven that face-to-face contact with a boar, plus tactile stimulus does improve sperm transport.

4. You should avoid late heat mating — failure to mate during a heat period means that your pig will have to go through a post breeding inflammatory response in the uterus to remove the non-fertilized sperm and this can cause bacterial infection of the reproductive organ.

Day 2

1. Fertilization rate is usually 100% if the female is mated to a fertile boar at the correct time.

2. Fertilization or union of sperm and egg occurs in the upper 1/3 of the oviduct to form the blastocysts.

3. The fertilised eggs (blastocysts) enter the uterus and begin to migrate and space themselves on the uterus horn.

Implication of this on your farm

1. To increase the number of sperms that are fertilised, where possible 2 different boars should be used to service a female pig at 12 hour intervals.

2. Preferably, use a proven fertile boar and a new one.

3. Don't raise or lower feeding levels within the first 30 days after breeding, instead provide a good, level plane of nutrition during and after breeding.

Days 11-16

1. The fertilised egg (blastocysts) stretch to 2-3 feet long and begin to attach to the uterine wall.

2. This is the most critical period during pregnancy, where most losses in litter size occurs due to the failure of the attachment of the blastocyst to the uterus.

3. On average, 16 eggs are shed at oestrus yet only about 10 to 12 are accounted for on most farms.

4. Research has shown that overcrowding is a major limiting factor

5. Other environmental stressors such as high temperatures and fighting as a result of mixing or regrouping animals can adversely influence implantation and embryo survival.

6. The presence of at least four blastocysts are required in order for pregnancy to` continue.

The implication of this on your farm

1. Your effort during this critical period should be to remove most stresses from your newly serviced female pigs. That is, to avoid under feeding, excessive temperature, forceful handling and any unnecessary moving of your pigs.

2. Minimize unnecessary stress by totally avoiding the mixing of female pigs until 30 days after fertilization. This is because implantation occurs between day 13 to

28 and during this time, any unnecessary stress such as sudden movement and bullying, etc. can result in embryo detachment and loss.

3. Please note, moving sows and gilts at any time during or following breeding greatly increases the chances of subsequent embryo mortality from transport stress and temperature changes.

4. Where possible, allow the animal to be on her own in an individual cell during this period

5. Avoid exposure to outside animals to minimise disease risk.

6. Feed intake should be reduced to the limit feeding level of 2 kg immediately after mating to avoid embryo loss due to high energy intake.

7. Farrowing less than five piglets is indicative of embryo death after the time of attachment.

Day 25-35

1. The 30-day mark is an important one during swine pregnancy, this is when skeletal development takes place.

2. This is when the piglets' bones are beginning to develop.

3. If there's a problem with the pregnancy before 30 days that causes all the piglets to die, the mother's body will reabsorb the babies and she would resume her normal heat cycles.

4. After 35 days, the babies can't be reabsorbed completely because their bones have begun to calcify. Instead, the sow will deliver mummified bodies of her babies.

5. Nutrients, waste, gases and certain antibodies cross the membranes between the dam and embryos blood systems.

The implication of this on your farm

1. As mentioned earlier, where possible, pregnant sows should be housed in individual cells with sufficient floor space. This will prevent disturbance, sudden movement and bullying.

2. The sow should rest and be quiet during this period when the fertilised eggs are implanting themselves unto the ovary wall.

3. Increase the calcium in the feed.

4. Improve the animal protein of the feed.

5. This may not be the good news that you wanted to hear but from the mummified bodies of your dead piglets you can guess what time their mortality took place post 35 days during the pregnancy.

Day 36-40

1. The foetal development period begins, sexes are determined.

2. Foetal orientation is determined; some are head to head; some are tail to tail and some are head to tail. At farrowing, about half are born tail first, and half are born head-first.

3. Calcification of the skeleton of dead foetal begins and deaths occurring after this point will result in mummification.

The implication of this on your farm

1. The sow should rest and be quiet during this period.

2. Avoid returning recently-served sows or gilts back to her previous group immediately.

3. Do not mix newly mated pig up with other non-familiar females

4. Farmer also needs to make sure that the floor is dry and not slippery, as slippery floors may lead to falling, causing accidental abortions.

5. Check your sows every 21 days to see if they come on it, even after 2 months into pregnancy.

Day 109 plus

1. The foetus now weighs about 2½ to 3 pounds with hair shafts.

2. Throughout gestation, the uterus gradually enlarges from about 2 to 3 pounds.

3. The piglet grows from the union of a microscopic sperm and egg into a fully formed individual weighing from 3 to 3½ pounds.

4. Sow loses up to 10 to 11% of their body weight at parturition or farrowing.

The implication of this to your farm

1. You should continue to provide the female with the required amount of energy and amino acids.

2. Providing additional feed to sows and gilts in late gestation will increase sow weight gain which might influence pig survivability during lactation.

3. Your objective of feeding your sow during pregnancy are first, so that she can produce an adequate number of piglets that are of acceptable body weight, secondly, so that the mammary glands are properly developed and produce high-quality colostrum and milk

4. A good way to determine how much feed to give to your sow is to feed them twice a day with as much food as she can finish up in thirty minutes of feeding. The advantage of doing this is to prevent the sow from getting too fat.

5. It is recommended that you feed your sow normally for the first three months of pregnancy and in the last month feed them ad libitum. Foetuses generally grow rapidly towards the end of pregnancy and nutrient requirements increase.

6. Treat your female pig for lice and mange.

7. Deworm your pig.

8. Increase observation of sows, check for the presence of milk and assist with farrowing.

17. Care and Management of Pregnant Sow

As a pig farmer, your overall goals for sow productivity can be summarised as:

- maximizes number of pigs per litter;

- optimizes pig birth weight;

- maximizes litters per year;

- maximizes lactation yield;

- optimizes longevity and lifetime productivity.

Sow's life on a pig farm is broken into the three phases:

1. Gestating a litter
2. Nursing a litter
3. Not pregnant but getting ready for the next litter

The longest of the three phases — gestation — could arguably be the most critical phase.

Now that you have successfully mated your pigs, you can confirm that she is pregnant by her failure to return to oestrus 3 weeks following the mating. The time period between mating and farrowing is known as gestation or pregnancy period.

Here are some basic facts about the life cycle of a pig.

Age at breeding — varies: for a gilt 220 days; for a boar about 7 months

Oestrus cycle — 18-24 days — three weeks

Gestation — 115 days — three months, three weeks and three days

Breeding season — generally none — poorer in the summer and early autumn

Slaughter weight — about 85 to 100kg at about 26 weeks of age

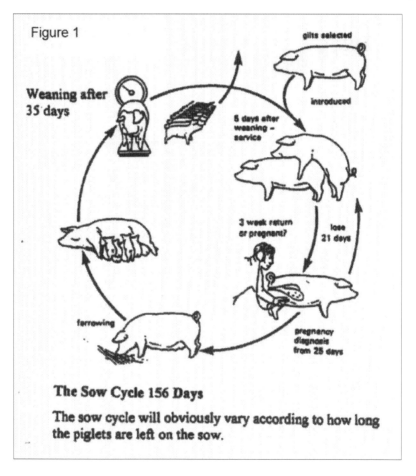

Source: https://www.britishloppig.org.uk/news-and-events/view/deerpark-pedigree-pigs

17.1 **HOUSING**

As mentioned earlier, after mating a sow needs to rest. She should be housed in an individual cell with sufficient floor space. This will prevent disturbance, sudden movement and bullying.

Farmers should provide restful and quiet surroundings for the newly mated pigs during the period when the fertilised eggs are implanting themselves unto the ovary wall. Recently-served sows or gilts should not be returned back to her previous group immediately or be mixed up with other non-familiar females that are awaiting service or those that are already pregnant.

Newly-served gilts are particularly more vulnerable; they could easily lose up to 2 piglets from their litter size through stress, lose 200 grams birth weight per pig or have lots of un-even litters.

Farmers also need to make sure that the floor is dry and not slippery, as slippery floors may lead to falling, causing acci-dental abortions.

17.2 **FEEDING**

During pregnancy, sows will definitely gain about two-thirds of their body weight. This will be from the fattening of the sow herself and from the embryos and embryonic fluid. Feeding is of particular importance and conversion of food into body weight is efficient and nutrient retention is also very high. Some studies suggest that high levels of feed intake are associated with proper embryonic development.

Nevertheless, it is not recommended that your sow should gain excessive weight during pregnancy or else they will be too heavy after farrowing and clumsy and piglets will be easily crushed.

You should feed your sow normally for the first three months of pregnancy and in the last month feed them ad libitum. Foetuses generally grow rapidly towards the end of pregnancy, and the nutrient requirements also increase. Finally, it is also important to promote increased appetite in sows as they will need this ability during lactation to eat their required nutrients.

Feed highly with bulky feeds from 4-5 days before and after farrowing by substituting with maize, watercress, ground legumes, which may help prevent constipation.

17.3 WHY YOU NEED TO PREVENT UNDER AND OVER-WEIGHT OF YOUR PIGS DURING PREGNANCY

Sows that are too thin during gestation are forced to draw on fat reserves from their own body to feed the piglets inside her — "milking off her back".

This may lead to the following:

- Early farrowing before the expected date
- Lower piglet weight and litter size
- Longer farrowing due to exhausted sows
- Lower milk production
- Poor ovulation, conception, litter numbers and the next lactation
- Increase of Interval between weaning and mating

Too fat sows in gestation may reversely induce the following disadvantages:

- Difficult and long farrowing (>4h)

- Increased stillborn piglets due to a reduced passage in the vagina

- Lower feed consumption in lactation leading to a high weight loss

- Feet troubles and early culling

17.4 WHY DO PIGLETS DIE BEFORE THEY ARE BORN

As mentioned earlier, a typical sow produces an average of 18 to 20 eggs during the heat and there is 100% fertilisation by the boar, then comes the question, why do most of our female pigs gives birth to 6 to 9 piglets on our farm?

Recent studies done in England revealed that the majority of your piglet loss happens before the piglets are born and that mortality in some farms even before birth can be as high as 40 per cent. Majority of this embryo loss occurs during the first two to three weeks following mating.

Factors associated with embryo loss include stage of pregnancy, disease, age of dam, genetic factors, nutrition, external environment, intrauterine environment, and stress-including heat stress.

The following recommendations should help to reduce embryo mortality:

1. Avoid late heat mating of sows- failure to mate means that pigs will have to go through a post-breeding inflammatory response in the uterus to remove the non-fertilized spermatozoa and this can cause bacterial infection of the reproductive organ and may affect the next batch of fertilised eggs.

2. Minimize unnecessary stress of mixing of female pigs after fertilization, implantation occurs between day 13 to 28. During this time, any unnecessary stress such as sudden movement and bullying and temperature following breeding can result in embryo detachment and loss.

3. Moving and transporting sows and gilts at any time during or following breeding greatly increases the chances of subsequent embryo mortality from transport stress and temperature changes.

4. Don't raise or lower feeding levels within the first 30 days after breeding, Instead provide a good, level plane of nutrition during and after breeding.

17.5 HOW CAN YOU IMPROVE THE LITTER SIZE OF YOUR FEMALE PIGS

As a pig farmer one of your key objectives is to have a large litter size on your farm.

Litter size is defined as the number of piglets born. It can be used to express the number of fully-formed individuals given birth to at farrowing.

Low litter size is a major problem for most African pig farmers. A commercial pig farmer should however be concerned when the gilts gave birth to less than 6 piglets and 8 piglets by a sow.

It is difficult to precisely work out the financial implication for a drop-in litter size, but we will try to determine the cost of achieving piglets on a typical Nigerian farm.

A sow will consume about N63, 875 ($182) worth of feed a year (2.5kg daily x N70 per kg of feed x 365 days), and she is expected to produce at least 16 piglets (8 piglets per litter x 2 litters per year) every 12 calendar months.

N63,875/16 piglets that means it costs N3,992 ($11) in feed alone to produce a piglet.

According to John Gadd, the author of A Practical Guide to Profit, UK studies have shown that the loss of just 2 piglets born per litter can reduce the amount of income that could be generated from the sow by as much as 15 to 20%. While these kinds of losses might not be obvious to the farmer, it can be the difference between a profitable farm and a mediocre farm.

Factors that affect gilt litter size on your farm

Serving your gilt too young — most new farmers buy gilts (especially the exotic breeds) and because of the size and the weight of the animal (not to mention the cost) they want to mate the gilt quickly. This is not the best for the pig as most hybrids or exotic pigs grow very quickly. When selecting gilts for breeding, "it is age not weight that matters". Age 7 to 8 months (or the 3rd heat of the gilts) is the critical factor that farmers must consider, not so much the weight, the size or the fat cover of the gilts.

Most exotic modern gilt can easily grow above their age especially when compared with the hybrid or popular breed. That means that though she may be heavy enough and even show vigorous signs of oestrus, if she is mated, she will have a poor conception rate or low first litter size due to immature sexual hormones and the fact that she is still growing.

If you are starting with exotic breed or oversized pig, you should avoid the temptation of rushing to mate your new gilt because you want to quickly get some pay back for the cost of procuring the gilt.

My advice to farmers is to buy gilt at 35–40 kg 3 to 4 months and raise it on your farm to 7 to 8 months so as to avoid any possibility of the seller farm 'forcing' the gilt sale before it reaches its proper age. And if you are not sure about the age of the gilts you bought, you should count the number of heats that she had on your farm and only mate at the 3rd heat.

Flushing in gilts

We mentioned flushing earlier. Flushing is important especially in gilts. It is a process that involves increasing the energy in the feed to stimulate the production of eggs in the female animal just before oestrus (7 to 10 days). Flushing can increase the number of eggs shed by gilt by one or two.

Flushing also encourages the 'feel-good' factor in the gilt. Most of the time, by the time your new sets of gilts arrive on your farm, they would have undergone transportation stress. In addition, they are stressed (from nervousness) with the new environment and some of them probably had quarrelsome fights on the way to your farm with the new sets of pigs that they were introduced to in the vehicle.

You should encourage your staff to off-load the gilts gently, settling them down and quietly into their pen. They should be provided with cool water and given a good high-nutrient feed that will also calm them down quickly into the 'feel good' factor which is so necessary for successful first litter formation.

Flushing in sows

Flushing also applies to sows. Sows that are in the lower than normal condition at weaning (i.e. loss lots of weight) do give poorer subsequent litter performance as well as poor re-service problems. Flushing can assist the sows to recover quickly, though it is expedient that farmers should improve the sow productivity by defending and protecting the sow from voracious piglets either by increasing the feed or by fostering the piglets.

Research has shown that high nutrient intake between weaning and service do help more eggs to be released closer together in time and/or it enables the womb surface (endometrium) to regain receptivity sooner.

Studies have also shown that for each 10 kg weight loss in lactation, subsequent litter size can be reduced by 1 pigs/litter.

The effect of friendly staff on sow productivity

Any pig that is harassed or stressed either through beating, bullying or humiliation rather than comfortable and contented is prone to poorer performance. Tender loving care from staff is particularly important in the lead-up to breeding gilts, and after mating. Farm staff that work closely with the pigs should do everything that they can to keep the sows calm and contented in a restful atmosphere once mating is over.

Contrary to stressing, experienced staff who show tender loving care to female pigs and encourages the production of reproductive hormones enjoy better litter sizes

Whereas staff that create fear and anxiety to female pigs tend to neutralize the pro-oestrus hormones and ultimately affect litter size.

17.6 IMPACTS OF YOUR STAFF BEHAVIOUR AND ATTITUDE ON YOUR LITTER SIZE

Here are the impacts of your staff behaviour and attitude on your litter size. That is causing fewer litter piglets:

- **Gilts** — poor and late heat detection, unkept and dirty floor, sudden noise, beating, bullying, lack of the 'Feel Good Factor', disease

- **Sows** — poor checking for returns, herd age profile, stress, discomfort, anxiety, genetics

- **Boars** — not monitoring boar records, overuse of favourite boar, not cleaning boar's sheath, poor nutrition, lack of exercise

You should do the following to reduce the pig stress on your farm

- Ensure that there is adequate space, especially fleeing space

- Watch out for the number of female pigs that you put together. It should be between 6 to 10 per pen

- Ensure evenness — if allowed, excited heavier gilts can become dominant and aggressive

- Keep gilt and sow separately

- Ensure adequate food and water access

Disease

Disease normally affects litter size after service. Call your veterinarian if you have stillborn, together with mummies.

Mycotoxins.

Studies have shown that various mycotoxins at very low levels may have a bearing on low litter size. Watch out for feed ingredients that are prone to aspergillus e.g. groundnut cake and grains, especially during the humid rainy season, always include antitoxin in the feed or stored grain. We will look at Mycotoxin in more details later in the book.

Genetic

This is the factor that most farmers always claim as the reason for their small litter size. While this is partly correct to some degree as all body functions implicated in litter size are under genetic control. However, if all your females are producing small litters, you should look at other factors, not focus on genetics alone which is out of your control.

As mentioned earlier in the essential attitude of successful farmer, you must have a winner's attitude, you should not be in a state of helplessness, you should always start by dealing with problems that are within your control and don't be overwhelmed with the ones that are not in your control. Always remember the quote from Francis of Assisi, *"Start by doing what's necessary; then do what's possible; and suddenly you are doing the impossible."*

17.7 HOW TO IMPROVE YOUR PIGLETS' BIRTHWEIGHTS

As a farmer, your goal should not only be to increase the number of pigs in your litters per sow but it should also be the birth weights of the piglets born alive on your farm.

According to John Gadd, studies have shown that the bigger the size of the litter the more the number of piglets that ultimately survive.

For example, a difference of 0.5 kg birthweight is equivalent to a weaning weight of 1 kg and 10kg at finisher.

Birth weight is important because it is an area that is within farmer's control. Birthweight is not determined by genetics but rather by how well your staff manage and treat the gilt or sow at the very early stage of the reproductive cycle.

What can you do on your farm to improve birth weight?

- Your staff need to make sure that they detect sow or gilt heat on time

- Where possible a female should be mated 2 times by a boar or 2 boars during the heat period

- After mating, staff should ensure that they provide rest and quiet place for the female pig to rest as this is the time for the gilt or sow to fertilise and implant the eggs

- Sow and gilt should be free from stress and sexual excitement from boar or other sow after mating

- Leaving sow to be on her own at the time is crucial, try not to mix sows at this time

- A relatively high nutrient intake between weaning and service is also beneficial. This may help more eggs to be released closer together in time and it also enables the womb surface (endometrium) to regain receptivity sooner

- Increase feed allowance (1.8 to maybe 3.0 kg) of this diet as pregnancy progresses

- Never let a sow nose-dive in lactation. This will impact on the next litter

17.8 HOW TO DIFFERENTIATE A HEALTHY AND A PIG IN DISTRESS DURING PREGNANCY

OBSERVATION	HEALTHY	DISTRESS
Appetite	She consumes all feed	She is off-feed feed refusal
Body condition	She is able to maintain it	She started losing weight
Response to stimulus	She stands up	Won't stand up apathetic or lethargic
Soundness and structure	Bearing weight evenly on all four legs	Lameness
Skin and cover	Short and smooth hair, pink skin	Long or rough hair yellow, pale or blue skin
Gestation	Able to maintain gestation mammary gland development	Abortion no mammary gland development
Body temperature	Normal: up to 101.4° F (38°C) in gestation up to 104° F (40°C) the day after farrowing	Fever: >101.4° F (>39°C) in gestation; >104° F (>40°C) the day after farrowing
Respiratory	Normal frequency: 13-20/min	Coughing, abnormal respiratory
Faeces	Manure is soft	frequency Scours
Urine	Long and strong urine stream	constipation Short urine, white urine

Source: A practical guide to profit by John Gadd

17.9 MANAGING FARROWING AND TAKING CARE OF NEW-BORN PIGLETS

Farrowing is the process where the sow gives birth to piglets. It also marks the end of the conception period in which the embryos have developed into baby pigs. Farrowing in pigs can range between 113 to 116 day without any serious consequences. Pigs that have large litters tend to have shorter gestation lengths compared to those with smaller and lighter litters.

It is therefore important for your farm to take note of the date that the female was mated, check whether she comes on heat again 3 weeks (21 days) after this. I would advise that you check out for heat again 42 days later to make sure she does not come on heat. Once these two heats are negative, then the date that the pig was originally mated should be recorded and farmer should add 112 days to that date. This is the expected week that sow will give birth.

As the farrowing date approaches, your staff needs to make some early preparations for the sow's farrowing. This is crucial for the survival of the piglets. You will begin to notice the clear signs of imminent birth. While complications are normally few during farrowing, it is advisable that a staff is on the ground to take care of the sows and the piglets if any problem arises.

Sow that has just farrowed piglets with placenta still hanging.   *The sow with new sets piglet'*

Preparation for farrowing

Two weeks before the farrowing:

- You should deworm and treat the pregnant female for external pests. This is to prevent the spread of this to the new piglets.

- You should wash the farrowing pen with detergent and disinfectant and put clean sow into a clean individual pen.

- Carefully wash the sow herself with soap and clean water with disinfectant and do this again 2 days before farrowing.

- Put adequate bedding material like wood shavings into the farrowing pen. Have enough bedding material for the sow to make a nest for the piglets.

- On the day of farrowing give the sow laxative food such as green fodder (like Gbure, water cress) instead of the normal feed. This prevents the risk of constipation.

Observing sow behaviour towards farrowing

There are a number of outward signs that is noticeable in the female pigs as she prepares to farrow.

1. She suddenly becomes nervous and expresses restless behaviour.

2. This will be accompanied by her instinctive nesting behaviour (pawing at floor), despite 6,000 years of domestication, this behaviour still occurs in pigs under confinement facilities with concrete flooring, so you need to put nesting or bedding materials out to encourage this behaviour.

3. Like their cousin in the wild, domestic pigs tend to farrow mostly during the night or evening.

4. Farmers would also notice slight muscular contractions of the flank, belly and tail even before the delivery begins.

5. The sow's breathing rate also increases or even doubles from a normal 25 to 30 per minute to as high as 80 per minute around five hours before delivery.

6. Before piglets can be delivered, the sow's cervix needs to dilate to allow passage of the piglets and each piglet will be positioned down the uterus toward the cervical opening. These events are controlled by complex changes in hormone levels in the sow.

7. As farrowing time draws nears, the sow's udder becomes more distended and firmer and milk can be seen on the teats.

8. As soon as you can detect that milk is abundantly available in the udder, you can be sure that the delivery of pigs is likely to be within six to eight hours.

9. As the unborn pigs move toward the cervical opening, the powerful contractions of the uterine muscles will break open the placental membranes which contain fluids.

10. Stained fluids with blood will start coming out from the vulva. This is the final sign that farrowing is about to start in less than two hours or less.

It is possible that some of these outward signs might not appear in some sows prior to farrowing, which is why a good record is important to get the timing right.

17.10 **WHAT IS THE ROLE OF OXYTOCIN?**

If you have been in the pig industry long enough, you would have heard about Oxytocin, but what is Oxytocin, what role does it plays in an animal physiology and how can you make sure that this complex hormonal activity during the farrowing and the nursing of the piglets goes well?

To understand this, we have to look again at the anatomy and the physiology of pigs to see what is happening hormonally within the female pigs as farrowing draws nearer.

- As farrowing draws nearer, the brain produces a hormone called prostaglandin which stops the production of progesterone, (progesterone is the hormone that is responsible for sustaining the pregnancy).

- Prostaglandin triggers the release of oxytocin into the bloodstream.

- Oxytocin is a hormone that causes contractions of smooth muscles in the milk glands (causing milk let down in female animals) and in the uterus (it causes the expulsion of pigs).

- Naturally, oxytocin can be stimulated in sow by your staff rubbing on the sow's udder (the same reflexes produced by the suckling of the nursing pigs). The oxytocin will cause the contractions for pig delivery.

- Oxytocin injections can be used to supplement the effects of naturally occurring oxytocin.

17.11 AVOID IMPROPER USE OF OXYTOCIN BY OBSERVING THESE GUIDELINES:

1. Your oxytocin injection will not induce the process of farrowing and should never be given before the sow has at least one piglet born. However, if you decide to do so, the stress that the injection will cause can interrupt or disturb a normal farrowing process.

2. You should only use oxytocin in your sows which appear to have stopped contractions before completion of delivery.

3. Routine use of oxytocin can result in increased stillbirths and other farrowing problems.

4. Always check the birth canal for a lodged pig before giving oxytocin. Failure to clear the passage could result in damage to the sow's uterus.

5. If oxytocin use is deemed to be necessary, inject one unit intramuscularly in the neck. Oxytocin acts rapidly, therefore, excessively large doses are wasteful and potentially dangerous to the sow.

6. Repeat the injection in 20 or 30 minutes if necessary.

17.12 DELIVERY OF PIGS

Farrowing happens all the time in the pig's world both domestically and in the wild and most sows are able to deliver their piglets with little or no help.

Delivery of pigs usually starts with muscular contractions of the uterus and this leads to the expelling of piglets from the uterus, through the dilated cervix and out the vulva. The tail of the sow will twitch a bit as the piglets move through the birth canal.

Delivery of the pig is considered normal whether the front feet and nose or the hind legs are first to exit the sow. The piglets sometimes have to travel more than five feet from the far end of the uterus to the vulva where the piglets come out especially if the mother is a mature sow. That is why some piglets are tired when they come out. The navel cord usually remains connected with the placenta and continues to supply enough oxygen for the piglets throughout the journey until they come out.

First come first served applies in piglet's world

The first-born pigs are usually the biggest and they usually select the juicy and robust teats with lots of colostrum that are close to the front of the sow and as a result they generally have greater survival rates.

Ideally, teats of your sow should be evenly spaced so that the milk produced is divided equally among all teats. However, front teats are spaced more widely than hind teats. This is why there is greater milk production and faster growth of pigs that usually suckle the front teats and again front teats are usually presented more fully to the piglets when the sow lies down to be nursed.

As expected, pigs located at the upper end of the uterus will usually be the last to be born and in the process of birth they could experience the detachment of the umbilical cord from the placenta, leading to loss of oxygen supply to the piglets. This may result in dead or weak piglets at birth.

On average, the total delivery time from the arrival of the first piglets to the last piglets is usually around two and one-half hours.

17.13 WHY SHOULD YOU HAVE STAFF ON STANDBY DURING FARROWING?

The role of your staff that is on standby is to detect and act upon problem farrowing. It is important that your staff do not over-react or interfere unnecessarily with a normal farrowing. Staff should only be concerned if the interval between the last piglet arrival exceeded 45 minutes or if the sow is having contractions without results, then the staff can check the birth canal for possible blockage.

Staff can do the following to help the sow:

1. Thoroughly wash and disinfect their hand and the sow's rear. This is necessary to keep pathogenic organisms from gaining entrance to the reproductive tract from outside.

2. Staff should apply Vaseline or any petroleum jelly on their hand and the vagina.

3. With a well-lubricated, gloved hand, he or she should carefully enter and search the reproductive tract for improperly presented (tail first or broadside) or extremely large pigs. Staff with the smallest hand is preferred to do this where possible.

4. Your staff should make every effort to prevent any damage to the inside of the sow.

5. A slight rotating movement of the hand may assist entry.

6. Some advantage may be gained by using the right hand if the sow is laying on her right side and vice versa.

7. While the hand is in the reproductive tract, if the piglet is located, your staff will need to determine the orientation or position and repositioned them slightly to allow them to enter the birth canal.

8. Time is important to prevent suffocation of the piglet.

9. If the sow stops straining and contracting before farrowing is completed, muscular exhaustion may be the problem. After a short rest, the sow may resume farrowing naturally or can be aided by injected oxytocin.

10. Keeping sows reasonably cool and out of direct sunlight may help prevent exhaustion.

Resuscitating piglets

Even after birth, staff can assist to resuscitate the piglets that appear to be dead at birth (stillborn). Your staff can do the following:

1. First, your staff should clear the mouth and nostrils of the pig with the fingers or a cloth.

2. Staff should hold pigs by their rear legs and gently but forcefully sling them in a downward arc. This will assist the piglets in clearing fluids from the lung and forcing air into the lungs.

3. Alternatively, a vigorous rubbing or massaging of the piglet's body can provide the stimulus needed to get the pig breathing on its own.

Your staff is also on standby during farrowing to detect and prevent sow losses. Loss of the sow is more important than the loss of one or more of your piglets during farrowing. Don't forget losing your sows during farrowing places the survival of all her piglets in doubt.

Sows may die during farrowing due to internal bleeding from haemorrhaging blood vessels in the uterus. You can drastically reduce the sow mortality by making certain that the farrow pen is cool and well ventilated.

You can aid cooling by soaking a towel in cool water and use it along the jaw, chest and udder of the sow, but do not pour water on the head of an over-heated sow during farrowing, as this may lead to shock and death.

Finally, recent studies indicate that having your staff around to attend and assist sows during farrowing can increase your piglet survival and the number of pigs weaned on you farm. Staff can quickly identify disadvantaged piglets and begin to assist them.

Prevent Chilling — you need to provide wood shavings to your farrowing quarters days before farrowing and make sure excess wind or draught is not blowing into the farrowing cell. Staff should closely monitor the sow and litter's responses to the zone heating to ensure their thermal needs are met.

17.14 CLEAN-UP OR EXPULSION OF THE PLACENTA

This final stage of the farrowing process is the expelling of the placenta. Failure to do this may result in severe complications: infections, possible lactation failure, rebreeding problems and death of the sow.

Some of the piglet's placenta are passed during delivery of each of the piglets but most will wait until after the farrowing is completed. Some are eaten by the sow, some argue that this is a bad practice as it might lead to sow eating the new-born piglets, but this is not our experience.

However, it is not healthy for placenta to be retained in the sow. If you cannot find the placenta and the after farrowing, the sow is showing signs of reduced appetite or elevated rectal temperatures, this may be the sign of a retained placenta.

17.15 MILK PRODUCTION IN SOWS

Milk production is a key function of the sow to successfully keep the farrowed piglets alive. The udder of a sow consists of mammary or milk producing tissue and teats which serve as canals to give the piglets access to the milk.

As mentioned earlier, front teats are spaced more widely than hind teats and as a result they have greater milk production and front teats are also usually presented more fully to the piglets when the sow lays down to be nursed, making it more accessible.

Piglets tend to fight the first week of life to choose their preferred teat, and they tend to stick to the preferred teat until they are weaned. Unfortunately, the smaller, weaker pigs are sometimes forced to nurse with the less productive rear teats and this can further reduce their chances for survival.

That is why it is important to select gilts with at least 12-14 functional evenly spaced teats for breeding. The presence of poorly performing nipples such as pin nipples, inverted nipples and nipples damaged by nipple necrosis will reduce the pigs' access to milk produced by the sow.

Other factors that can affect milk production are nutrition, environmental temperature, genetics, mould toxins, diseases and other factors.

The amount of milk produced by your sow and the quality of the composition will ultimately determine the survival and the growth of your piglets. Milk yield will continue to increase until three weeks after farrowing and it then begins to decline.

Sow will require 4 to 5 kg of feed to produce sufficient milk for the piglets without the excessive weight losses.

Piglets are efficient converters of milk to body weight gain at around 3 to 4kg of milk to 1kg of body weight.

Each batch of milk produced by the sow at a time "milk let-down period" only lasts for 20 or 30 seconds but this occurs every one hour.

Piglets are nursed more frequently during the day (when there is light) than at night (dark periods). That means that you can improve the sow's milk yield by exposing sow to longer light on your farm. More milk produced by the sow and consumed by the piglets should result in greater survival and heavier weights of pigs.

Sows which are underfed or ration-fed and who are always hungrily awaiting feeding may not allow piglets to nurse for extended periods of time.

Colostrum milk contains a greater concentration of immuno-globulin proteins increasing the percent of solids and total protein in the milk.

Poor production of milk is found more frequently:

- in fat sows and gilts,
- during extremely hot temperatures,
- in sow fed diets without laxatives,
- in concrete floored farrowing houses using contaminated wood shavings for bedding.

17.16 ACCIDENTAL KILLING OF THE PIGLETS BY THE SOW

Immediately after birth it is normal for the mother to do the following:

- Eat the afterbirth. This is normal.

- Become aggressive towards their litters especially the inexperienced young gilts.

- Become frightened by the new-born piglets and try to avoid them and start biting.

- This hysteria generally subsides in a few hours.

- Test the sow by placing only one piglet with her and watching her reaction.

- In the meantime, keep the rest of the piglets warm in a box.

- For mother that is not settled use tranquilizers or force her to drink a bottle of beer. This should calm the sow down and make her fall asleep enough for the piglets to be able to drink milk without being attacked.

17.17 OTHER POST-FARROWING PROBLEMS

a. One problem that could happen during or after farrowing involves savaging, or the attempts of sows to bite or kill newborn pigs. Savaging tends to occur more in overly fat sows or inexperienced gilts and in certain breeds and family lines. As mentioned earlier, tranquilizers or a bottle of beer may be needed for extreme cases, removal of newborn pigs to a warm box until farrowing is complete may also solve the problem. In severe cases, sows which continue to bite their pigs should be culled from the herd.

b. Lack of appetite, sickness, hypogalactia and constipation are frequently found at the same time in the farrowing house.

c.   Sows which fail to form a stool by 24 to 48 hours after farrowing should receive a prescribed injectable or oral veterinary laxative, or the feed should be top dressed with two tablespoons of Epsom salts (magnesium sulphate) or potassium chloride.

d.   Lack of appetite in the sow is a symptom of sickness and/or constipation. If the sow is sick, the rectal temperature will often be elevated. Frequently, the sow's rectal temperature rises to 41 degrees C) after farrowing veterinary attention is advisable.

e.   Improve appetite and feed intake by using more palatable rations, more frequent feedings, or cooler environmental temperatures.

f.   Check the flow rate of water nipples and the quality of water because water intake and feed intake are closely related.

g.   Sow lameness is caused by rough flooring and can damage foot pads or cause cuts and scrapes. Slippery flooring causes injuries and may discourage sows from attempting to get up, eat and move about.

h.   Observations of the general activity level of the sow can indicate discomfort and the potential for poor sow performance.

i.   Sows which rarely get up or eat and drink may be sick or lame and often do not produce adequate milk yields. It is a good idea to make sure that all sows get up every time you feed them.

17.18 COMMON FARROWING ILLNESSES

Metritis — inflammation of the uterus is suggested by a whitish-yellow and/or foul-smelling discharge from the vagina.

This could be an indication that delivery was not complete. Check and remove if there are any piglets remaining inside.

Mastitis — inflammation of the udder may affect one or more teats hence decreasing milk production and the piglets may starve. Check the temperature of the sow. Treat the sow immediately if temperature is above 39.5°C. Give a 5cc injection of oxytocin and an antibiotic. Review the treatment after 24 hours if the treatment has no effect.

Constipation is brought about when the sows stop eating shortly before farrowing. The sow become restless and neglects her newborn piglets. Ease constipation by feeding laxatives such as castor oil or Epsom salt dissolved in water. In order to prevent constipation before farrowing, one or two tablespoons of Epsom salts should be mixed with the feed each day and extra leafy green foods should be given.

Checklist of days after farrowing

Time (Day)	Management Item
1	Limit sow feed intake to 3-4 lbs.
1-2	Check udders for signs of lactation failure or mastitis. Equalize litters by transferring pigs of same age into smaller litters.
2-7	Gradually increase sow feed intake by 2 pounds per day as long as the sow continues to increase intake
Weaning	Check sows for appetite, rectal temperature, constipation and milk flow (observe nursing of pigs)
	Reduce feed intake to 4-6 lbs. except in extremely thin sows.
	Deworm and treat for lice and mange.

18. Care of the new-born piglets

In the last few chapters, we focused on farrowing from the mother's perspective, i.e. the gilts and the sow. Now we will look at farrowing from the piglet's perspective.

At birth, piglets are born into a hostile bacterial environment, that is your farm. Unfortunately, piglets do not have adequate body fat or sufficient glycogen reserves in their body to maintain body heat for long, so they begin to suffer if they are starved of feed or left in a cold environment for too long.

Immediately after farrowing, it is important that each of your piglets receive colostrum to provide immediate and temporary protection against common bacterial infections. Antibodies in the sow's milk are the best protection against these bacteria.

Piglets get most of their energy and antibodies for the first few days from colostrum and they also require a warm, dry environment — an ambient temperature of about 35 centigrade.

Proper nutrition of the sow, including a laxative ration prior to and following farrowing; maintaining proper environmental temperature; and freedom from contagious disease organisms all help to ensure normal milk production.

Baby pigs may struggle to nurse because of a hostile sow, especially among large litter of pigs, or among small or otherwise weak pigs or death of the sow, or failure of the sow to have sufficient milk. Other ways baby pigs can get antibodies are by being bottle-fed colostrum; they can also be foster-nursed by another newly farrowed sow.

It is good insurance to feed the piglets with some colostrum before you transfer them to a foster sow. Sow milk replacers are nutritionally adequate for newborn pigs, but they lack antibodies; they contain no antibiotics, which will help to control growth of unfavourable bacteria.

18.1 WHAT IS COLOSTRUM

As mentioned earlier, piglets are born with insufficient antibodies in their body to defend themselves against the hostile bacteria and particularly the viruses that surround the environment of your farm. It is important for the piglets to obtain protection from these pathogens from their mother's first batch of milk that contains immunoglobulins, known as colostrum.

Colostrum is rich in disease-preventing immunoglobulins; the very first batch of colostrum produced after farrowing is the richest and best, but it declines as the hour passes by.

Ensuring that your piglets get a good dose of colostrum, especially from the piglet's sow, is probably the single most important thing that your staff can do to guarantee your piglet's survival and long-term health.

Immunoglobulins have a large molecule size and the cells lining of the newborn piglets` gut is able to absorb it as soon as they are born, however, these cells lining begins to reduce their absorptive areas within 6 hours of farrowing and may be fully closed within 12-16 hours.

That is why it is so important that you ensure that all piglets are drinking sufficient colostrum immediately after they are born. Typically, the piglets that are born last are at a severe disadvantage. Not only will they be weaker and weary because they have had to travel longer in the sow's uterus but the time wasted during the journey means that they are in danger of 'missing the immunity window'.

While those that are born earlier usually enjoy as much as an additional 30 mg/ml of antibodies, the piglets that came last and are suckling poorly might only achieve 4 to 6 mg/ml during this immunity window. Not to mention the fact that the longer it takes to farrow the weaker are usually the last to be born.

To be blunt, it means your last-born piglets have already begun to die as soon as the farrowing process commences". That is why it is very important to make sure that your experienced staff is around during farrowing and he or she can make sure that the piglets that are born last or the weaker piglets are placed on the sow's nipple as soon as they arrive to start obtaining as much intake of colostrum that they can.

As colostrum is also very rich in quickly-absorbed energy, large consumption of it helps piglets to defends themselves against cold and it gives them enough energy to move away quickly from overlaying by the sow.

Studies have shown that sow normally produces between 1200 to 1900 g/day of milk. Total intake by the newborns is variable but is probably 200 — 450g/piglet (range 100-1400g/day within the first 24 hours of life) so with more than 8 new borns there may not be enough for all the piglets and it is the weaker piglets that will first suffer. We would advise that so as not to disturb your piglets from suckling colostrum, you should avoid teeth clipping during the first 3 days as it is bound to deter suckling.

Factors that determine the quality of colostrum

Studies have also shown that the quality of colostrum varies due to:

1. The age of the sow, colostrum quality peaks at the second litters and begins to drop after six litters

2. The quality also drops if the sow has been sick or previously exposed to pathogen challenges.

3. The quality of the gilt`s colostrum is below that of her colostrum of a more mature sow

4. Good nutrition also has an effect on colostrum quality. The sow needs to be properly fed with protein, especially leading up to farrowing, especially sows that look a little below par.

Colostrum substitutes

Alternatively, colostrum substitutes, mostly derived from cow colostrum, as mentioned earlier, getting a good dose of colostrum, especially from the piglet's dam, is probably the single most important factor related to a piglet's survival and long-term health.

The strong, early-born piglets get to the udder hours before their later-born litter mates and go from teat to teat taking the best colostrum. Thus, disadvantaged piglets often need assistance to obtain enough colostrum.

Below are some methods to ensure piglets obtain an adequate dose of colostrum.

- Make sure the pen is warm so that the piglets can stay warm and active.

- Split suckle — remove some of the piglets from litter especially the largest, strongest piglets for a one-hour period during the morning and again in the afternoon, leaving the small piglets on the sow to suckle the mother without being bullied.

- Give the sow one unit of oxytocin each time the largest piglets are removed.

- Collect colostrum from the sow. To milk a sow, remove all her piglets for one hour, then give her 1ml of oxytocin, wait one or two minutes, then strip her teats (front teats are better because they produce more milk) to obtain colostrum.

- Give the colostrum to the piglets via a syringe.

- Cow colostrum also can be used and may be more easily obtained.

18.2 FEEDING PIGLETS WITH ADDITIONAL NUTRIENTS — POST COLOSTRUMS,

As earlier mentioned, many liveborn piglets die because they starve. Weak piglets are most affected because they cannot compete very well for milk and not eating well means that they are most vulnerable to chilling. You can improve their survival rate by giving a supplemental source of nutrients the first few hours of life.

Post colostrums — you should provide weak piglets with 10 to 15 ml of milk every four hours during the first day or two following farrowing. The economic benefit of providing supplemental milk to piglets is to improve the preweaning survival rate of piglets on your farm, every little helps,

Mother's milk is always the best. It is important that the first dose of milk suckled by the piglets' afterbirth is colostrum. Colostrum from the sow is best but obtaining manually is time consuming.

Commercial milk replacers will only be very useful for the piglets after the piglets have received an adequate dose of colostrum directly or indirectly from the sow.

You can use a syringe to give the supplemental milk to the piglets.

When you are rearing motherless or weak piglets manually, it is very important that they first receive colostrum straight after birth to build up their natural resistance. However, if the sow dies whilst farrowing, the colostrum will have to be taken from another farrowing sow for the piglets. Without colostrum, the chance of the piglets' survival is very small.

Cow's or goat's milk can be given to the piglets but preferably after the piglets have taken colostrum. Cow's or goat's milk should not be diluted, as sow's milk is very concentrated, the milk should be warmed up to slightly above body temperature ($37° - 40°C$) in a pan that is lowered into a larger pan containing boiling water.

When you are feeding pig manually, they should be fed at regular intervals 5 times a day for the first two days, for about 10 minutes each time. This could be reduced to four times a day on the third and on the fourth day.

After 14 days, you can reduce the frequency but increase the quantity of milk at each feed and gradually change over to more solid feed, so that by the age of about three weeks they should be able to take regular feed like chick mash or broiler starter.

However, if no nutritious feed is available then they should continue on milk for a while longer. There should be a continuous supply of water, which should be boiled to avoid any contamination.

Staff compounding feed *Feeding piglets with milk and with creep feed*

18.3 HOW TO FEED YOUR SOW DURING LACTATION.

Sows need not be fed for 12-24 hours after farrowing, but water should be continuously available. Feeding greens and vegetables as first post-farrow feeding is good for sows and the amount of feed fed to sows should be gradually increased until the maximal feed level is reached. Sows that are thin at farrow may benefit from generous feeding in the early post-farrow.

Sows' milk does not contain enough iron for baby pigs. Iron must be given to piglets within their first 3 or 4 days to prevent anaemia. Piglets can be supplied with iron by giving them iron injections (iron dextran in the ham or heavy neck muscle). When piglets are about 1 week old, start feeding them with starter feed (about 20% protein) in a shallow pan.

Generally, males tend to gain protein faster than females when fed comparable diets over the same amount of time. While females tend to accumulate fat more than males.

18.4 CREEP FEEDING

We pig farmers talk a lot about creep feed but what does it mean on our farm?

Creep feeding is usually recommended at about 14 days of age for piglets. This is usually when the amount of milk produced by the sow has reached its peak and will begin to drop. This also correspond to when the nutritional demand by the piglets is also increasing which means that sufficient nutrients will not be available to sustain the maximal piglet growth.

Here are ways to improve creep feed intake:

- Start your creep feeding with a proper diet that is as rich as the poultry chick mash. The complexity and palatability of the diet is a big factor that can affect success of creep feeding. Piglets will consume more of a diet that has several speciality ingredients (so you can add more of this to the chick mash, fish meal, milk, baby feed etc. to make it more palatable) rather than a simpler one that contains palm kernel cake, corn bran, etc.

- The feed should be provided to the piglets in a mini-pellet form or as a wet mash.

- Make sure there is fresh clean water at all times. There is a strong correlation between drinking and eating. Piglets that have access to fresh water eat more feed than those who don't.

- Keep the feed fresh by increasing the frequency of offering to five or more in a day, as mentioned earlier pigs suckle the mother every hour.

- Piglets must be attracted to the feed, which means feed must have a smell that appeals to the piglets nose sensory. Your feed must smell better and appealing than the surroundings. Anytime you bring it in afresh, they will be attracted to it.

- Only offer the piglets just the right amount that they will finish at a time and feed them several times daily (about 5 times) to mimic the way the sow milk is released to them.

- Store the remaining feed in a facility or room separate from pigs.

- Make sure you remove stale or uneaten feed from the farrowing quarters daily and clean the feed trough to prevent contamination.

- Make the feed easily accessible to all the piglets. You can sprinkle small quantities on the floor or in a shallow pan when introducing the creep feed.

18.5 HOW TO TAKE CARE OF PIGLETS FROM DAY 3 TO WEANING

Good care and management of your farm during farrowing has a major influence on the number of liveborn piglets that are born are eventually weaned and on how well they perform in their later stages of production.

Studies have shown that over 40 % of the mortality in pig production occur in the first four weeks of life.

A successful farmer therefore needs to understand some of the physical characteristics of newborn piglets that makes them more vulnerable than other types of pigs on the farm.

Piglets are born without any antibody protection; their bodies also have no hair and there is also very small fat energy on their skin. That means that they cannot regulate internal body temperature or cope with cold environments.

Your farm's first responsibility after farrowing is to prevent anything that can lead to reduction in milk production in your sow and consumption of milk by piglets. You need to block cold from draughts from broken walls, insulate concrete floors, or provide warmth to counter any drop-in environment temperature especially during harmattan or rainy season. Keep the pen clean to prevent exposure to disease organisms that can compromise the health and well-being of the newborn piglets.

The piglets that the sow gave birth on your farm to can be categorise into two broad categories:

- Normal piglets
- Underprivileged or weak piglets.

Normal piglets

Normal piglets are those piglets that are born quickly, get on their feet within a minute or two, look for the nipples and start suckling in about 15 minutes after birth. They will probably move from teat to teat, taking a disproportionately large share of the most concentrated, immunoglobulin-rich colostrum. If your sow is a good mother and the farrowing environment is adequate, normal piglets thrive without much help from staff.

Underprivileged or weak piglets

Underprivileged or weak piglets are those weakened by the challenges of the birth process.

- These are piglets that are located at the upper end of the uterus. They will usually be the last to be born and in the process of birth they could experience the detachment of the umbilical cord from the placenta leading to loss of oxygen supply to the piglets.

- Piglets that were stillbirths during farrowing but were revived.

- Piglets that experiences excessive physical trauma during farrowing.

- The longer a sow takes to farrow the greater the chance these problems will appear.

- Lightweight piglets, especially those weighing less than 1kg at birth, are much less likely to survive to weaning than heavier piglets.

- Piglets with spread out legs is a common congenital defect observed in underprivileged piglets.

- Another type of underprivileged piglet are piglets that are shivering at birth. Often these piglets are seen shivering and huddled with litter mates, because their thermal requirements have not been met e.g. lack of insulator like wood shavings on a cold concrete floor during the harmattan.

Underprivileged piglets are also slow in getting on their feet and to the udder. Their weakened state compromises their ability to compete with stronger, normal litter mates for access to teats during the first hours after birth. This reduces their intake of colostrum.

Prevent Chilling — The farrowing quarters need to provide wood shavings days before farrowing and make sure wind is not blowing into the farrowing pen. Staff should closely monitor the sow and litter's responses to the zone heating to ensure their thermal needs are met.

18.6   CROSS FOSTERING

Cross fostering is the most effective way to reduce within-litter piglet weight variation. The primary purpose of cross fostering is to reduce the weight variation within the litter and to more evenly match the number of piglets with the sow's ability to raise them. Ultimately, this is determined by the number of functional teats that the sow has.

Below are important tips to ensure good results from cross fostering.

- Ensure piglets that will be cross fostered consume colostrum from their own mother. Prior to cross fostering, piglets should be allowed to remain with their mother for at least four to six hours following birth before they are cross fostered. Otherwise, it is likely the fostered piglets will not consume an adequate amount of colostrum, especially if they are fostered to a sow which farrowed one to two days previously.

- Farmers should try and cross foster piglets before they are 24 to 48 hours old. Piglets normally establish teat fidelity (preference for a particular teat) within the first few days after birth and will almost always suckle at the same teat or pair of teats until weaning. It is an advantage for piglets to establish teat fidelity, because it reduces competition and fighting at the udder. When teat fidelity is not established, piglets fight more throughout lactation and have poorer weight gains. Cross fostering after teat fidelity is established is disruptive and induces fighting between resident and fostered piglets.

- Match sow and piglets, choose small, docile sows with small, slender nipples of medium length to raise below-average-weight piglets.

- Observe for the presence of disease problems in the farrowing quarters before cross fostering. This is important to reduce the spread of disease. Avoid moving a healthy piglet to a diseased litter or vice-versa.

- Transfer males rather than females if you are going to use the female piglets as a replacement gilt later. This is to improve accuracy and traceability of female selection later.

18.7 POST-FARROWING ROUTINE

There are lots of Post-Farrowing Routines that piglets go through once farrowing has taken place, this includes carrying out the following activities: clipping teeth, clipping and treating the umbilical cord, iron administration, tail docking, identification, treating splay legged piglets, providing supplemental nutrients, and castration.

Equipment

Have all the equipment you need to process piglets.

Supplies and equipment needed to process piglets as described in this fact sheet are:

- Disinfectant, such as Lysol

- Antiseptic, such as tamed iodine

- Wound spray

- Supplemental iron

- Cotton wool

- Syringe and needle 2ml, 5ml, 10ml

- Ear tags and applicator

- Adhesive, elastic or duct tape cut in 1/2 to 3/4 inch strips

- Castration knife or scalpel

- Shallow container for disinfectant in which to put the cutting edge of instruments between uses

Avoid transferring disease — During the post-farrowing routine, care should be taken not to spread disease around the farm. Disease spread can be prevented by processing sick litters last, cleaning and disinfecting the box and dipping instruments into a disinfectant after you have processed each piglet. Use new syringes and needle for each batch.

Staff Safety — You should be careful when removing piglets from the sows. Sows are very protective of their piglets and they often try to bite or grab you to protect their litter.

Restraining a Piglet

Hold the piglet so you can cut the teeth and umbilical cord and administer iron in very rapid succession without changing your grip.

Umbilical Cord Care — The umbilical cord, which enables the foetus to obtain nutrients from the dam and expel wastes during pregnancy, usually does not require much attention. If the cord is dry and shrivelled, it is not necessary to treat. Just cut it off, leaving one to three inches of cord.

However, if there is excess bleeding from the umbilical cord, then tie it off immediately with string. This is to prevent bacteria and viruses from travelling up the cord after the piglet is born and cause infection.

Piglet Teeth Clipping

As in the wild, the newborn piglets are born with eight needle teeth, sometimes referred to as wolf teeth, located on the sides of the upper and lower jaws. While these teeth are useful for fending and killing small vertebrates in the wild, it is of no positive use on your farm and it is advisable to clip these teeth within 72 hours after birth to reduce the chance piglets lacerating each other during sibling fighting or to injure the sow's udder when competing for nipples. The 3 days after birth is to ensure that this activity does not disrupt the piglets from consuming the much-needed colostrum.

1. You should use sharp blades to prevent the teeth from being crushed, which could lead to infection.

2. Only cut away one-half of the tooth otherwise infection might set in or the gum be injured, and the piglet may not nurse well.

3. Avoid cutting the piglet's gum or tongue.

4. Cut the teeth off flat and not at an angle.

5. For your health and safety, wear protective glasses or goggles to protect your eyes from flying pieces of teeth.

6. Hold the piglet and place the side cutters parallel to the gum and cut off one-half of the two lower teeth at once. Turn the side cutters over and cut the two upper teeth. Repeat on the other side of the mouth.

Tail Docking

The undocked tail is a very convenient target for tail biting or cannibalism. This is to reduce tail biting, and is usually done within about 24 hours after birth. From our experience tail biting among pigs is not very common in Nigeria, so might not be necessary.

Supplemental Iron

Iron deficiency anaemia is very common in nursing piglets and it may appear in piglets within 7-10 days after birth.

Causes of anaemia in piglet

1. Low iron reserves in the body of new-born piglet
2. Also low iron in sow's colostrum and milk
3. Lack of contact with iron in the soil, wild piglets normally pick iron from the soil after birthThe rapid growth rate of piglets

On the farm, iron can be administered by injection. Administering of iron to piglets via injection guarantees the quantity of iron that reaches critical tissues.

Administer 200mg of iron injection to piglets while they are one to three days old and again at weaning. Injectable iron products are available in both the 100 and 200mg of iron/ml concentrations. Read the label carefully to learn the iron concentration of the product you are using. Do not overdose, as too much iron can be toxic.

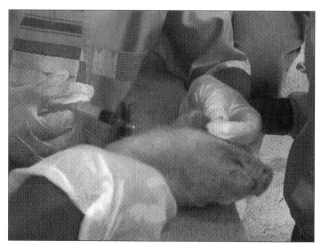

Piglets receiving iron injection

How to administer iron injection

a. Use a clean syringe for each litter.

b. Withdraw iron solution from its container, using a 14 or 16-gauge (large diameter) needle which is left inserted in bottle. The idea is to avoid using a contaminated needle to draw iron from the bottle every time that you need to administer an injection. Otherwise, foreign matter and pathogens will likely be introduced into the bottle.

c. After filling the syringe, use a 1/2 inch needle to inject iron into the piglet's muscle.

d. If there are air bubbles in the syringe, point the needle up, tap the syringe and push the air out.

e. If the injection site is dirty, wipe it clean with an antiseptic before injecting.

f. Inject iron into the neck or thigh muscle.

g. In countries where ham tissue is a premium product, many of the pig farms in such countries don't administer drugs via the thigh muscle because of the fear that it will devalue the meat to the buyer.

h. **Injecting.** Be careful not to inject into the spinal area. Pull or roll back the skin with your finger or bend the piglet's neck sideways prior to inserting the needle.

i. Insert the needle perpendicular to site and inject.

Medication routes in pigs

There are many routes of medication which can be practically used in pigs.

Medication by Injection

Intramuscular

Inject into the muscle behind the ear.

Iron injection in piglets used to be administered into the hind leg muscles. In countries where ham is a premium product, this should be avoided

Subcutaneous

Extremely difficult to find a true area in the pig with subcutaneous tissue. The skin is closely applied to the fat and muscle layer. It is possible in the inner thigh as shown, at the point of the shoulder and in the peri-anal region. The needle needs to be inserted at a low angle as shown.

Medication via the Oral route

Oral manual

Oral dosing using a syringe — very useful for administration of oral vaccines or anti-coccidiostat medication.

A stomach tube can be passed into the stomach and can be very useful in the administration of warm colostrum in weak piglets.

Medication can be administered via tablets which can be disguised in apple, grapes or small sweets. This can be very useful in boars or pet pigs

How to manage the Splay-legged Piglets

As mentioned earlier, some piglets are born splay-legged piglets. They tend to appear normal except when they attempt to stand, their hind legs (and sometimes front legs) extend sideways. While the condition can be a congenital disease among premature litters with a 113 day or shorter gestation period, a slippery floor in the farrowing quarters can also contribute to the number of spayed-legged piglets. The mortality rate in piglets with the back splayed legs can be reduced by taping the legs soon after birth to prevent them from extending sideways.

Use either elastic wrapping tape, adhesive tape, or duct tape. Apply tape to the rear legs allowing a two-inch gap between legs so the piglet can stand properly. Avoid wrapping the tape too tightly to restrict circulation of blood and be sure to remove the tape a few days later.

Abscesses

Pigs are prone to subcutaneous abscesses which can be very large — containing 6 litres of purulent material for example. The abscess can be released once the contents are fluid, which is assessed by inserting a clean needle into the softest part of the lump and drawing back with a 10 ml syringe to reveal a yellow creamy liquid. If the abscess contents are fluid, release using a cross-cut at the bottom of the abscess, not at the point. It is essential that the skin wound does not heal too fast as the abscess will reappear. The cut at the bottom allows adequate drainage; no pocket of abscess should be left. Flush with running water 2-3 times daily. If necessary, inject with routine antibiotics to reduce secondary infection. In the early stages of an abscess, possibly injecting with lincomycin may clear the infection. Review causes of fighting among stock to try and eliminate the cause of the abscess. However, pigs will fight when housed together and abscessation is an inevitable consequence.

Castration

Castration is the surgical removal of the two testicles. This is a routine management practice for male piglets destined for slaughter and will never be used for breeding. The testicles produce sperm and encourages the production of the male hormone, testosterone.

Pork from male pigs that are not castrated at slaughter do have an odour during cooking that many customers find very offensive.

The best time to castrate a piglet is between 14 to 21 days of age. Young piglets are easier to hold or restrain, bleed less from surgery, and have antibody protection from the sow's colostrum and milk.

Staff should examine each piglet carefully before castrating to identify those with a scrotal hernia. A piglet with a scrotal hernia has a loop of intestine in its scrotum and when the piglet is opened up the intestine becomes visible and unless you are trained to repair hernias and have surgical equipment to pack and suture the wound it should not be attempted.

One staff member should hold the piglet upright so the scrotum is down to see if the scrotum is uniform in size, or hold the piglet with its head down and squeeze the back legs together to lift the testicles. If there is an enlargement in one or both halves of the scrotum, the piglet probably has a hernia. Do not castrate the piglet unless you are trained to repair hernias. The piglet's intestines will be forced open through the incision. Sometimes the testicle is removed before a scrotal hernia is discovered. If this happens, the herniation must be repaired by suturing immediately. Most scrotal hernias are genetic in origin. Do not keep replacement animals from any litter in which one or more piglets was herniated.

If one or both testicles are not found, the piglet may be a cryptorchid. This means that the testicle(s) failed to descend through the inguinal canal from the abdomen during development. When this condition is noticed, ear notch or mark the piglet and make a record of it. Often, the testicle(s) will descend to a normal position as the piglet grows.

The piglet should be castrated after the testicle presents itself. If one testicle has descended at the time of castration, it should be removed. Use either a surgical knife or sharp blade to castrate. The instrument of choice must be sharp and disinfected. If the scrotum is dirty, clean it and the surrounding area with a cotton swab soaked in a mild disinfectant.

Castration Method for Two People Using a Knife

1. One person holds the piglet by the rear legs while another does the castrating.
2. With one hand, tighten the skin over the scrotum to help expose the testicle and the site for the incision.

3. With the castration knife, make two incisions about as long as the testicles near the centre of each.

4. Cut deeply enough to go through the outside body skin. It does not matter whether you cut through the white membrane (tunica vaginalis), which surrounds the testicle, or not.

5. Squeeze, or pop, the testicles through the incision.

6. Enlarge the incision slightly at the end closest to the tail if the testicle will not pop out.

7. Pull out the end of the testicle which is toward the tail at a right angle to the length of the body, roll the blood vessel and vas deference 5 times and cut the cord close to the incision.

8. Do not pull straight up on the testicle.

9. Repeat the procedure for the second testicle.

10. Spray the wound with an antiseptic.

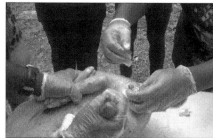

Pig Castration

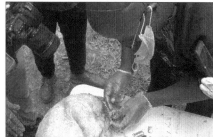

With the castration knife, make incisions to remove the testicle

Post-Castration Care

Observe castrated animals for excess bleeding or the presence of tissue or intestines (hernia). Apply pressure to the wound for about two minutes to stop any bleeding. Cut off any cord that may be protruding from the incision as this may serve as a wick for infection, but make sure it is not intestine.

If intestines protrude and they are black or torn, it is usually best to euthanise or kill the piglet.

Methods of Euthanasia for Baby Pigs

Euthanizing animals is an unpleasant but necessary part of livestock farming. As farmers, you may often have to euthanize your piglets because they are sick and suffering with little-or-no chance of recovery. Some piglets should be euthanized because if left to live they become a source of infection for their pen or littermates.

Blunt Mechanical Trauma

Place the piglet on the ground and apply a quick, firm blow with a blunt instrument, such as a hammer, to the piglet's head. The point to aim for is where two imaginary lines, drawn from the base of each ear to the opposite eye, cross. Alternatively, hold the piglet by its hind legs and forcefully hit the piglet's head against a hard surface such as concrete. Immediately repeat the above procedures if there is any possibility that the animal is still alive.

Farm managers need to be sensitive to the dislike many people have to euthanizing animals and ensure they assign the task to someone who is comfortable with the job.

Caring for your farm medical equipment

Proper equipment care will help ensure that piglets will be processed with minimal discomfort and complications from infection. After each use, place equipment such as side cutters and scalpel blade in a bowl of non-irritating disinfectant. Do this rather than laying equipment on the platform after they have been used to process each piglet. Change the disinfectant after about every ten litters. Before moving to another farrowing room to process, clean and disinfect the cart and equipment. Also, check needles to ensure they are not bent or blunt on the end. Replace needles after they have been used on 30-50 piglets or earlier if damaged. Dispose of needles in a sharps container.

Records

We recommend that you collect as much information about your farm, however, you should not only collect production records for collection's sake but should use these to identify strengths and weaknesses of your operation.

Records that should be kept in the farrowing quarters include:

- birth date,
- number of piglets born alive and dead,
- date and cause of death of piglets,
- pedigree information,
- number of piglets weaned,
- and piglet (or litter) weaning weight.

For example, if your farm is experiencing problems in the farrowing quarters. Such as small litter, hernia, splayed-leg etc., these problems will continue to propagate if accurate records are not kept. This is because most reproductive traits are heritable.

Record keeping will allow you to identify superior sows and boar and make sure they are retained on the farm. This could also lead to successive improvements of performance on the farm which should lead to fewer problems. For example, identifying the boar that produces large litters can help you to maximise the usage of such boar.

In addition, accurate records will help management identify people who are doing a good job (who can then be rewarded) and accurate records also help identify weak areas that the staff can work to improve.

Remarks on anything unusual or wrong with the piglets should be noted as well. In addition, you may want to record feed intake during lactation. Medications given to animals should be recorded to ensure treatment protocols and withdrawal periods are followed.

While you can use cards, clipboards, mobile phones or other recording devices near each farrowing crate or pen, you should endeavour to have a computer on your farm that you can translate this information to.

18.8 **DAILY PIGLET OBSERVATION**

- Closely observe each of your piglets at least twice daily for evidence of adequate milk production by the sow.

- Careful observation of your piglet's behaviour and body condition is the best method of determining if a sow is milking well.

- Lactation failure must be treated aggressively and the litter may need to be given supplemental milk as the sow is recovering.

- Healthy, well-nourished piglets run around and play, especially when the sow rises to eat. For the first few days of their lives, piglets do little more than eat and sleep. Milk is frequently seen around their mouths. However, in a few days they begin to be active away from the udder. These activities are delayed in piglets that are sick or undernourished.

- In the normal sow, milk ejection from the teats starts about one to three minutes following initiation of nursing behaviour (which occurs about once each hour in early lactation) when oxytocin is released and milk let-down occurs.

- The piglets will nurse steadily for about 30 seconds then gradually quit. Piglets nursing a sow with lactation failure will spend more time at the udder, including fighting, and will be less content.

- If the piglets' needle teeth have not been clipped, they can inflict severe damage to the faces and snouts of litter mates and sometimes to the sow's udder.

- Well-nourished piglets have tight, shiny skin and a thrifty look, i.e., "bloom".

- Piglets go from having less than 1% body fat at birth to about 10% by 10 days of age. Much of that fat is stored just under the skin. It is that rapid accumulation of subcutaneous fat that gives piglets tight, shiny skin and a thrifty look. Piglets that are not performing well have loose skin, look depressed, and have a "hairy" appearance.

18.9   PREVENTING PIGLETS' ENCOUNTERING DISEASE AGENTS

As mentioned earlier, preventing piglets from primary prevention involves managing the following four basic areas:

1. Make sure that you source your weaners and replacement breeding stock from a good source.

2. Manage the movement of people, vehicles, materials, and pigs to and from your farm.

3. Ensure the layout of your farm does not encourage the transfer of disease from within i.e. from older pigs to most vulnerable pigs e.g. piglets.

4. Maintain regular cleaning of the farrowing quarters and the sow.

To be a profitable pig farmer, you should divert more energy and resources to primary and secondary prevention techniques mentioned above and don't over depend on the less effective and more costly approach of using drugs to treat sick piglets.

Even with all of this, some piglets will die of disease and the causes can be broadly classified as those occurring regularly (endemic) or only occasionally (epidemic).

The causes will vary by farm, the typical endemic disease will cause problems continually and contribute to a low-level "normal" piglet mortality of 5-15%. Colibacillosis and Coccidiosis are often endemic diseases.

In contrast, a disease such as transmissible Gastroenteritis can cause an epidemic of piglet losses up to 100% and last for many weeks.

Diagnosis.

Determining the cause of piglet losses is not easy because few diseases produce signs that are unique to the causative agent. For example, baby pig scours can be caused by a bacteria, virus, or parasite and you cannot distinguish between them by the nature of the scours. Your veterinarian can assist you in obtaining a diagnosis and recommending treatment. It's expensive and wasteful to begin treating if you're unsure of the cause of the disease so it is important to obtain a diagnosis and treat accordingly. For the experienced farmer, some diseases which occur regularly on the farm can be recognized by farm managers and treatment instituted as soon as the signs are recognized. However, if the piglets do not respond to treatment, then contact your veterinarian to reassess the situation and check the diagnosis.

Treatment.

Appropriate treatment will vary depending on the cause of the disease. Provided the organisms are sensitive, antibiotics will usually alleviate a bacterial infection; however, antibiotics will not affect viruses or parasites. Sometimes antibiotics are recommended to help prevent secondary infection when the primary infection is a virus or parasite. In these cases, the antibiotics do not affect the organism causing the disease, they just help ensure that bacteria do not take advantage of the weakened piglet. Treatments for individual diseases are discussed below. Remember that all drugs must be administered according to label directions unless your veterinarian has directed you to do otherwise.

18.10 **COMMON DISEASES IN PIGLETS**

Clostridial Infections. The disease is caused when Clostridium perfringens, which is a normal inhabitant in the large intestine, becomes established in the small intestine. This usually occurs when the piglet has had insufficient intake of colostrum. Piglets usually develop a foul-smelling diarrhoea and many will die. It is more commonly seen in piglets less than seven days old. Oral ampicillin is commonly recommended.

Congenital Tremor. Most pig farmers have seen newborn pigs with tremors and shaking muscles. It tends to come and go sporadically but seems to be more common in gilt herds, where 80% of litters can have affected piglets. Affected piglets must be assisted to suckle and provided for until they grow out of the disease in a few weeks.

Greasy Pig Disease. (Exudative Dermatitis). Greasy pig disease is often a problem in newly established gilt herds. The causative bacterium, Staphylococcus hyicus, infects the skin of a piglet and produces a toxin that damages its liver and kidneys. A piglet is usually infected at, or soon after, birth. Lacerations on the side of the face, made by unclipped needle-teeth as piglets scramble for the best teat on the sows' udders, are thought to be the site where the bacterium often first infects the piglet. The first clinical signs appear between 4 to 35 days when small dark spots appear on the side of the face. Then, brown scales develop on the underside of the piglet which, in serious cases, spread to cover the whole piglet. Severely affected piglets usually die and survivors do poorly. Affected herds can suffer decreased growth performance for 12 months. The disease is readily recognized by its typical appearance, and treatment is most successful when started as soon as signs appear.

Before antibiotic treatment is started, affected live piglets should be submitted to a laboratory to determine the antibiotic sensitivity of Staphylococcus Hyicus. Greasy pig disease is difficult to control unless mange is first eliminated. The mange mites damage the skin and allow Staphylococcus Hyicus to enter. Affected piglets should be given electrolytes orally because they become dehydrated rapidly. The disease can be prevented by removing any sharp edges in the farrowing crate that may lacerate the piglets, cutting needle teeth, spraying the udder of the sow with an iodine-based disinfectant, adopt an all-in/all out policy for the farrowing house and ensure the room is thoroughly disinfected and dry before sows enter.

Glasser's Disease. Glasser's Disease is caused by Hemophilus parasuis which is present in most herds. The disease usually affects weaned pigs, but suckling piglets can be affected. Often the heaviest, best looking piglets die. Pigs are fevered, depressed, slow to rise, lack appetite, and have swollen joints. Some have nervous signs such as tremors. Before they die, the skin often turns blue and the eyes are reddened. Hemophilus parasuis is sensitive to a wide range of antibiotics including the penicillins, tetracyclines, and ceftiofur. It is best to start treatment as early as possible and a combination of injectable and water medication is usually indicated.

Parasites

Porcine Reproductive and Respiratory Syndrome (PRRS). PRRS is usually only seen in unweaned piglets when the disease first infects a naive herd. Piglets may cough, sneeze, and have diarrhea, conjunctivitis, and difficulty breathing. Signs in individual herds will vary because of the effects of different secondary infections. Individual piglets should be rehydrated and treated with antibiotics to control secondary infections.

Tetanus. Tetanus is rare in piglets but sometimes the causative bacterium, Clostridium tetani, will infect piglets when they are castrated. Because the incubation period is 1-10 weeks, signs are rarely seen until the pigs are at least two weeks old. Affected piglets are stiff, have an erect tail, and facial muscle spasms. Managers should review castration and other processing procedures to ensure they are using hygienic techniques.

18.11 AFRICAN SWINE FEVER

African Swine Fever (ASF) is a highly contagious haemorrhagic viral disease of domestic and wild pigs, which is responsible for serious economic and production losses in pig industry .

It is caused by a large DNA virus which also infects ticks of the genus Ornithodoros.

The tick will ingest the virus when taking a blood meal and then pass it on when feeding on susceptible animals.

The virus is found in all body fluids and tissues of infected domestic pigs.

It is a transboundary animal disease and can be spread by live or dead pigs, domestic or wild, and pork products.

History of the Disease

This disease is endemic to some sub-Saharan regions of Africa. The region between the equator and northern Transvaal has seen major outbreaks of this disease. Sporadic incidences of African Swine Fever outbreak have occurred outside the sub-Saharan region. The disease is also prevalent outside Africa; in Sardinia, Italy, in particular, where it is mostly found in wild pigs.

Transmission

- Direct contact with infected pig or wild pig.

- The virus mainly spreads through their mouth and nose.

- The blood of an infected pig that is injured during a pig fight, can also cause the virus to spread Indirect transmission through infected vector tick.

- Transmission can also occur via contaminated feed and objects such as shoes, clothes, vehicles, knives, equipment etc., due to the high environmental resistance of ASF virus.

- Contaminated sites can hold the virus for up to one month.

- Blood, feces, salted dried ham, frozen carcass, and boned meat are other mediums through which the virus is transmitted.

- At times, the food given to pigs gets mixed with leftovers of an infected pig, which eventually leads to transmission of this virus to healthy individuals.

- virus is able to survive in uncooked and cured pork and pork products for months

- The introduction of new animals or pork products from infected herds, into a herd is the most likely source of infection

- The virus is very resistant in the environment, surviving for months

- Recovered animals remain infective for at least 6 months

- The virus is inactivated by approved disinfectants

Clinical signs

Acute forms of ASF are characterised by

- high fever, depression, anorexia and loss of appetite, redness of skin on ears, abdomen and legs.

- Pregnant sows will abort, cyanosis, vomiting, bleeding from the nose and rectum, diarrhoea and death within 6- 10 days.

- In severe cases, a farmer might lose his entire stock.

Chronic forms are caused by less virulent viruses, and produce less serious clinical signs that can last longer.

- Mortality rate in the chronic form may still reach 70%

- Chronic disease symptoms include loss of weight, intermittent fever, respiratory problems, skin ulcers and joint problems.

- Different types of pig may have varying susceptibility to ASF virus infection. African wild pigs may be infected without showing clinical signs allowing them to act as reservoirs.

Prevention and control

- Currently there is no approved vaccine for ASF and no treatment.

- Prevention in countries free of the disease depends on implementation of appropriate import policies and biosecurity measures.

- Ensuring that neither infected live pigs nor pork products are introduced into areas free of ASF.

During outbreaks, early detection and humane killing of animals (with proper disposal of carcases and waste); thorough cleansing and disinfection strict biosecurity measures on farms can help reduce the spread of the disease.

Public health risk

- ASF is not a risk to human health.

- ASF is a disease listed in the World Organisation for Animal Health (OIE) Terrestrial Animal Health Code and must be reported to the OIE.

19. How to manage your pigs during and after weaning

Weaning is a stressful experience for young piglets, affecting them both socially and physiologically. So, it is your responsibilities as a farmer to make sure that weaning is not more stressful than it should be and should not lead to severe growth checks and even deaths.

This is important to you because any slow growth at this point will impact your farm performance and reduce your profitability. While we do not advise that you wean your pigs before 6 weeks. The earlier you wean your pig (i.e. the shorter the suckling period), the more sophisticated the housing, feeding and management skills that will be required to raise the piglets.

From our experience on most farms in Africa, we often see poor nutrition among piglets. While this is not done deliberately most farms give their piglets incorrect nutrition (same cheap feed given to adult pigs) as the piglets transit over this crucial period. Our second observation is that farmers do not provide these expensive, high-quality feed in a clean manner to the piglets e.g. poorly cleaned piglet troughs.

It is important that the staff that you assigned to raising weaners pay close attention to what happens when they wean piglets.

Managing piglets on the farm

19.1 WHAT HAPPENS WHEN YOU WEAN YOUR PIGLETS?

As we have reiterated several times throughout this book, the more a farmer knows about what really does happen behind the scenes, especially with the anatomy and the physiology of a piglet, the more he or she can assist and protect the animal.

First of all, nature never intended for piglets to be removed suddenly from their mother and especially not at such an early age as 5 weeks. In the wild, weaning is a gradual process that takes at least 13 to 17 weeks, The duration allows the piglet gut to become accustomed to digesting solid food little by little.

This gradual process also allows the bacterial and chemical pathways in the piglet's digestive system sufficient time to adjust and change from dealing with just (liquid) milk to dealing with (solid) plant roots, acorns, mast, grass and weeds, apples and the soil bacteria and fungi ingested with it. And while this adjustment is taking place in the piglets' stomach, there is always time for piglets to have a quick mother's milk from the sow nearby to help level out any inconsistencies in the feed or in the process.

However, the recent practice of weaning abruptly between 4 to 5 weeks put a tremendous strain on the piglet's digestive system at such a young age. It is your responsibility to understand what the piglet is going through first and, having understood the challenge, you should do whatever you can to assist the piglets to manage and counteract the suddenness of these changes.

19.2 WHAT HAPPENS IN A NORMAL PIGLET BEFORE WEANING?

- At 3-weeks-old, the piglet's stomach still serves as both a reservoir for the milk suckle by the piglets and piglet's stomach can hold about 0.2 litres and a pre-digestive and it serves as a mixing tank.

- Sow produces milk every 35 to 45 minutes. The milk is released in response to the suckling stimulus by the piglets into the udder cisterns, and it switches off within a few minutes of suckling.

- Piglets only gets an hourly 'ration' of about 150-200 cc no matter how long and vigorously they suckle.

- This makes sense because the stomach of the unweaned piglet is not very elastic and can only hold 0.2 litre.

- The stomach walls of the piglets will liberate both digestive enzymes and hydrochloric acid to start pre-digesting proteins and carbohydrates. The acid also helps to kill pathogenic bacteria which are involuntarily eaten along with the food.

- The sow's milk already contains nutrients in the right form and within 35 minutes the pre-digestive (enzymes) and sanitation (acids) processes finishes and the stomach contents enter the small intestine free of potentially damaging organisms the piglet may have eaten

19.3 WHAT HAPPENS TO PIGLETS DURING WEANING?

- During weaning, the mother is removed from the pig-lets. That means that the regular 45 minutes of feeding on mother's milk automatically stops and as a result the piglets gets hungry and look around naturally for the mother's nipples, but the mother is nowhere to be found.

- By the end of the first two hours of waiting and looking for mum and breast, all the feed in the piglet's whole digestive system is empty. That is, all feed in the stom-ach, the duodenum and the small intestine has moved on and its contents have been digested and absorbed.

- Though the piglets could see the solid food that your staff placed in front of them but the piglet does not con-sider it as food. The piglet is probably thinking this is not wet and it doesn't taste or feel like milk. It is also not warm like the mother's milk, so the piglets think the mother will soon arrive. That is, the proper food is still coming.

- By the end of next 2 hours, all the piglets that are still waiting are now extremely hungry and ravenous.

- In addition to all of these, we should also remember that during weaning, piglets are often regrouped according to size and sex and are moved to new and strange sur-roundings with other piglets where they will spend the next few days establishing a new pecking order and ad-justing to the new environment. All of these have the effect of reducing feed intake and imposing a nutrition-al stress on the piglet at a very crucial stage in its devel-opment.

- After a while, some of the piglets that are waiting for milk, get bolder or hungrier. Piglets in the same pen will begin to taste and eat some of the solid food provided. Eventually, the piglet also tries a bit of the solid food and waits.

- This is how animals determine safe or poisonous feed in the wild. They eat a bit and wait a while to check if it is poisonous or not.

- Eventually, the piglet is convinced that this strange but palatable solid feed is ok, though not as good as the sow's milk, but by this time the piglet is so hungry that it overeats to remove the hunger pangs that it is experiencing. The new and solid food is rushed through the piglet's digestive system.

- However, because the food does not stay long enough in the stomach or duodenum of the piglets, it is not sufficiently pre-digested or sufficiently washed with acid to eliminate the hostile bacteria before reaching the small intestine.

- The food therefore arrives too soon and is not well digested as it enters the small intestine with the wrong chemical signatures for absorption, and is also loaded with damaging bacteria.

- The ingesta therefore forms a traffic jam blockage at the intestine creating a breeding ground for bacteria in the digestive system. These pathogens quickly proliferate and their toxins destroy the delicate absorptive structures — the villi — which covers the cells in the small intestine of the piglets and, as a result, the small intestine refuses to accept those not pre-digested sufficiently.

- In the bid to protect itself, the intestine will liberate lots of fluid to liquefy the undigested feed in the intestine and to stimulates bowel movements to flush the blockage down the gut. This is what scouring (diarrhoea) is — it is a lavatory-flushing operation to help cleanse the gut of potentially lethal material but this causes piglet scours / dehydrates.

- The trouble is that when this is happening in a small piglet of 4 to 6 kg that has only a limited amount of water in its bloodstream and body cells to 'flush the lavatory' it leads to extreme dehydration.

- As the piglet loses water, the blood thickens unless the water can be quickly replaced. Blood is then unable to convey nutrient energy to the muscles or remove toxins via the venous system to the organs (liver, kidneys).

- With thickened blood the piglet is starved of muscle energy (gets sluggish) and also gets cold (shivering).

- It already starts to poison itself with the accumulating toxins (feels very ill).

19.4 HOW CAN FARMER MINIMISE POST WEANING STRESS

1. Delay the weaning until the piglet reaches at least 6 to 8 weeks and gradually introduce creep feed. This will allow the piglets to grow accustomed to sufficient solid feed, while still having access to mother's milk. Mother's milk is not only the best but also the cheapest and most affordable.

2. Also, at 6 to 8 weeks, pigs are of a size and age that they can fend for themselves under average farm conditions.

3. In addition, the sow's milk production starts to fall by 6 to 8 weeks, therefore it is uneconomic to feed the piglets only the sow's milk beyond this stage. Fortunately, by this age and weight, pigs are becoming accustomed to dry feed and can better adjust to temperature changes and stress. However, a high standard of hygiene must still be maintained.

4. You should expect that piglets will engorge after weaning, so you should provide a good quality pre-digestive food which will be easy to digest e.g. chick mash or broiler starter, milk or milk waste for the first 3 days of weaning and then gradually begin to mix it with other pig feed ingredients.

5. Predigest means that it has been processed a bit outside the animal, by cooking, soaking, fermenting, drying, etc. before it is fed to the pig. This means that it doesn't need to remain in either the stomach or duodenum for the necessary 35-40 minutes for normal processing as it is already part digested.

6. Have electrolyte solution available and plenty of clean fresh water.

7. Go through the farm daily in the morning before the staff disturb the pigs, starting from the piglets. As soon as looseness or yellow excreta is noted on the floor of the weaner pen, an electrolyte solution should be provided as an additive to the normal water supply.

8. Add minerals and trace elements in a far more absorbable organic form into the feed e.g. in the form of chick or piglets' premix.

9. Farmers can make locally pre-digested feed by subjecting feed to heat treatment. Cook or ferment your feed

before giving it to weaners to make it more easily digested.

10. Try and make the food exceptionally palatable (texture, flavour and smell) for weaners to dissuade holding off eating solid food.

11. Improve the freshness by increasing the frequency of feeding from 3 to 6 times a day for piglets, instead of piling all the feed at one go. Piglets tend to always eat fresh feed when served and forage away when full.

12. Keep your weaner warm — Chills and draughts raise stress (anxiety, worry) and generate low-level hormone reactions which dampen down both appetite and digestive competence.

13. Always check the lying pattern of the pigs both at the warmest and coldest time of the day. Try not to disturb the animal. Take a torch and move quietly to detect resting patterns and satisfactory breathing.

14. Feed and water trough hygiene is vital. A good farm will clean the trough after every feed properly and remove stale uneaten food.

15. Recent research work suggests that the pigs settle together more quickly with a night's weaning as they rest throughout the night more than those weaned during morning hours.

19.5 WHAT TO LOOK OUT FOR TO DETECT IF SOMETHING IS WRONG WITH YOUR WEANERS

Your weaners are always talking to you as a farmer. Blessed is the farmer that is vigilant enough to hear and respond to their cry promptly.

- Appearance — alert or depressed
- Body condition — normal or thin
- Abdominal shape — round or gaunt
- Skin — sleek/'polished' or dry
- Hair standing proud/gingery in white breeds
- Appetite — feeding at the feeder or hanging back
- Dehydration — sunken eyes
- Lying position — supine or semi-sternum
- Even, quiet breathing — listen last thing at night
- Huddling

Lying pattern as an indicator of comfort

Too cold — Lie on the floor with their legs tucked under their body to reduce floor contact. Lie huddles with other pigs. Lie close to a wall. Pigs may shiver. The pigs may become hairy. With larger pigs they seem unable to adopt this tucked position for very long and tend to lie semi-recumbent with their legs tucked into their body.

Comfortable

Within a group of pigs there will be a selection of lying patterns. The main group of pigs will sleep together in a pile. However, other pigs will be lying spread out but with maximum contact with the floor. These separated pigs will be the more dominant pigs. The lower order pigs will lie on the edge of the main group. Pigs sleep with legs stretched out from the body.

Too hot

- Pigs will be panting > 40 per minute
- Pigs are generally dirty.
- Lie away from other pigs, sometimes against a cold wall.
- They do not sleep closely together
- Lie in any wet/cooler area

Pigs will dig into earth/bedded floors.

19.6 HOW DOES DISEASE GET TO YOUR PIGS?

HOW ORGANISMS CAN ENTER AND LEAVE THE PIG

As a livestock farmer, you will have heard words like biosecurity and the need to keep the farm not only physically clean but hygienically clean, but many of us are not very clear what the fuss is all about. In our mind we think that if pigs in the wild can survive in the mud or dirty water, what is the problem?

In this section, we will try to simplify the complex anatomical and physiological activities and battle that takes place all the time in the body of every animal including your pig. We will draw our analogy from modern warfare and try to link the similarities between what goes on inside your pig body.

Invasion

On your farm, a pig's body is continually invaded by foreign bodies through the skin, nose, eyes, mouth, etc.

An enormous variety of these organisms exist all around your farm, in the air, feed or water. There are some that can survive and even develop in the body of people or animals. If the organism can cause infection in your pig's body, it is called **an infectious agent**.

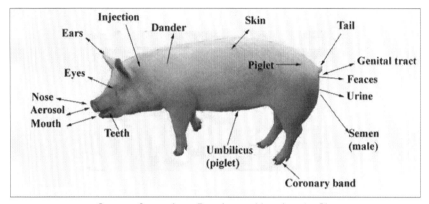

Routes of organisms Entering and Leaving the Pig
source: https://www.bing.com/th?id=OIP.cUxB03zSSVp2FhviS1FYdwHaKE&pid=Api&rs=1

Infectious agents which cause infection and illness are called **pathogens**. Disease is caused by either the pathogens or the toxins that they produce.

The common pig pathogens include the following:

- Virus — viruses invade living cells; this pathogen needs structures in the pig cells to reproduce. Viruses can survive or form a resistant cyst for months in tropical temperatures and can also multiply outside the host.

- Bacteria are single cell organisms; they are considered more primitive than animal or plant cells. They persist for up to several weeks and can multiply outside the host

- Fungi — A group of organisms which include yeast, moulds, and mushrooms.

- Protozoa — area single cell organisms, they can form a resistant cyst which can survive for months.

- Helminths are worms (roundworms, flukes or tapeworms). Often male and female must meet in a host to reproduce, and sometimes they multiply in intermediate hosts. It often has a complex lifecycle with a development in the environment or intermediate hosts.

Infection transmission routes

Feed-borne infections: infections which can be transmitted through eating feed containing the pathogen.

Vector-borne infections: infections transmitted through vectors — biological vector, that is a vector in which the pathogen goes through a development before further transmission is possible (e.g. mosquitos, tsetse fly, body louse).

Water-borne infections: infections which can be transmitted through drinking water which contains the pathogen.

Water-washed infections: infections caused by pathogens whose transmission can be prevented by improving personal hygiene. Infections can have either direct or indirect transmission routes.

Pig survival mechanism

Like all mammals, the pig's body has a range of mechanisms that prevent a pathogen from causing infection.

For example, the epithelial cells on the skin serve as the safety shield of the animal body. It protects the body by being a barrier between the internal cells and the dirt and microbes that are always in the farm environment. However, an open wound (e.g. insect bite, cut, abrasion) can make this barrier ineffective.

Once the body defence system has been breached and pathogens invade, a firefight commences. The next barriers are mechanisms that react to the pathogen, and try to counter its development. A variety of soldiers are called upon by the pig body to deal with the pathogen enemy, which has already invaded healthy cells in the animal's tissue, might be reproducing inside them and sometimes almost emerging to take overall control of the pig's body cell territory.

The reconnaissance

As the pathogen bursts forth through the epithelia cells into the body, Helper T cells swings into action and act as scout. Helper T cells are always on watch in the pig's body, to identify any pathogens and send a message to the Headquarter, i.e. the brain, that particular foreign invaders have invaded the animal body. Helper T cells do not make toxins or fight invaders themselves. Instead, they are like team coordinators. The chemical messages that they send serve as instructions to the other immune system cells in the pig body e.g. to produce Killer-T cells and B-cells and make sure the fight stays under control.

The resistance

Once the first line of defence is infected or damaged, Helper T cells call for help by releasing chemicals to attract macrophages. These chemicals also open spaces between blood vessel cells that allow macrophages to squeeze between the spaces to get to the action.

Macrophages are a kind of white blood cell. In times of peace they live peacefully in the bone marrow 'which is like the barracks'. They are usually the first cells at the scene of infection. They are the forward defence screen, i.e. the body natural killer cells. Macrophages are cell-eating machines. First, the macrophage surrounds the unwanted particle e.g. viruses and bacteria, and suck them in. Then, the macrophage breaks it down and the leftover material is then pushed out of the cell as waste. Not only do macrophages keep the body clean of debris and invaders, they also call for backup when an infection is too big for them to handle alone.

However, the ferocity of macrophage resistance can be undermined if the pig on your farm is suffering from other infections or is malnourished, stressed, or fatigued. For example, the gilt in your farm have a higher risk of infection when pregnant which further weakens the macrophage's resistance.

Macrophages deal with some, not all, of the invaders, especially bacteria, fungi, cells invaded by viruses and cancer cells. Thus, they identify the enemy that they cannot handle and liaise with the Helper T cells to mobilise the assistance of B cells.

Rapid Reaction troops

While this is going on in the battle front, the brain (HQ) is busy pulling together and sends rapid reaction troops — Killer T cells, in response to the antigen alarm that was earlier sent. T-cells are a type of white blood cell that works with macrophages. Unlike macrophages that can attack any invading cell or virus, each T-cell can fight only one type of virus. There is a tendency to think that this means macrophages are stronger than T-cells, but they aren't. Instead, T-cells are like a special forces' unit or targeted scud missile that fight only one kind of virus that might be attacking your pig's body.

Killer T-cells find and destroy infected cells that have been turned into virus-making factories. To do this they need to tell the difference between the infected cells and healthy cells with the help of special molecules called antigens. Killer T-cells are able to find the cells with viruses and destroy them.

The primary defence force

The primary defence force of the body is the B cells. They are like the heavily armed troops. The armament being antibodies. These are specific and targeted antibodies for specific antigens — in the same way that an army uses different weapons to deal with different challenges — anti-aircraft, anti-tank, mines, machine guns, etc.

Unlike T-cells and macrophage cells, B-cells don't kill viruses themselves. The B-cell sweeps up the leftover viruses after the T-**cell** attack. They make important molecules called antibodies. These molecules trap specific invading viruses and bacteria. Without this line of defence, your pig's body would not be able to finish fighting most infection.

Many of these B-cells quickly turn into Plasma cells. Plasma cells make and release antibodies that connect to the same antigen as the original B-cell receptor. Plasma cells make thousands of antibodies per second, which spread throughout the pig's body, trapping any viruses they see along the way.

Even after the animal's body has fought off the infection, some antibodies stay in the pigs' blood. So that if that virus tries to infect again, the pig's immune system will recognise the pathogen and make antibodies which will attack the pathogen. This is called active immunity.

The battle commences

After the build-up in response to attack by disease (during which time all the troops involved need all the help you — the rest of the civilian population /government (farmer) edicts — can give them by reducing stress, giving good quality feed and water, keeping things clean, not overstocking and managing warmth and ventilation well) while the heavy duty B cells start tearing into the antigen invaders. Each B cell 'regiment' recognises and reacts to only one specific antigen by destroying the body cells harbouring the enemy antigen (such as a virus) or neutralising the virus itself.

Battle over

When the battle is over and the pig's body wins, another form of Helper T cell has been in reserve, called Suppressor T cells takes over the logistics and intelligence corps. These detect that the battle has been won and stand down most of the troops. Without it the various troops, by now in full fighting mood, could begin attacking healthy body cells, too — not just only those occupied by the enemy.

In summary, the heavily and specifically armed B cells recognise and react to only one form of virus enemy, and Memory B cells and some T cells stay in the body waiting for any re-invasion of the antigen 'enemy' i.e. if there is re-exposure to the same antigen, or invader.

19.7 WHAT CAN YOU DO AS A FARMER TO ASSIST THE PIGS IN THIS BATTLE?

While your pig is trying to heal from pathogens that have attacked the body, your key objective as a farmer should be to empower your pig to fight on and protect the pigs from other external attacks. By doing this you will allow your pigs to divert more nutrients into growth and production and use your feed to fortify its immune shield.

- Minimize buying in of stock from many sources, more sources more challenges

- Keep visitors away

- Adopt All in All Out and batch rearing for your grower and finisher

- Provide good feed to your pigs and clean water

- Establish strict reliable vehicle sanitation and driver discipline

- Never allow casual disposal of pigs around the farm boundary

- Incinerate all casualties

- Put in place a complete biosecurity system

- Implement vermin control/bird control

In addition to the list above you should also carry out the following on the farm:

- Realise how important it is to wash weaner's pen regularly with water, detergent and disinfectant

- Treat scour (diarrhoea) promptly and swiftly clean area soiled with diarrhoea as soon as it is noticed

- Check all diets are adequately provided with zinc, especially organic zinc

- Make sure there is sufficient ventilation in your pen

- Ensure that your slurry drainage flows out of the unit to the nearest exit

- Site dung heaps should not be close to the weaner pen

- Never allow farm staff to consume pork/meat products on-farm

- Replenish the water in your foot dips frequently and use the correct disinfectant

- If you have more than one farm unit, do not exchange tools/vehicles, etc., and change your clothes when visiting

- Keep domestic and farm animals out, especially sheep and chickens

19.8 WHAT ARE THE STRESSES ON YOUR FARM AND HOW DO THEY IMPACT YOUR PROFITABILITY?

Stress is the total of all the biological reactions of pigs to any adverse stimuli.

These stimuli can be physical, mental or emotional — those which disturb the smooth functioning (stability) of the pig's metabolism.

What triggers the stress in a pig is called a Stressor. It can be an individual or an action (collectively called stimuli) which disturbs this stability.

When an animal is stressed, information about the stressor goes to the brain and the brain instructs the body within a millisecond either to 'flight/fear' or to be 'depression, anxiety, worry'.

For example, in the wild when a pig sees a predator like a lion which presents a sudden threat to the animal, the brain quickly activates the Autonomic Nervous System (ANS). The immediate effect of this is to increase the availability of energy, increase heart and respiratory rate while putting digestion and reproductive on hold — all of this is done by hormonal activity. The pig can then either fight or flee the threat. Once the threat is deemed over, the activating hormones quickly reduce and disappear, so the effect can be of short duration.

Now you can begin to appreciate why most wild pigs, especially in Africa, tend to be small in size. One of the reasons is that they have more predators in Africa than prey, unlike their European counterpart which are bigger in size because they have fewer predators and more prey. Less stress means they can grow bigger.

On your farm you too can increase the amount of stress that your pig is exposed to through overcrowding, overstocking, bullying, regular torment from staff, wound and injury, temperature, discomfort, disease challenge and uncaring and overworked staff behaviour. In this situation and with this kind of threat, the pig thinks that it is under attack and its brain activates ANS.

However, this hormone produced by the pig to respond to this stress negatively affects the organs in the body which deal with growth, especially protein formation which is important to the farmer. Less food conversion means less meat is formed from the food.

Such stress also affects the body's immune system and the animal's ability to defend itself against disease; and the animal reproduction, the ability to have piglets. For example, ovulation, and the implantation of the embryo, are particularly vulnerable to the strains caused by stress of incorrect nutrition, lack of rest and quiet after service, and unfavourable conditions at farrowing.

19.9 THINGS THAT YOU CAN DO TO DETECT AND ALSO REDUCE STRESS ON YOUR PIG FARM

These are some things that you can do on your farm to reduce stress on your pigs:

- As much as possible, your staff should avoid wearing white coats or overalls on the farm (as the reflection of the sun on the white cloth affect the eyes of the pig). Your staff should preferably wear green or dark blue clothes

- As much as possible reduce all unnecessary noise (especially abrupt noise) on your farm, encourage your staff to do everything quietly

- They should move slowly and gently, not aggressively when moving through your pen

- No bullying or beating of the pig of any kind is permitted by staff on the farm

- No humiliation or intimidation of pigs is permitted especially the boar

- Quietly observe your pigs under their normal behaviour patterns

- You should do your inspection every week, but your manager should do this daily

- Check stocking density: Check, check, check. Stocking density quickly gets out of control as your pig increases in size

- Attend to water: Ensure that water flow rate is up to standard and the ease of access is adequate

- Check that any materials e.g., wooden shavings, straw, etc. are still adequate and not fouled

- Maintenance of floor quality (slipperiness, gaps/holes, roughness) must all be checked during the stress audit

- Review conditions during mating or implantation: Far too many sows are stressed during the 7-28-day period post-service. They need rest and quiet, freedom from aggression or discouragement from aggressing others. They need to be adequately well fed and they need to be kept out of draughts and excessive warmth

- Open doors to your pen quietly and listen before entering

- Listen to the breathing, for restlessness, wheezing, (light, irritant sneezing) and for laboured respiration/ coughing.)

- Observe your pigs when they are unaware that you are doing so

- Look out for their resting pattern, huddling (piling)

- Do not enter until you have looked at as many areas as possible before the pigs disturb themselves

- A good time to detect problems is last thing at night with a torch or first thing in the morning before the staff come in to disturb the pigs

- Observe them also when the pigs stir up

- At the same time look for stiffness/lameness/reluctance to move

- In weaner pen and farrowing rooms, look for piglets which are lying awkwardly/ lifting their undersides in the semi-sternum posture. This is advance warning of digestive upsets

- Look out also for yellowish stained excreta on the floor, also a sign of diarrhoea

- In the farrowing pen, palpate the sow's udders, feeling for warmth, unusual conditions/discomfort

- Check the feeder and watering troughs for stale food, contamination, cleanliness

- Check evidence of feed wastage on the floor

- Are pigs 'nosing' and not eating the food in the troughs? This is a sign of nutritional dissatisfaction from hunger to unpalatability

- Get as many nursing sows to stand

- Condition score those that do and check legs/sores/rubbing

- Check water adequacy i.e. colour of urine

- Check for discharges

- For group-housed weaners, growers and gilts, let them move past you and study gait and alertness

- Check their water supply

- Check too much queuing disturbance during feeding

19.10 LEARN TO LISTEN TO YOUR PIGS

Like piglets, pigs communicate regularly with the farmer all the time. You need to keep vigilant, use all your five senses (sight, sound, hearing, smell, and touch) while you are on your farm and also pay close attention to pig body language and actions (behaviour) as well as watch for their bodily functions and be ready to pick up the messages quickly.

- Vocal hunger — a sort of low 'grizzle'

- Thirst — a more urgent, demanding high-pitched clamour coupled with their bright yellow urine

- You can literarily smell when scouring (diarrhoea) is about to commence. The pig will sometimes lie in the semi-sternum position with its lower body lifted off the ground supported by the forelegs, possibly because with disturbed intestines it feels better if it lifts its belly off the ground

- If your nose is very sensitive, you will notice the acrid smell of incipient scour before it actually occurs — it is better to nip scours in the bud before an outbreak by taking advance action just in case

- Constipation could be caused by lack of water or digestible fibre. If it is lack of water, you will see visible signs. It is a distinct yellow urine in sows and a slowdown in excreting body toxins

Constipation is an involuntary means of communication. Farmers and staff should be in the habit of noticing dung consistency — pig dung should deform slightly as it hits the floor and be easy to compress with a light touch of the boot, if recently excreted by the pigs

- When it is too cold — your pigs huddle (piling) together very closely

- Abnormal behaviour such as your pig urinating in the `wrong` place (e.g. where it normally eat or rests, a place that they would naturally keep dry and comfortable) is a sign that the whole of the pig cell (or room) stench and the pig cannot differentiate toilet from bedroom, though it might look clean to your naked eyes

- Sometimes pregnant sow may deliberately wet their resting place in order to cool themselves. This is a sign that the cell environment is too hot or overly exposed to direct sunlight. They wet the floor so that the evaporation of moisture from the floor surface will cool them. The remedy is to improve the ventilation in the pen by making sure the wall of your pen is not too tall and to have water troughs or a shower system

- When your pig starts tail biting, ear biting or any form of cannibalism, this is usually sign of boredom and they are looking for something to do or overcrowding or a stuffy atmosphere or over exposure to too much direct sunlight where there is no shade

- Pigs are sentient beings — inquisitive and explorative — so giving them something to do will certainly help or distract them. If you have plantain or pawpaw plantation on your farm, you can chop the stem into 1-foot lengths and throw it into your pig cell, they like to push it around and eat until it becomes a sponge. This is called 'environmental enrichment' — the scientists' euphemism for just giving them something to do!

- Bar chewing is a sign of boredom. You can alleviate this by giving stalled sow culprits a little more food for a week or so with a fibre additive or a gut-filler like a little rice bran or pam kernel cake.

- Sluggards or laziness. If your pig's slow to come to, feed this is unusual. Something could be wrong or starting to develop.

Once you have identified the animal that needs attention, you spray mark all of them and start medication or attending to them. You do not need to wait for scouring or problems to appear.

20. Managing Growth Rate in Pigs

Now that you have successfully weaned your pigs, managing their growth rate is your next objective, to get them to market weight as quickly and as cost effective as possible.

Growth is the progressive increase in size of a living thing on the farm. This translate into the rate of increase in body weight of a pig for a unit in time, e.g. grams per day (g/day) or kg per week (kg/wk).

Variation in live weight is usually evident at birth.

As mentioned earlier, light birth weight piglets are disadvantaged compared to their heavier contemporaries and they are particularly at risk in the early days following birth.

Light piglets are more susceptible to cold and are less able to compete with bigger piglets for access to teats and, as a consequence, there is a reduction in the amount of colostrum and nutrient that they consume. All these factors do not only further keep them lighter but also increase the risk of preweaning mortality from crushing, starvation, and/or disease.

It is therefore very important for you as a farmer to measure the growth rate in grams from birth through to weaning, because it is at this stage that profit and loss is often determined.

a. Birthweights. Ensure that you manage your gilts or sows very well during pregnancy so that they could give you litters with good birthweight. Studies have shown that pigs that are 500g heavier at birth translate into 10 kg heavier by 106 kg.

b. Show more tender loving care to the small and weak piglets that you have in your litter so that they can catch up. Studies have shown that 50% of runt pigs can reach 7 kg at weaning if fed and managed selectively.

c. Make sure that there is adequate trough space for all the piglets. Most fighting happens at the feeding troughs

d. Feeder gap space — Where possible unrestricted access to food all through the grower's life is a major influence on uniform growth within a group. Overcrowded pigs are not only more stressed as it affects their ability to convert food efficiently, but the submissive ones are likely to eat less food than the dominants and so they start to lag behind in weight-for-age terms.

e. Genetics has its place in growth — The quality of sow's lines influences variability in both growth and grading.

f. Mating sows to more than one male line may increase variation similarly.

g. Good environment is important. Too hot, too cold, incorrect ventilation all affect variation.

h. The amount of feed that pigs actually eat (not the amount given to the pig) can affect growth. If 2 cells are given the same amount of feed, the actual feed intake can vary by 20% within a cell and by a similar amount between pens, due to the attention of the staff, e.g. an increase in frequency, evenly spreading of feed, etc.

i.   Water provision. Accessibility can be as important as adequacy, as mentioned earlier. The more water pigs drink, the more feed they eat.

j.   Seasonal effects. Studies around the world have shown that carcass weights are lower in the summer months than winter. It is easy to see why pigs that are in sub-Saharan Africa (with 12 months of summer) might struggle a bit with weight.

k.   Health. Good health reduces the spread of weights within pens.

20.1 HOW TO PREVENT POOR RATE OF GROWTH OF PIGS ON FARM

There are many causes of poor rate of growth of pigs that you need to watch out for.

If your farm is experiencing a slow up in growth, you should check the following on your farm:

- Check stocking density — see if there are too many pigs in a pen. The pen might be suitable when the pigs are small piglets but as they grow in size, the number of pigs might have outgrown the pen. You might need to remove some pigs from the pen.

- Check feed accessibility — check how easy is it for each of the pigs to access food. Are all the pigs having access to feed and also water at the same time during feeding?

- Check for challenging behaviour — Are there signs of challenging behaviour like bullying or tail biting among the pigs?

- Check for unevenness — is the size of pigs very different? If distinctly obvious, then split the pen into two but try to avoid re-mixing two new sets of pigs together as this will lead to a fresh fight for dominance.

- Check for ectoparasite — Is there a build-up of mange on your pig's body causing continuous stress and scratching that can affect food utilisation?

- Check for worms — When last were your pigs dewormed?

- Check the feed — Check the feed, the nutrient. Is it ok, is it palatable and is the texture ok for the pigs? Also check for moulds and other contamination.

- You should also keep freshness of feed at the back of your mind.

- Check the pen environment for draught, cold or excessive direct sunlight.

- Housing change — check if the new house's environment is too cold.

21. Care and Management of breeding Boar

The importance of the boar on your farm cannot be overemphasised; the boar is responsible for the production of forty to fifty times more piglets than a sow. Nearly half of the genetic potential of the piglet on your farm is determined by the boar(s) on your farm.

With this statistic, it is important that you give more priority to the management of boars that you newly introduced into your farm so that they can achieve maximum reproductive efficiency. A boar must be ready, able, willing and fit to serve a sow on heat. This can only be possible if his housing need is met, feed is adequate and his condition is not neglected or overworked.

Good reproductive and nutritional management of a boar pays dividends through an increased number of piglets farrowed and weaned.

21.1 PRACTICES THAT CAN HELP YOU TO MAXIMIZE FERTILITY AND LONGEVITY OF YOUR BOAR

The following boar management practices should help your farm to maximize fertility and longevity.

Your boar should be evaluated for reproductive soundness, using the following:

Boar evaluation criteria

Boars should be evaluated from 6 months of age on the following criteria:

1. Behaviour

Bring your gilt that is in standing heat into your boar's pen and observe the following:

- **Libido:** Observe the boar's aggressiveness and desire to mate.

- **Mounting:** Good boars must have the ability to mount correctly. Some boars may be interested in mounting but lameness, arthritis, or injury may prevent success.

- **Mating:** Observe the boar's ability to erect the penis and properly enter the gilt.

2. Examine the boar's penis for normal size and condition.

Typical penis abnormalities that you must avoid should include:

- adhered or tied penis,
- limp penis,
- infantile penis,
- coiling of the penis in the diverticulum.

These conditions may be heritable, and boars exhibiting these problems should not be used to produce breeding stock.

3. Check the quality of semen produced.

Some boars may mate but fail to produce sperm cells. To be sure your pig is not firing empty bullets, you should take semen from young boars and submit to a check under the microscope.

The simplest way to collect semen from a boar is to allow the boar to mount a gilt in standing heat.

- First place a rubber glove (latex) on one hand and after the boar begins to extend his penis, grasp firmly the corkscrew end of his penis and bring the penis gradually forward once extended ejaculation begins.

- Collect the entire ejaculate into a wide-mouth container covered with a double layer of cheesecloth to separate the gel fraction.

- The volume of semen obtained is quite variable between boars but averages generally between 200-250 millilitres (about 1 cup).

- If the sperm concentration is high, the semen will be milky in appearance. Boars with watery or bloody semen should be evaluated by a reproduction specialist.

- If you look at the sperm under the microscope, usually 70 to 80 percent of the sperm should be motile immediately after collection.

- Low sperm motility is not a serious matter unless the condition persists for several months.

- Boars that produce semen with no sperm or only a few sperm should be rechecked several times at weekly intervals. If the condition persists, the boar should be culled. The first ejaculate of a new boar may not provide an accurate test and should not be used for evaluation.

4. Test Mating.

Ultimately, the best way to test the soundness of a boar on the farm is to allow him to mount and mate two or three gilts and carefully check after 21 days whether the sow or gilt returns to oestrus.

But please note, a new boar may have temporary infertility due to transportation stress, exposure to conditions or microorganisms on the new farm. High environmental temperatures, illness, lameness, or injuries causing high body temperature can alter sperm motility. All of these can reduce fertility for up to 8 weeks.

21.2 HOW TO SELECT A BOAR FOR YOUR FARM

The search for a boar for your farm should begin well before it is required.

Allow the boar at least three to five weeks to settle into his new home before expecting him to begin work.

You should invest in good quality boar; the offspring of a superior boar will need less feeding to reach marketing stage and will obtain higher grades (and thus prices) than a genetically poor boar.

Avoid the following features in the genetic make-up of your boar

Hydrocephalus	This is when a large amount of fluid accumulates on the brain. Symptoms are an enlarged heart and fits
Umbilical hernia	Common in piglets caused by a recessive gene
Scrotal hernia	The intestines protrude into the scrotum
Cryptorchidism	When one or both testicles do not descend into the scrotum after birth. If both testicles are retained, the animal will be sterile

Hermaphroditism	Double-sexed. These pigs show the characteristics of both sexes to varying degrees. Such animals are sterile.
Other deformities	May occur in the legs, skin, ears and metabolism. In addition, the farmer should not select a boar from a sow that has had a history of reproductive failures

21.3 HOW TO WELCOME NEW BOAR TO YOUR FARM

If the boar that you bought is still young (under seven months old), the boar should be housed for the first month away from the sight and smells of sows and gilts on heat to avoid frustration.

He should be dewormed and given a mange wash or spray on arrival.

This settling in period is the best time for you and your staff to get to know the boar and vice versa. So that you can work together as a team towards the same goal.

22. Fattening your pig for the market

Once piglets have been weaned from their mum, it is a good time for you to decide which of the pigs will be selected for breeding using the parameters that we stated in the previous chapters and the rest of the pigs will automatically be for fattening.

Fattening pigs involves raising or buying batches of young pigs (usually weaners around 12-20 kg each) and feeding them to market weight of 70 to 100kg.

The key factor that will determine your success in fattening is market timing. This means that you need to acquire your young pigs at the right time so that they reach market weigh at the right time when opportunity for profit is favourable i.e. when the farm gate price of pigs is at its peak.

Based on historical performance, profit will be higher during the festive season from November to December than any other months. Therefore, it is advisable to bring your weaner in or start raising your weaner pigs from around May up to December to get the best price. Generally speaking the higher the farm gate price per kg you can get for your pigs the better the profits per head of pigs sold.

Apart from the end of the year festive period, you should also check other festive periods like Easter and wedding periods of the community that prefer pork meat. We will talk more about this in the marketing chapter.

Let us reiterate the situation where fattening production system is best suitable, the advantages and the disadvantages of raising pigs for fattening that we mentioned earlier.

Fattening production system is best suitable on farms where:

- There is a shortage of skilful labour to manager the complexity of sow-herd management

- There is abundant space to accommodate weaners

- Pig feed ingredients are readily available and affordable for farmers e.g. close to food factory or the farm has a large expanse of arable crop

- The operator has good connection with abattoir or slaughtering houses

- Have an adequate capital to prevent such losses and even sell on credit

- The operator's ability to use various marketing techniques

- Operator is up to date with the meat industry and keep up with the market

Advantages:

- Rate of capital turn-over is relatively fast with fattening compared to farrow-finish operations. For example, with the breeder stock, the period from start-up to first sales is approximately 1 year whereas fattening is only 4 to 6 months.

- Specialised labour not required e.g. detecting heat and farrowing and demanding management needed by breeding herds and new-born pigs are not required for fattening.

- Requires less labour and management — two staff can handle 100 grower pigs

- Produces lots of pig waste that can be processed or used as a fertiliser.

- Has a flexibility to shut-down business at the end of each cycle — the cost for stopping a fattening operation is relatively smaller and the loss associated with shutting down is the cost of idle buildings and equipment. Unlike a sow-litter operation, which is more complicated.

Disadvantages:

- Significant expenses of regularly buying large quantity of pig's feed which accounts for over 80% of total production costs.

- Likely to stock poor quality pigs if pigs are purchased from different farms, which may lead to unknown health status, variations in growth performance and increased medication costs, biosecurity threat, and high mortality rate.

- Lack of uniformity when you amass young pigs from various sources.

- The volatility in pig feed means that the profit is determined and highly influenced by current market prices. It may be at a loss may if the feed price goes up and the selling price of pig remains stagnant.

- Supplier may become competitor, combine farrow to wean and to finish as a system type of choice due to the lack of market for their piglets.

22.1 HOW TO FEED YOUR FATTENING PIGS — EITHER AD LIB. OR BY RATIONING

1. Ad lib
2. Rationing

Ad lib is the feeding management through which pigs are offered as much food as they want. That is, they always have feed in their feeding trough at their disposal 24/7.

The advantages of ad lib feeding are:

- Pigs grow faster

- There is a quicker turnover of pigs

- Easier to manager as feed is always available in the feeding trough. Staff do not need to adhere to feeding time.

- There is less competition for feed among pig thereby reducing bullying and tail biting at feeding trough.

The disadvantage is the high cost of food and sometimes wastage of the feed.

Rationing feeding entails offering the animals limited amounts of feed, normally lower than the amount that they are able to eat (the feed is not available 24 hours a day).

The advantages of rationing feeding are:

- Lower cost of food, though slower growth rate

- Good management needed to ensure that feeding times are adhere to by staff

- No sophisticated feeding equipment

- Less waste of feed

Your preferred approach will depend on the market that you are catering to meet, for example, if you have a target weight, volume and tight schedule that you need to meet on a regularly basis you might consider ad lib feeding to guarantee that you meet the order. But make sure the price that you are selling your pig for reflects the effort.

However, if the requirement of the market that you are targeting is not as rigorous, for example if you are supplying an open market, then ration feeding is your preferred option.

22.2 THINGS TO BEAR IN MIND WHEN FEEDING YOUR FATTENERS

Here are some points that you need to bear in mind when feeding fatteners, irrespective of the option you choose:

- Pigs are very greedy animals and will eat large amounts of food if they are fed ad lib.

- Pig feeding is a balance between feeding ad lib. (in order to achieve the best growth) and rationing (to achieve the best prices).

- Rationing reduces the amount of meal eaten by the pig and thus the cost of the finished animal; but in return the pig stays longer on the farm which is an additional cost on the fixed asset.

- Pigs are slaughtered while they are still growing. That means your feed is used for growth of the organs, the meat and the fat production all at the same time. For live pig sales you do not have to worry about this as you sell all of these together as a whole.

- Where possible you should feed your pig with scientifically formulated and balanced meal or pellet that is high in protein and the essential amino acids (especially lysine).

- However, to save cost, you can also buy all the ingredients required locally and mix your own rations on the farm. This will definitely reduce the cost of rations but make sure that you have a sound knowledge of pig nutrition (or get a good feed formula from your feed nutritionist) and make sure the final feed contains all the required ingredients.

- The period from birth to 15 kg is when a pig is most efficient at converting feed. Less than 3 kg of feed is required for every 1 kg the pig gains. Your pig should, therefore, be encouraged to eat as much as possible at this stage and the feed should be of the highest quality.

- The piglets should be offered a high protein creep feed from one week old and should have free access to this.

- After the creep feed, the feed should be changed to a slightly lower protein grower's meal — again offered ad lib.

- Young pigs under 45kg weight have mostly meat (and not lots of fat). Meat deposition is mostly taking place. At this stage, your pig should be fed ad lib. For every 1 kg the pig gains, only 3 kg or less needs to be fed.

- From 45 kg to 70 kg, however, the energy from the food goes increasingly into laying down fat. At this stage, it is wise for you to switch from ad lib to ration feeding. This means that your pigs are given as much feed as they can finish in two thirty-minute feeding sessions.

- It is generally accepted that pigs up to 45 kg need a diet containing 18% crude protein then, after that weight, the pigs can be put onto a 15 — 16 % crude protein diet.

- Since 70% of the cost of raising a pig is feeding, it makes sense to ensure that feed is doing the job required.

- You can know how much the pigs need in this system by putting a little in the troughs and then topping up twice more during the thirty-minute feeding session. By the end of the session, only a few mouthfuls of food should remain. You eventually will know how much to put in at the start of feeding sessions.

- The optimum feed allowance is usually between 2.5 to 3 kg per pig.

- Lower than this fails to use the pig's potential to form lean meat and higher than this will just put fat on the pigs.

- Between 70 to 85 kg is where most fat deposition takes place.

- Feeding frequency — It is sometimes worth feeding pigs that are between 8 — 12 weeks old three or more times daily. This is particularly so if the pigs are backward and light for their age. With older pigs, there seems to be no advantage in feeding more than twice daily.

- Once a day feeding is not recommended as it tends to lead to insufficient feed to pigs or waste of feed.

- Pigs grow well on pellets but it is thought that this is due to the pellets being heated during compression and thus partially "cooked". This makes the pellets more digestible than ordinary dry meal.

- Pigs prefer wet feed and they consume it more easily than pellets.

- Feeding dry meal is wasteful as particles of the feed float around in the air and are breathed in by the pigs.

- Adding water to the meal in the ratio of 1-part meal with 2 parts water renders meal into a mash and reduces this waste.

22.3 **HOUSING**

To reduce the overall cost of housing, fattening pigs should be raised in groups of 10 to 20.

1. As mentioned earlier, pigs in the wild tend to flock in groups not larger than 20. If you keep more than this number of pigs together, the pigs will spend more time than normal fighting and bullying each other. This will translate into pigs with even larger variations in weights, as well as the fact that it will be taking them longer time for some of them to reach market weight.

2. Pigs in a group of 20 or less will quickly establish a pecking order or social status which will remain in place as long as they are together.

3. The most dominant pigs are probably the biggest and will become the authority pig in the group and they tend to eat the most so become larger and heavier than the other pigs.

4. There will always be some variation in the weights of pigs being fattened for this reason.

5. Whenever practical, male growers should always be penned separately from gilts except if the male is castrated.

6. Male pigs will eat, on average, half a kilogram more than gilts and will steal the gilt's food if they are fed together.

7. Male growers also run to fat quicker too, so it is a good idea not to allow them access to more food than their ration allows.

8. There should be a sleeping area and a dunging area with adequate feed trough space for the number of pigs in each pen.

9. There must also be enough water trough space or drinking nipples for the pigs.

10. Pigs can be fattened in relatively simple buildings if the climate is suitable. It is far more profitable to attend to the daily management of the pigs themselves than to build big pigs palaces.

11. The whole of the sleeping and feeding area can be roofed with thatch or asbestos sheets and it is a good idea to insulate the latter.

12. Ventilation is all important to keep the house cool in summer, warm in winter and free of noxious gases at all times.

22.4 TRANSPORTING YOUR FATTENED PIGS TO THE MARKET

1. Your fattened pigs should be loaded and unloaded when being transported to market in such a way that no injury or suffering is caused.

2. The floor of the transporter must be slip free and preferably fitted with a grid.

3. The sides of the transporter should be strong enough to withstand the considerable pressure it will experience from the pigs.

4. Hot weather and humidity are deadly to pigs as they have no sweat glands. Allow maximum airflow through the transporter under these conditions.

5. Any truck can break down. Be prepared!

6. Fattened pigs that show signs of porcine stress syndrome (PSS) during transportation must be allowed to rest or they will die. The signs of PSS include suddenly lying down, panting and trembling. The skin of these pigs often takes on a red, blotchy appearance.

7. Most of your fattened pigs which have been penned are not used to exercise. Merely climbing the ramp to the transporter can make their heart beat abnormally and these pigs will lie down to rest. This should bring the heart rate back to a more acceptable level.

8. A trained driver will deliver more pigs in better condition to the abattoir than an untrained driver.

9. Spend time with your drivers. Teach them how to pull away smoothly, brake slowly and corner without throwing the animals to one side.

10. Also spend time to teach your staff, who load the animals, to be patient and calm.

11. Pigs seldom fight when they are transported.

12. Try and group animals which know one another in order to help avoid fights.

13. Every farmer knows that pigs do not eagerly jump out of the transporting lorry! However, paying attention to small details can make the trip to the market run relatively smoothly.

14. Add vitamins and electrolytes or anti-stress medications to the drinking water at least two days before transportation and continue 3-5 days after arrival.

15. Transport the pigs during the coldest part of the day. The vehicle should be well ventilated and protected against direct sunlight.

16. . The pigs should not be handled roughly. Place beddings of straw or grasses at the flooring of the vehicle to protect the legs and feet of the animals.

17. Do not mix big and small animals.

18. Do not feed the pigs during transport. Drinking water should be given during long trips.

22.5 WHAT TO DO WHEN YOU ARE BRINGING A NEW SET OF WEANERS TO YOUR FARM

1. Clean and disinfect the pens prior to their arrival.

2. Make sure the pen is dry.

3. Maintain a warm pen environment of 21-24 degrees centigrade for the first few days after arrival.

4. Group pigs according to their sizes not ages. Separate weak ones.

5. Restrict feeding for the first few days after arrival to avoid digestive problems.

6. Do not immediately change the kind of feed given from the supplier.

22.6 HOW TO MINIMIZE FIGHTING AMONG NEWLY MIXED PIGLETS

1. Do not use a pen where some of the weaners are already housed.

2. Preferably use a pen that is new to all the piglets that you wish to put together.

3. Give the piglets "toys" like balls or "1-foot length" banana or plantain stem to keep them busy.

4. Spray with cresol or iodine especially around the ears and tail.

5. Preferably mix pigs towards the evening so that they can settle into the night.

6. General stability is reached after 48 hours.

7. Provide feeding trough where all pigs can eat at the same time.

8. The pens should be regularly cleaned.

9. Bathe or spray the animals, especially during hot weather (27 degrees).

10. Follow the proper feeding guide based on its nutritional requirements.

22.7 BEWARE OF MYCOTOXIN IN YOUR PIG FEED

Mycotoxin is a hidden thief in pig production and it is therefore important that you understand the factors on your farm that can contribute to mycotoxin production and the impact that this can have on your pigs and how to minimise the risk posed to the pig in your farm.

Mycotoxins are leftover toxic chemical products produced by organisms of fungal origin.

Fungi include moulds, mildews, rusts, yeasts and mushrooms. As an organism, they lack chlorophyll, leaves, true stems and roots. They reproduce by growing spores on dead organic matter or parasites.

Mould is the coating or discolouration caused by various fungi that develop in a damp atmosphere on the surface of stored food and fabrics, etc. For example, where humidity is very high during the rainy season especially in the forest and semi forest.

The mould fungus may be harmless or even dead but they still leave mycotoxin (poisonous) residues behind, commonly in stored and mixed feed, and especially in mouldy grain.

Even when the grain is eventually processed, while it may destroy the moulds, it still leaves mycotoxin residues behind. Mycotoxin only need to be present in very small quantities in the feed to cause problems in pigs such as infertility, anoestrus, prolapse, false pregnancies and embryo mortality; poor growth and vomiting. They can pass through sow's milk and remain behind in any slaughtered carcass.

There are some conditions that increase the chance of mycotoxins occurring in your pig feed, they include:

- storage of moist grain (grain with more than 13% moisture) — this is common in West Africa, especially where grains are harvested during the rainy season and are not allowed to dry properly.

- storage in damp, warm conditions (relative humidity more than 80%) — storing grains in a humid environment on the farm.

- storing feed in damaged or leaking feed bins.

- Keeping feed that is in a bag on a bare floor or on the wall can increase moulding of feed. Feed should be stored on the farm on a rack and away from the wall.

- storing feed where there are fluctuating temperatures.

- liquid feeding if it encourages growth of fungi.

- poor storage hygiene.

- damaged or broken grains are more susceptible to mould growth.

22.8 WHY IS MYCOTOXINS EFFECT SO PREVALENT?

Mycotoxin is very important because many pig farms are suffering from problems that emanate from using mycotoxin infected grains and feed ingredients and the farmers are not aware that mycotoxin is one of the main cause of problems on their farm such as infertility, anoestrus, prolapse, false pregnancies and embryo mortality; poor growth and vomiting.

Mycotoxin has become a bigger problem in many farms because:

- Global climate change has resulted in unusual weather patterns, with increased frequency of drought, flooding and temperature extremes. These changes in weather all increase the chance of mycotoxin contamination of feed grains.

- Majority of the sub-Saharan countries like Nigeria use maize and groundnut at high inclusion levels as a cheaper alternative to soya meal and fishmeal, these two ingredients are the primary suspect ingredients in a pig's diet, for example many feed samples of maize have as much as 153 ppm and 200 ppm in groundnut.

- In addition, there is an increased use of by-products such as brewery waste, rice and corn and wheat bran as an alternative feed ingredient to reduce feed costs. This factory waste often has a high degree of mycotoxin contamination.

- Increased mixture of crops grown under different climatic conditions e.g. savannah in the north and humid southwest which, when mixed together, can result in a wide spectrum of mycotoxin presence, made more acute in their effects on the pig.

- Poor harvesting method and substandard storage facilities which crack the protective grain pericarp before any drying process takes place and allows surface moulds to gain entry.

- Leaky feed containers with poor ventilation especially in the humid areas of the country.

- Keeping feed that is in a bag on a bare floor or on the wall can increase moulding of feed. Feed should be stored on the farm on a rack and away from the wall.

There is no reliable treatment for mycotoxicosis apart from the removal of suspect food or partial substitution of mycotoxin-free food to reduce the contamination.

Certain feeds are more likely sources than others — although harvesting and subsequent storage conditions can influence the degree of contamination of any crop.

22.9 HOW DO YOU KNOW IF YOU HAVE A MYCOTOXIN PROBLEM?

The following symptoms have all been associated with mycotoxins, but of course some of them could be due to other causes.

- Problem with breeding herd — Anoestrus, abortion, vulva swelling, vaginal prolapse, pseudo-pregnancy, increased weight loss in lactation, stillbirths, low viability piglets, splay legs, agalactia, udder oedema, reduced libido.

- Finishing and breeding herd — Reduced appetite, vomiting, rectal prolapse, liver and kidney damage, reduced feed intake, noticeably poor growth rate, scouring, respiratory oedema, skin irritation, increased water intake, immunosuppression

- Small pigs — Relatively mild outbreaks from 3 to 35 kg. lasting between 4 to 8 weeks and raised production cost by 8%.

- And severe outbreaks lasting 4 to 5 weeks and raised production costs by 24%.

- Note this 'hidden' cost so often not appreciated because it doesn't become obvious until slaughter.

23. Biosecurity

Biosecurity involves everything which needs to be done to protect a farm, its livestock and its workers from disease.

Biosecurity measures should be used to avoid the entry of pathogens into your herd or farm (external biosecurity) and to prevent the spread of disease to uninfected animals within a herd or farm and to other farms, when the pathogen is already present (internal biosecurity).

In this section, we will concentrate mainly on the effective and affordable measures that we as pig farmers can implement to deter infectious diseases from increasing and spreading should they gain a foothold on our farm; and to eliminate those present as much as possible.

It is worth noting that no farm can ever be sterile, so the target is not to turn our farm into a sterile surgical theatre room (over sterile farm has its disadvantage too) rather our goal is to reduce the level of pathogens on our farm to that which is low enough for our pigs' own defence mechanisms to cope and deal with those remaining.

26.1 **HOW MUCH ARE WE LOSING TO POOR HYGIENE**

As an experienced pig farmer, I know pig farmers talk a lot about biosecurity but to fully appreciate the damage that poor hygiene is doing to our farm, we need to see the cost implication on our pig performance and ultimately our profit.

I know most of my readers are entrepreneurial farmers and as business minded people if cleanliness (which is next to Godliness) did not move us to go that extra mile in our hygiene, the amount that we are losing from poor hygiene will make us sit tighter.

According to the research done on the UK pig farms, poor hygiene reduces food conversion in pigs by up to 30% that means of the 3 kg daily feed @ N70 per kg = N210 (0.65USDollar), 30% (0.20USD) of this is wasted within the body of your pig as the feed is used to fight pathogens picked up from poor hygiene, instead of converting the feed to muscle and more weight. This is particularly important because the feed cost is 60 to 70% of our running cost and recently the cost of feed is skyrocketing.

The research also reveals that poor hygiene on pig farms also affects your sows or gilt making them to farrow 2 fewer pigs per sow per litter.

Let us look closely at the financial implication of this statement on your farm. If your animal gives birth to 9 litters twice a year = 18, you have already lost 4 piglets per year to poor hygiene. And assuming the cost of weaner is N8000 — N1,500 worth of feed that the piglets consume for 8 weeks before weaning). That means a farmer is losing = N6,500 x 4 = N26,000 ($7.4 USD) per sow per annum.

The research concluded with the fact that the greatest loss is the subclinical disease — the low-level sickness that is invisible disease and that it possibly costs farmers more, over a period of say 2 years than a major outbreak.

26.2 WHAT CAN WE DO TO PROTECT OUR FARM FROM THESE LOSSES?

Segregation is the first and most important steps for pig farmers. It involves keeping potentially infected and sick animals and materials away from uninfected animals.

This is in line with a Yoruba adage that says, "If the wall is not cracked, a lizard cannot enter the house through the crack".

The logic behind this is that if a pathogen is prevented from entering a farm holding, no infection can take place.

No animals or materials infected with pathogens should enter or leave a pig pen: this includes not only infected pigs e.g. piglets with diarrhoea or pneumonia, but also humans, e.g. pig buyers or your staff who may be infected.

As a farmer you should control the entry of pigs from outside farms, implement quarantine for newly purchased animals, limit the number of sources of your animal, fence your farm area and control access for people especially the pig buyers, as well as birds and rodents, provide footwear and clothing to be worn only on the farm.

Cleaning is the most effective step in biosecurity that we can all afford. Materials (e.g., vehicles, equipment), that have to enter (or leave) the farm must be thoroughly cleaned to remove visible dirt. By doing this you will remove most of the pathogens that contaminate the materials. You should also avoid borrowing farm equipment from another farm to use on your farm, this includes a measuring scale from pig buyer.

The importance of regular and thorough cleaning of the pig pen floors and walls cannot be over emphasised. Manure needs to be scraped from the floor and the walls, it should also be swept, and washed with broom or brushes from the pig pens every day.

Most pathogen contamination on physical objects are contained in faecal material, urine or secretions that adhere to the surface of the floor and the walls; cleaning with soap should remove most of the contaminating pathogen.

It is important to clean the pen thoroughly first before disinfection. All the organic matter in the pen has to be removed by scraping the surface using brushes and broom with water and soap or detergent, rinsing it with clean water and allowing to dry. Use of a dilute detergent solution can help remove faecal material.

Let us look at the impact of cleaning and disinfectant on our pig pen.

Typical Total Viable Counts (TVC) of bacteria on your grower pen is estimated below:

- Immediately after pigs out 50,000,000

- After scraping and plain water washing 20,000,000

- Washing with hot and heavy-duty detergent 100.000
- After disinfection 1,000

Source: Waddilove (1999)

The table shows that each biosecurity activity does impact on the number of bacteria drastically. You will notice that after scraping and plain water washing and washing with heavy duty detergent the TVC goes down drastically even before using the disinfectant.

Cleaning is effective because when we are cleaning our pen floor, most of the excreta, faeces and feed that is on the floor or wall are often dried on, they are strongly adherent and greasy. To illustrate the state of this waste on the floor, you can imagine finishing a dinner of Eba or any starchy food and greasy soup at home with some friends and instead of washing up the food plates you decided to leave the waste on the plate overnight. Washing this plate in the morning will require that you scrape with metal sponge to get rid of the starch and grease that would have glued to the plate, pouring cold water on it will probably not be enough, you might need to add a detergent and soak it and use metal sponge to make it easier to clean. That is why daily scraping, washing and use of detergent is important during your pen cleaning.

Disinfection.

Disinfectant is "the application of chemical intended to destroy the infectious or parasitic agents of animal diseases."

Most disinfections are only effective when performed consistently and correctly and it should be regarded as the last step in biosecurity, and it will only be effective after comprehensive cleaning.

Contrary to many of farmer's assumptions, disinfectants will not necessarily penetrate dirt in sufficiently high concentrations if the floor or wall is not thoroughly cleansed, neither will the disinfectant be present long enough to kill the bacteria. In addition, the effect of many disinfectant's power is inactivated by organic materials, such as wood or faecal material.

This shows that cleaning is as important, if not more important than disinfection, however both are required to keep your farm safe.

After cleaning and disinfecting, materials or vehicles should be allowed to dry before reuse. If you are re-populating a pig pen with new sets of pigs, a minimum 3 days down-time should be applied to ensure sufficient time for drying.

Other good practices that you must imbibe on your farm:

- New pigs introduced must be free of disease.

- The use of quarantine is very important.

- Newly purchased pigs should be kept for a minimum number of days in a quarantine pen.

- Age-segregated rearing should be encouraged and buildings designed so that co-mingling among groups of pigs of different health status can easily be avoided.

- An all-in-all-out management system.

- Proper fencing and measures to control contact with birds, rodents, cats and dogs should be promoted.

- It is important to develop protocols for the farm, to which visitors must strictly adhere; with confined pigs, it is possible to control access for vehicles and people, including drivers and feed providers.

- Authorized visitors, particularly those dealing with pigs — including other farmers — should be provided with specific clothing and clean footwear by the farm being visited and should wash their hands upon entry.

- All instruments or equipment that is likely to come into contact with pigs should be assigned to the farm and kept clean.

- There should be regular and thorough cleaning of the pig unit.

- Manure should be removed from the pens every day, unless there are slatted floors or an equivalent.

- After thorough cleaning, the use of disinfectant should be promoted.

- The physical location of herds should be planned to maintain adequate distances from neighbouring farms and frequently used roads.

- Training and updating of staff by veterinarians and technicians specialized in disease control is necessary.

- Focus on the control of feedstuffs, water and wildlife and human visitors.

- Slaughterhouses are another important element in the marketing chain where all three elements of biosecurity must be implemented, with a major focus on biocontainment.

Pigs are susceptible to a wide range of diseases that affect productivity and, de facto, the producer's income.

26.3 **TRANSMITTERS OF PATHOGENS ON A PIG FARM**

- The role of people (staff and pig buyers and transporters) as transmitters of pathogens to pigs has been carefully studied.

- People can transport pathogens on footwear, clothing, hands, etc.

- People can carry viruses on their nasal mucosae (nasal carriers) without being infected, and shed pathogens when they are sick or carriers with no clinical signs.

- Pig workers must be aware of their own potential role in the spread of disease, as they have physical contact with pigs — including those that are clinically affected — in their daily work.

- Pig feed, including swill feeding, and drinking-water.

- Pig manure and bedding.

- Disposal of pig manure must be considered when designing and implementing biosecurity programmes, as manure may contain pathogenic organisms, leading to faecal-oral-transmitted diseases.

- The potential for disease transmission by people, vehicles and/or equipment, feed, bedding material or manure will be affected by temperature: cold temperatures enhance the survival of pathogens, whereas exposure to sunlight and drying tends to reduce survival.

- Birds, bats, rodents, feral and wild pigs and stray/domestic animals are a particular risk for disease spread in open piggeries.

- Rodents, particularly rats and mice, commonly live in close contact with pigs and are involved in endemic disease transmission in pig operations. Rodents may roam the countryside looking for new food sources when pig houses are emptied, and return when they are repopulated, when they can re-contaminate incoming pigs.

- Ticks are unable to travel to pigs, but pigs can be in contact with ticks when they graze or sleep in tick-infested areas. ASF is a good example of a tick-borne virus; its control requires knowledge of both the arthropod and the host's behaviour.

- Flies are attracted to organic matter, such as manure and carcasses, and can mechanically spread pathogens such as TGE and Streptococcus suis as they fly between farms.

26.4 WORKER'S AND VISITOR'S HYGIENE PROTOCOL

- Workers and visitors must strictly observe farm protocols to minimize the risk of bringing in diseases; the aim is to keep visitors away from pigs as much as possible. All people entering the farm, including the farmer and salaried workers, should not have been in contact with other pigs recently.

- Another effective option is to have foot dip, with disinfectant water available to remove all visible organic material, followed by disinfection. Disinfectant mats or buckets will not work if there is manure present on footwear.

- Visitors to farms should always be asked whether they have recently been to potentially contaminated places, such as pig farms, slaughterhouses. If they have, they should not be admitted to the farm unless all appropriate protection measures are taken.

- A visitor log book, in which visitors record their last exposure to pigs, is a useful tool for implementation of this measure.

- Salaried workers working with the herd should have no contact with other pigs, i.e., they should not keep pigs at their own homes.

- Visitors, including other farmers and pig workers, should be provided with specific clothing and clean footwear by the farm being visited, and should wash their hands-on entry.

- Where possible, a dedicated building should be located at the entrance, where workers and visitors can change clothing or put on/take off overalls and boots.

- In the context of the pandemic H1N1 2009 crisis, infected people can transmit the virus to pigs, so it is critical that people with respiratory illness symptoms are kept away from farms until they have recovered, and any fomite they may have contaminated must be disinfected before entry to farms.

- All instruments or equipment that are likely to come into contact with pigs, such as restraint snares, needles and scalpels, should be assigned to the farm and kept clean. They should not be transported from farm to farm; if they have to be, they should be cleaned and disinfected.

- Pig farmers should practise regular pest and rodent control, by having a cat on the farm or by keeping the surroundings of the pig unit clean.

26.5 REDUCING HEALTH RISKS FOR FARM STAFF

- Cover all wounds with a coloured waterproof dressing promptly

- Report all accidents to the farm manager

- Tell your line manager if you have diarrhoea or vomiting and do not work with animals

- Avoid touching your nose and mouth, picking your nose, biting your fingernails and licking your fingers

- Wash hands

- Regularly wash your hands, particularly after treating any sick pigs

- Wash your hands before eating, drinking or going to the toilet

- To avoid injury always move animals appropriately, for example using a pig board.

- Always use extreme caution when moving adult boars or a sow and her litter

- When pressure washing wear suitable protective clothing — protect your eyes, face and hands in particular.

- Health and safety face masks

- When handling dust environments ensure that you wear face masks to protect your respiratory system.

- Wear gloves when handling sick pigs — especially when the condition is contagious to other pigs or is zoonotic

- If you participate in a post-mortem or handle blood wear gloves

- Medicine fridge — Needles, medicines and syringes

- Ensure that all needles are covered. Store medicines and syringes appropriately. Dispose of all used needles, syringes and medicine bottles in a sharps container

- If staff are going to eat at the farm, provide suitable facilities where food can be stored and eaten cleanly. Do not allow pig food products onto the farm

- Ensure that there is sufficient light to work safely among the pigs — minimum of 50 lux

26.6 EFFECTIVE HAND WASHING GUIDELINES

In the research conducted in the UK, they discovered that:

"62% of men and 40% of women do not wash their hands after using the toilet".

"80% of communicable diseases are spread by touch. Handbags, keyboards, phones and kitchen chopping boards have all been found to have more than 200% more faecal bacteria than a toilet seat."

"Washing your hands prevents 30% of diarrhoea related illnesses".

The World Health Organisation provide the following guidance for washing hands correctly:

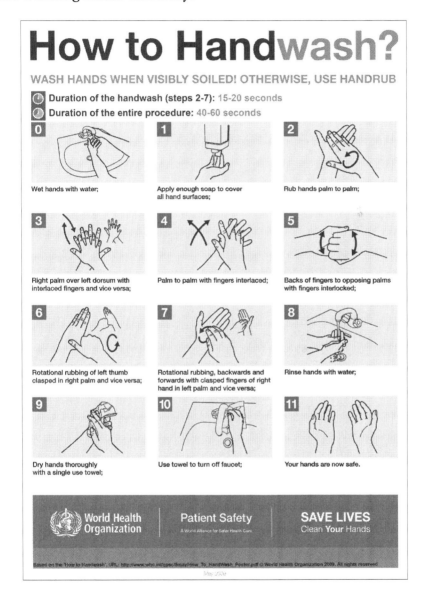

24. Pig management

I like this quote as it summarises the whole activity of a pig farmer:

"The animals of the farm should be regarded as living factories that are continuously converting their feed into products useful to man. A fact of great economic importance is that a large part of the food they consume is of such character that humans cannot directly utilise it themselves". — Henry and Morison in Feed and Feeding.

Management of pigs is more than just raising pigs, it involves taking into account variable seasonal factors, fluctuating markets and declining terms of trade. The most successful pig farmers have a good knowledge of market requirements, matching product quality to suit.

There are many factors that determine the productivity and profitability of a pig enterprise. These include:

1. The supply and quality of feedstuffs
2. The use of the most appropriate genetics
3. Ensuring high health standards
4. Optimising housing or environmental conditions
5. Meeting quality assurance requirements

6. Having a sound knowledge of market requirements

As we mentioned earlier, with the rising trend of middle-class pig farmers and managers, a commercial pig farm needs to become a business-orientated farm. Its progress should be measured by profit, not necessarily by physical performance.

A commercial farmer must develop better management skills so as to be able to make better decisions and good choices between alternatives.

Pig management is therefore "making decisions to increase profits", "making use of the best of available resources" and "using, managing and allocating resources".

These decisions will be determined firstly, based on the goals of the proprietor, secondly, that there are sufficient resources such as land, labour and capital that can be used or allocated to achieve the goals. Thirdly, that the resources to be used or allocated imply more than one possible use.

As a result, a commercial pig farmer is no longer just a pig farmer that takes care of pigs. This includes controlling their breeding, herding and feeding, protecting from diseases and where necessary, housing them in order to get a useful product. But also a business manager, who daily makes different decisions, such as making choices, for example, should I start with breeder pigs or weaners? how to best use the resources that are available in the setup, the construction and the production, the selection of the most appropriate approach e.g. intensive or free range, and deciding where and whom to sell their produce and at what prices.

As a trainer, pig farmers never stop complaining about the market and how it lets them down, but it is important for pig farmers to understand that like other businesses we do not work in a vacuum. Rather, we operate within a dynamic and constantly changing environment caused by:

1. Changing prices: Prices of inputs e.g. feed ingredients, medication, etc. and outputs such as the price of pig and pork meat are constantly changing in line with supply and demand and market forces. Though changes in the prices of products are outside the control of the farmer, it does affect farm's profitability.

2. Changing resource availability: The quantity available of any input has a direct impact on farm profitability e.g. rise in grain cost such as maize, soya, groundnut cake, and farmers will constantly need to reassess in relation to the resources available e.g. should we part substitute the maize with cassava? Should I use brewery waste, etc.?

3. Changing technical relationships: The relationship between inputs and outputs changes as technological advances are made. For example, should I invest in expensive exotic breeds that will give me faster growth and depend on extensive use of 100% expensive concentrate or should I use hybrids, a cross between exotic and popular breed), that will grow not as fast as an exotic breed but more than popular breeds but will eat locally affordable and available feed ingredients? What impact will these two decisions have on the farm's profitability.

4. Changing institutional/social relations: With the recent favourable disposition of the government and the Bank of Agriculture towards farming, should I expand my farm or maintain the current production? Should I expand my production based on the current demand by Shoprite and all other supermarkets? And what will the impact of the new ECOWAS flexible single currency 'Eco' has on my business?

24.1 TYPICAL PIT FALLS OF MANY NEW FARMERS

Studies of pig farmers in Nigeria have shown that pig farmers are more educated than other livestock or arable farmers in Nigeria. They are dedicated, hard-working, courageous, resilient, good-humoured, they do care for their animals within the bounds of convenience and cost, and many outside influences, such as volatile cost of feed and static price of pork and sometimes glut market with zero assistant from the government.

From my experience of interacting and visiting many pig farms in Nigeria, here is a summary of the typical pitfalls that I saw many farmers falling into:

- Ignorance of the core fundamentals of pig production. Typically, many people rarely study or research in great depth on the business that they are doing. If you are reading this book you are definitely not in that category.

- Poor recording and measuring of information or things well enough on paper or (recording) in the piggery (monitoring devices/controls).

- Some experienced farmers think they know everything about piggery and they have nothing new to learn but their experience is often the factor that is holding them back.

- The newcomer to the industries assumes that pig production is too easy.

- People are not observant enough. Most of the new ideas can be picked up through observation.

- Some farmers overwhelm themselves with daily chores on the farm with little time to think strategically.

- Some are absentee farmers that put their whole investment on somebody they just met.

- Overstocking, trying to cram lots of pigs into a minimal space.

- Not measuring or monitoring the growth of their pigs.

- Over investing in the fixed asset at the expense of the operational cost.

- Wastage, especially food, and not realising the many, hidden ways of wasting it.

- Poor recruitment and training of labour.

- Pushing gilts into production too impatiently at 6 months or first two heats.

- Not using the veterinarian properly.

- Slow to espouse business partnerships/linkages/collaboration.

- Not joining or supporting producer discussion groups.

- Falling behind in biosecurity requirements.

- Not treating pig production sufficiently as a business.

- Not realising how mycotoxins are 'hidden thieves.'

- Not spotting where or when to invest, i.e. poor prioritisation.

- Tending to delay spending completely rather than spending an affordable amount in the right place and at the right time. "A stitch in time may save nine."

Quite a long list. Even so, I find many people commit at least 30% of these shortfalls. Please go back through this list again and think hard where you may be adrift.

24.2 HOW SHOULD A MANAGER OR OWNER SPEND HIS OR HER TIME OM THE FARM?

1. Look at every pen of pigs once a day — two hours/day, plus 30 minutes/day to check on water equipment and feed

2. Go through the farm record and update it once a day — one hour/day

3. Go through farm finance, especially the farm cash flow against budget — 2 hours/week.

4. Think through ways in which money can be saved, or better, redirected into areas which give a more promising return

5. Go through the state of the flock to see if they are growing to target

6. Brief all staff formally each day — 15-20 minutes. Not only does this help to ensure that the right things at the sharp end are being done in good time, but it is also a useful finger on the unit's pulse, both where pigs and people are concerned

7. Plan and explore marketing opportunities — 5 hours/week

8. Plan and explore new feed source — 5 hours/week

9. Supervise the weekly composition of pig feed — 2 hours/week

24.3 THE REAL PRIORITY OF A PIG FARMER MANAGER

Selling your output effectively: The priority manager involves keeping a very sharp eye on selling your pigs to the outlet which can influence the farm income in the most positive. As a good manager, your job is to make it easy for the consumer, middle men, processor or retail outlets to buy your pigs, which means maximising the output of exactly the right quality of animal which the buyer needs, on time and deliveries at the minimal cost to the farm enterprise.

Cost control — You must manipulate productivity correctly so as to maximise profit. It is not necessarily the farm which spends the most money which makes the most profit. Control of costs is a vital management area in any business. The ways in which money can be saved, or better, redirected into areas which give a more promising return is the key role of a farm manager.

Astute at spending capital, especially on the big three, which include precision feeding, reducing disease and accurate environment control. An investment of one monetary unit on facilities which improve each one of these will yield never less than a threefold return on each, and that's a huge hike in income.

Delegate duty to staff — While farm managers need to do little manual work so as not to lose touch, many managers tend to overdo these chores. For a manager, manual work must not be done at the expense of key areas mentioned above. They should never allow themselves to get caught up in an increasing spiral of manual work. Sometimes the owner or proprietor measure a manager's work and expect them to be seeing working the chores. I hope as many proprietors are reading this book as the manager. Manager should carefully delegate the farm chores to staff.

Be profit minded — some managers are still very much output-minded to the exclusion of all else. To get the manager off these mindsets, the proprietor can offer a low wage but a 10% share of the profits. This will teach the manager how to effectively manipulate output so as to maximise profit. This means if they get this right they too will be well-rewarded, but also the owner — 9 times more.

Recruit and train sufficient staff for your farm — too many pig farms are understaffed. This means the farm is always short in the number of staff available to do the work. Cleaning, repairs and maintenance tasks in particular and the manager often has to assist to ensure the work-flow comes back somewhere near on-schedule again. Proprietors and managers should sit down and work out the cost-effectiveness of such a policy. Your staff should be trained as professionals– it is too important a job to leave to half-knowledge about peripheral tasks because he or she is busy at something else which also won't wait.

24.5 WHAT IS THE ROLE OF THE VETERINARIAN ON YOUR FARM?

At present, the role of the veterinarian in most farms in Africa could be described as that of a fire brigade, where the veterinarian is called upon to treat an individual animal or in an outbreak of disease. On most occasions, the damage is already done or the help is too late.

This problem is further exacerbated by the current price of pigs (the cheapest meat in many countries) and the size of many farms in most African countries (most of which are small, less than 100 pigs), as a consequence, most farms cannot afford the cost of a continuous veterinary service, especially where the government support for veterinary service is low.

But I believe that the role of veterinarians should be that of preventative medicine. This include caring for the wellbeing/welfare of the pigs, maintaining good medicine protocols and helping to ensure efficient production of consistently high-quality pig meat. When there are epidemics they should research on the life cycle of a specific disease agent, ensure specific control measures are put in place to control and even eliminate the disease from the farm. It is a shame that by now with so many veterinarian and scientist in Nigeria, a breed that is genetically designed for Nigeria has not been engineered. I am aware that to achieve this, African countries will require more veterinarians that specialise in pig production. Research has shown that there are a limited number of pig specialist veterinarians worldwide and it is even fewer in Africa.

24.6 WHAT YOU SHOULD EXPECT FROM YOUR VETERINARIAN

- Disease recognition
- A confidant to share concerns
- An enthusiast to provide information and drive
- Source of information
- Second pair of eyes to see common-sense failings
- Independence of opinion
- Training resource

24.7 STEP BY STEP PROCEDURE TO CLINICAL EXAMINATION OF YOUR PIG

This is sometimes not easy especially for indigenous or popular breed, as they are not used to being handled. They become very vocal when caught and will not settle easily. Ideally you should try and assess your pig as much as possible from a distance before handling the animal.

1. Make contact with your pig both vocally and physically. Pigs do not like surprises, as you enter the pig cell to assess the animal's body condition.

2. Pigs like to be scratched particularly behind the ear and along the back, it will calm them down.

3. Check the head of the pig for any discharges from the nose, eyes, mouth.

4. When handling the head, be on the watch out and make sure that the pig does not try and bite.

5. Take the rectal temperature normal 39C (102.5F).

6. Examine and note the mucosa colour of the external genitalia.

7. Palpate the lumbar muscles of the pig.

8. Some pigs may allow abdominal palpation.

9. Examine the mammary glands. Pigs also like to be rubbed on the underside.

10. Look for any abnormalities to the abdomen and chest.

11. It may be possible to examine the legs starting at the hind legs and moving to the fore. Pigs do not like having their feet touched.

12. Palpation of the limbs should start at the top and work down the limb.

13. Other examinations are possible after the initial examination is complete.

24.8 MANAGING RISK IN A PIG FARM

Risk management is an important component of any business.

This is even more important in pig farming, as you will be mak-ing decisions every day that affect your farming operations. Many of the factors that affect the decisions that you are making cannot be predicted with complete accuracy; this is risk. Your risk is having to produce without complete certainty about what will happen to your production.

Your risk as a pig farmer increases as you expand and move towards becoming a commercial. In order to generate more profit and become competitive it is therefore important that you have a good understanding of the farming environment, understand risk and have risk management skills to better anticipate problems and reduce consequences.

Sources of risk

The most common sources of risk in farming can be divided into five areas:

1. production
2. marketing
3. financial
4. institutional
5. human

Production and technical risk

Pig performance depends on biological processes that are affected by the quality of the breeder pig, the quality and storage of feed and the quality of the housing and the staff managing the farm. For example, severe weather such as too much heat in summer could lead to low conception among the gilts and sows and reduced litter size, while too much and prolonged harmattan cold could lead to shivering, pneumonia and death in piglets. Outbreaks of diseases such as African Swine Fever could also cause major yield losses on a pig farm. The risk is that farmers are having to produce without complete certainty about what will happen to their production.

Marketing risk — prices and costs

Changes in prices of pigs and pork meat are beyond the control of any individual farmer. The price of farm products is affected by the supply of a product, demand for the product, and the cost of production.

For example, supply of a product is affected by a combination of production decisions made by farmers as a group and other factors that influence yields. Whereas demand for a product is affected by consumer preference, consumers' level of income, the strength of the general economy, and the supply and price of competing products and finally cost of production of a unit of product depends on both input costs and yield. This makes it highly variable. Although input costs tend to be less variable than output prices. When combined with yield variations the cost of production becomes a serious source of risk.

As you will see later in the marketing section, sometimes price movements follow seasonal or cyclical trends that can be predicted by farmers, however sometimes supply or demand will change unexpectedly and, in turn, affect the market price.

Financial risk

As we discussed earlier in the book, financial risk occurs when money is borrowed to finance the farm business. This risk can be caused by uncertainty about future interest rates, a lender's willingness and ability to continue to provide funds when needed, and the ability of the farmer to generate the income necessary for loan repayment. Lower than expected prices, combined with low yields, can make debt repayment difficult and even lead to the sale of the farm.

Institutional risk

Institutional risk refers to unpredictable changes in the provision of services from institutions that support farming. As we will see later in the marketing section, that there are many stakeholders and institutions that are involved in pig and pork meat marketing. Some are informal e.g. other farmers, feed suppliers, local pig assemblers, middlemen, etc. and formal, which include banks, cooperatives, Research Institutions, etc.

Part of institutional risk is the uncertainty of government policy affecting farming, such as subsidies, opening up the border for imported meat, meat quality regulations, rules for animal waste disposal and quarantine levies. We are yet to see how the new ECOWAS "Eco" will affect trade in regional coutries. These are examples of decisions taken by governments that can have a major impact on the farm business.

Human and personal risk

Human risk refers to the risks to the farm business caused by illness or death and the personal situation of the farm family or proprietor. Accidents, illness and death can disrupt farm performance. In many sub-Saharan countries, labour migration away from rural areas is another common occurrence. Migration can cause labour shortages for the farm.

All the risks identified above are frequently interrelated. For example, the ability to repay debts depends on levels of production and the prices received for produce sold. Financing of production depends on the ability to borrow capital and the ability of the lender to supply capital in time.

Decision making process

Decisions about your farm will be made in the context of your goals and objectives. This will ultimately guide and influence the decisions that the farmer makes.

Once the goals are set you will look at the different ways to achieve the goals; you will evaluate the different alternatives; select the best alternative; plan for implementation; and review and evaluate the consequences of the action. This is called the decision-making cycle

Risk management strategies are used to reduce the chance of a "bad" outcome occurring. To do this, you need to identify the possible sources of risk; realize the possible outcomes; decide on alternative strategies available; assess the consequences of each possible outcome; and evaluate the trade-offs between the cost of the risk and the gains that can be made.

At the end of the day, your personal attitudes regarding risk will be based on your personal feelings rather than information presented to you to help them make more rational decisions.

Farmers' attitudes toward risk, this can be divided into three types:

1. risk-averse
2. risk-neutral;
3. risk-takers

Risk averse — If you are risk-averse, you will try to avoid taking risks. You are more cautious individual with preferences for less risky sources of income. In general, you will sacrifice some amount of income to reduce the chance of low income and losses. As a risk averter you will seek to be compensated for the risk taken by receiving a higher return than would normally be obtained if there were no risk.

Risk taker — If you are a risk-taker, you will be open to more risky business options. Unlike the risk-averse, you will choose the alternative that gives some chance of a higher outcome, even though you may have to accept an initial lower outcome. When faced with the choice, risk-taking farmers tend to prefer to take the chance to make gains rather than protecting themselves from potential losses. Even so, risk-taking farmers are still influenced by the return they could receive.

Risk-neutral lies between the risk-averse and risk-taking positions.

24.9 CHECKLIST FOR POSSIBLE RISKS ON A PIG FARM

Risk Factors	Possible Actions Checklist
Disease Biosecurity	• Footdip • Use of detergent and disinfectant • Correct use of the veterinary and medication • Managing collection especially from buyer • Vermin and birds • Awareness of local disease situation
Staffing/labour Work flow.	• Training and Motivation of staff • Your own contribution i.e. time spent on management rather than helping out manually: measuring, checking, forecasting, quotations, record analysis, updating yourself, talking to others.
Food quality	• Home-mix / complete feeds? Wet v. dry? • Good Knowledge of raw materials and nutrition. • Dialogue with nutritionist and veterinarian (e.g. current immune levels). Wastage, spoilage (mycotoxins). Feed and raw material analysis. Availability and correct use of by-products. Water adequacy.

Risk Factors	Possible Actions Checklist
Housing	• Adequacy, internal monitoring (measurements), especially ventilation and power saving, use of consultant. • Repairs and renovations. Fire risk. Provision of cheap overflow accommodation. Understanding basic technology – air movement/ pig behaviour.
Records	Avoiding non-superfluous data. Action on data available (action lists). Graphics not numbers. Staff motivation. Outside inputting help e.g. accounts and tax help, and secretarial assistance
Productivity	Diagnostic records, use of consultant in interpretation. Understanding and using the New Terminology.
Reducing exploitation by suppliers and buyers	Diversification, i.e. contract processing, farm shop exploitation by (with other foods), local brands, pork joint ventures, home mixing/wet feeding, commodity buying, internet buying (buying 'clubs'), Farmers' Markets (in future, Farmers' Supermarkets) i.e. open always

25. Feeding your pigs for less

As we have reiterated throughout this book, it is always good for farmer to understand why pigs behave the way they do and to try to mimic this behaviour to your farm's advantage instead of working against it.

Pigs' feeding behaviours have developed through evolution and ultimately, the way that the animal has adapted towards different specific feed sources is one of the key reasons why they survived evolution and why they have retained their form and function.

Historically, the earliest forms of land-based animal were large amphibians. These amphibians continued to feed on vertebrate in the sea such as fish, but later some began to eat alternative feed types such as vertebrates on the land and as such they became carnivorous. Some also began to consume plant sources and so they became herbivorous. At last, some animal like pigs developed the ability to consume both plant and animal and became omnivores.

Pigs are non-ruminants, which means that they have a simpler digestive system unlike sheep, cattle and horses. Food enters the stomach via the oesophagus. Once food has been processed it passes out of the stomach into the small intestine. As a result, pigs cannot graze exclusively on pasture, in the way cattle or sheep do, but they can graze to some degree with the right plant species.

However, unlike human, pig digestive system is well suited to benefit from cellulose and lignin because pig has an organ, known as the caecum, that is attached to the large intestine, which allows a longer digestion period for the cellulose from plant cell walls to be properly broken down and absorbed before exiting the pig. This organ is important in herbivore's digestive system to break down raw plants, however pigs, though omnivore, benefit from this organ's presence.

Pig feed is similar to human food. It is composed mainly of protein, carbohydrates, lipids (fats), minerals, vitamins and water.

All the local feed ingredients that you have in mind to feed your pigs such as Palm Kernel Cake, Soya Meal, Groundnut Cake, Maize, Fish Meal, Brewery waste, Cassava have different constituents and they have a different quantity of each of the nutrients mentioned above. Some have more of a particular nutrient than the others. For example, ingredients such as legumes, soya, groundnut or animal muscle tissue such as fish and meat have relatively more protein and lower carbohydrate than other feed ingredients, whereas feed ingredients such as sorghum, maize, wheat, cassava, yam, potatoes contain relatively high levels of carbohydrate and lower levels of protein.

Good feed is necessary for pig's growth, body maintenance and the production of meat and milk.

Pigs grow fast and are more prolific than other domesticated livestock species. They offer more meat per breeding female of any domestic animal. Your goal as a pig farmer is to convert affordable feedstuffs into edible pork for high quality food proteins.

During the first four months in the life of a pig, the muscle tissue and the bones of the skeleton develop faster than the fat tissues; after four months of age, this process is reversed and muscle which forms the lean meat develops slower than the fat. This explains why pigs can be fed meal ad lib. (as much as they can eat) up to 40kg of weight but have to be rationed in the later stages of production.

Feedstuff consumed by pigs gets digested in the body. In the process, the nutrients are absorbed by the body for its growth and maintenance. For better growth and production perfor-mance of the pigs the feedstuff should contain the following nutrients:

- Fibre
- Water
- Protein / essential amino acids
- Cabohydrate
- Vitamins
- Minerals
- Salt
- Feed additives
- Some essential fatty acid.

25.1 FIBRE

Fibre is an essential component of pig diets and it is vital for optimal health and digestion. Dietary fibre improves pig health by assisting in the maturation of the gut wall and promoting the growth of lactic acid bacteria, the "good bacteria". It also suppresses the multiplication of disease-causing bacteria like

E. coli and Salmonella thereby lowering the pH in the pig intestines just like the probiotics. Inadequate fibre levels in pig diet can have a negative effect on gut health leading to higher incidence of diarrhoea especially in piglets.

As mentioned earlier, pigs have an organ known as the caecum, that is attached to the large intestine, which allows the digestion and the absorption of fibres, e.g. the cellulose from plant cell walls. In the pig digestive system, cellulose is fermented by bacteria to produce short-chain fatty acids that can be used as an energy source by the pig.

Dietary fibre also reduces stress and behavioural problems in pigs. This is especially important given that most pig farming in Africa is intensive farming. Studies have shown that intensive system of farming can be quite stressful on pigs and has detrimental effects on production.

Fibre is also used to bulk pig feed; bulk density of feed plays an important role not only in the energy utilisation of pigs because it affects feed intake and the ability of pigs to consume sufficient energy to maintain growth. But it also affects the weight of the gastro-intestinal tract of pigs, thereby affecting the amount of energy necessary for maintenance. For example, sows appear to be less stressed and to move around less if they are physically and nutritionally satisfied.

In addition, young animals with an immature immune system are more vulnerable to pathogens, weaning stress and the associated change in nutrient source is known to increase digestive upsets. Studies have shown that fibre helps to improve piglet gut maturation, i.e. performance, health and development and good gut maturation means that feed efficiency can be optimized in the growing and finishing phases.

A recent trial in weaned piglets shows that corn bran, rice bran and wheat bran had a positive effect on gut maturity. Fibre also improved the intestinal barrier function, meaning that pigs fed these diets had a greater level of protection against digestive disorders.

While the benefits of including fibrous ingredients in pig diets are not always mentioned in normal diet formulations, the evidences point to the fact that high fibre diets are good for pigs and should be used more.

A better understanding of these dynamics will lead to sustainable use of fibrous ingredients in pig diets. For example, pigs can extract up to 25% of the energy they need from fibre fermentation products. This would mean that grains in their diets could be reduced.

However, weaners must not be given diets that contain more than 2 per cent fibre because young pigs cannot easily digest it (they may scour) and the high fibre also restricts the intake of required nutrients in piglets due to their small stomach capacity. In summer months, pigs need diets that are low in fibre because their body generates more heat during fibre digestion. If low feed intakes are a problem, higher amounts of fat can be used in diets because fat is easily digested.

Sources of by-products of grains include rice polish, rice meal, wheat bran, rice bran etc.

25.2 WATER

Water is one of the most impotant nutrients consumed by the pig during the course of its life. Like all animals, pigs need water for various reasons in the body. Water controls the body's metabolic functions, adjusts body temperature, transports nutrients to body tissues, removes metabolic waste, promotes the production of milk and, of course, contributes to growth and production.

Pigs should therefore have free and convenient access to water prior to weaning. The amount required varies with age, type of feed, environmental temperature, status of lactation, fever, high urinary output (as well as from high salt or protein intake), or diarrhoea. Normally, growing pigs consume 2–3 kg of water for every one kg of dry feed. Lactating sows consume more water because of the high-water content of the milk they produce. Water restriction reduces performance and milk production and may result in death if the restriction is severe.

Water quality is important. Water should be relatively free of microbial contamination; if not, chlorination may be necessary. Contrary to many local beliefs, only clean drinking water should be given to a pig. Dirty water is the source of many pathogens that causes a number of diseases in pigs in Africa.

Pigs consume most of their water by drinking, that means even when you give them wet feed, the pig should still be given fresh clean water. A pig at birth is made up of approximately 80% water, and even at a market pig of 70 to 90kg, pigs still consist of approximately 50% water. Studies have shown that a pig can lose almost all its fat and half its protein and still live; however, when it loses one-tenth of water in her body she will die.

Feed intake and growth performance are therefore strongly correlated with water intake. When pigs are thirsty they do not eat feed until their thirst is satisfied. Long term lack of water intake leads to constipation and salt poisoning.

Water deprivation usually occurs in pig farms through farmer's negligence, for example,

1. If the well or borehole water pump breaks down and is not quickly repaired.

2. The owner depends on staff to draw or fetch well water manually for the pigs, instead of completing the plumbing work.

3. If there is blockage of water pipe and nipple drinkers due to soil or debris or sediments from the well or borehole water blocking the nipple.

4. When pigs refuse to drink because the water is too hot e.g. if your water storage tank is in the sun without cover, especially the metal tank.

Here are some signs that tell you that your pigs are having water deprivation:

*   Initially thirst, constipation, skin irritation and lack of appetite.

*   Nervous signs include ear twitching, aimless wandering, bumping into objects, dog-sitting, falling over sideways and apparent deafness and blindness.

*   Nervous signs also follow, especially when unrestricted water is suddenly available after a period without water.

*   Affected pigs may move round in a circle using one foot as a pivot and may convulse.

*   Convulsions re-occur with remarkable regularity at approximately seven-minute intervals.

When a farmer discovers that there has been water deprivation to the pigs on the farm, water should be reintroduced gradually to pigs especially if they have been without water for more than 24 hours. Electrolytes in water can also help to rehydrate the affected animals. Pigs showing nervous signs need to be placed in a darkened area with bedding material to help prevent injuries.

Minimum daily water requirement for pigs

Body weight of pig (kg)	Daily water requirement (litres)
Newly weaned	1.0 to 1.5
Up to 20kg	1.5 to 2
20 to 40kg	2 to 5
Finishing pig up to 100kg	5 to 8
Sows and gilts	15 to 30
Boars	5 to 8

Source : Handbook of Animal Husbandry, ICAR Delhi

Water is a critical nutrient that is quite often overlooked but it has a significant impact on every phase of pork production.

25.3 **PROTEIN**

Protein is different to energy. Pigs need protein to grow and most importantly, to develop muscle tissue (muscles contain chiefly protein and water). Protein is made up of amino acids, the 'building blocks' of protein, linked together in chains. Amino acids contain nitrogen and this is what distinguishes them from other food groups such as fat and carbohydrates. The amino acids and their balance with each other in protein is very important in pig nutrition, more important than just the level of protein.

Protein is particularly important for pigs. If protein is not included in their diet, there is a strong tendency for animals to not thrive, and often cannibalism may follow.

- Protein is important to build new tissues for growth and reproduction.

- Protein also repairs worn out tissues and helps in production of milk.

- Protein is needed for growth, maintenance and production.

- Protein provides energy.

- Lack of protein in diet leads to loss of weight.

Source of protein

Protein is available in both plant and animal sources.

Plant source: groundnut cake (GNC), soya bean meals, cotton seed oil cake, sunflower meal etc. Soybean remains the most important and preferred source of high-quality vegetable protein for animal feed manufacturers. Soybean meal, which is the by-product of oil extraction, has a high crude protein content of 44 to 50 percent and a high level of inclusion (30-40 percent) is used in high performance pig diets.

In West Africa, especially where groundnut is cultivated for its oil and for human consumption. After oil extraction the resulting groundnut cake contains 35 to 40% protein of medium biological value.

Animal source: Meat meal, fish meal, blood meal, bone meal, dried milk, whey milk. Fishmeal provides a good source of quality protein for pig. Compared with other sources of plant protein and cereals, fishmeal can also provide a good nutritional source of calcium and phosphorus in animal diets.

When formulating diets, it is necessary to take into account how your pigs are growing at each stage of their lives. As they grow older, they put on a proportionally greater amount of fat and less lean meat than younger pigs. It can be put this way, lighter pigs have less fat relative to lean meat than heavier pigs. Therefore, younger pigs need a diet higher in amino acids than older pigs so they can grow proportionally more muscle tissue.

It has been known for decades that the growth and development of muscle of pigs essentially requires dietary supply of protein, or amino acids (AAs), to be exact. There are 20 to 25 different amino acids found in proteins. They serve as building blocks for protein biosynthesis; pigs can synthesize about 10 of these, enough for their metabolic needs, however the following ten must always be included in a pig's diet: Lysine, Isoleucine, Leucine, Methionine, Phenylalanine, Threonine, Valine, Arginine, Histidine and Tryptophan

Among these essential AAs, Lysine is the most important amino acid in pig feed because it is the most deficient AA in nearly all typical swine diets based on cereal grains. Without enough lysine in the diet, the other amino acids cannot combine correctly to form muscle protein. Lysine supplementation increases the nitrogen retention and protein deposit and improves the growth performance of the growing and finishing pigs.

For this reason, lysine is usually called the first-limiting amino acid. This means that the amount of protein (for example, muscle) that animals can make is limited by the amount of lysine in their diet.

Fish meal is high in Lysine, while of the vegetable proteins, soybeans have the highest proportion of Lysine.

Category of pig	Protein requirement (% of total required feed)
Suckling piglets (creep ration)	22%
Weaner (grower ration)	18 to 20%
Breeding boar and pregnant sow (finished ration)	15%

Source : Handbook of Animal Husbandry , ICAR Delhi

25.4 BALANCING CARBOHYDRATE AND PROTEIN

Pigs need both energy and protein (amino acids) to grow. However, there is a correct balance between the amount of energy in a diet and the amount of protein.

Pigs need enough energy to allow the lysine and amino acids to be used in building muscle tissue. If there is too much energy in the diet and it is not balanced with lysine, pigs will convert the oversupply of energy into fat.

On the other hand, too much lysine can be just as costly not only in the additional cost but with the fact that excess protein can be broken down into non-essential amino acids or be lost in urine.

Generally, the lysine/energy ratio required is related to weight and age. As pigs get older, their need for lysine falls. This is because heavier pigs cannot grow as high a proportion of muscle tissue as lighter pigs and a greater proportion of the food energy is required for maintenance rather than growth.

25.5 CARBOHYDRATES

Pigs need energy for maintenance and for growth and reproduction. Pigs need energy just to keep their bodily functions working. The amount of energy needed will vary according to the climate, the environment, the age and weight of the pigs, and whether they are breeding or not. For example, pigs growing in temperate regions where there is cold weather will use more energy to keep themselves warm through shivering. This means they must eat more if they are to keep growing as there is less energy left over for growth compared with pigs in Africa where it is hot. They are therefore able to use a larger portion of their feed for maintenance.

Pigs get all their energy from feed, but not all of it is digested. Some energy will pass through and be lost in faeces, while some will be lost as gas. So digestible energy is the energy in the diet that is digested and available to the pig.

Some feed ingredients are more digestible than others. Growing pigs do not digest plants with high fibre well, so feeding them with high fibre ingredients like rice bran, wheat bran and corn bran will be less digestible than ingredients with low fibre e.g. whole maize and wheat. By comparison, the digestible energy in fats and oils is very high and pigs waste very little derived from them.

Carbohydrates constitute about 70% of total required feed per day. Pigs require large quantities of energy and moderate quantities of protein (15 to 25%) for growth and development.

Energy requirements are determined by the weight of the pig, its growth rate, the amount required for maintenance and its stage in the reproductive cycle. The energy requirements is higher in lactating sow, for example, the survival of the piglet in the first 2 to 3 days of life is highly dependent on a regular supply of energy and if the sow's nutrition is inadequate leading to poor quality milk, the susceptibility to disease and piglet mortality rises.

In the newly weaned pig, the quality and availability of carbo-hydrates and other energy sources are vital if a healthy rapid growing pig is to be produced. Within 12 to 24 hours after weaning most pigs become energy deficient for a short period, which affects the degree of villus atrophy and the rate of their regeneration. The immune system also does not respond efficiently and the results are more disease or a greater incidence.

Popular sources of carbohydrate in Africa include cereals like rice, maize, oats, wheat, grain, sorghum and barley etc. ad tuber crops like cassava, yam, potato etc.

25.6 **VITAMIN**

These essential substances play important roles in regulating many biochemical processes in the body. Most of the locally available feedstuffs used in pig diets contain various amounts of most vitamins; however, the relative availability of these can vary substantially. However, it is difficult to accurately calculate and factor any of these vitamin's contribution from the pig feed. To overcome this, farmers always add vitamin supplement to the diet (in the form of premix for pigs) that contains most of the useful vitamins. This is relatively inexpensive and it is a good form of insurance against the risk of vitamin deficiencies and should help reduce the effects of disease and environmental stresses on pig performance. If deficiency problems do occur, you may need to add more of the deficient vitamin.

Vitamins (A, D, E, K, B complex and C) are needed in minute quantity for absorption and utilization of different feed nutrients.

Deficiency of vitamins in feed causes a number of ailments in pigs including poor growth, weakness, anaemia, low production of milk, etc. Vitamins are obtained mainly from different green forages. Some of the vitamins are also produced in the body (digestive system). External supply of small quantities of vitamins especially during pregnancy and lactation help better growth of piglets and increase milk production.

Mixtures of required vitamins and minerals e.g. premix, are readily available in a pack in most feed shops or veterinary chemists.

25.7 **MINERALS**

Minerals are essential compounds that provide the elements used to maintain the animal's bone structure and regulate many biochemical processes. The main mineral elements in diet formulation, considered individually, are sodium, calcium and phosphorus. Iron, zinc, copper and manganese are also required but only in trace amounts. Usually, these trace elements are added to the diet as a mineral premix.

Minerals are essential in formation of bone, blood, teeth muscle and milk.

It helps in maintenance of normal fluid level in the body.

Supply of minerals in feed is essential especially during the time of pregnancy and lactation in order to stimulate normal growth of piglets, increased milk yield and to prevent disease like milk fever.

Mineral mixture can be purchased from the feed mill or veterinary or pharmacy clinic. It is required only in small quantities, say 1 to 2 teaspoonfuls per pig per day.

Iron and phosphorus should be added separately as sow's milk is deficient in iron.

Factors that are responsible for mineral deficiencies in pigs are:

- Pigs are fed mainly cereal grains or industrial by-products (rice bran, wheat bran, corn bran, etc.). Minerals such as calcium are relatively low in these feeds.

- Pigs that do not consume large amounts of roughage are prone to mineral deficiencies.

- Pig reproduce at a younger age while they are still growing than any other classes of livestock. For this reason, mineral requirements are higher in pigs.

- Pigs are fed to grow at a maximum rate for an early market, before they become mature.

Salt is an essential item in pig ration. A higher amount of salt may lead to toxicity. An amount of 5grm/day is adequate. Deficiency may lead to birth of hairless pigs.

Pigs suffering from salt poisoning can be severely affected and in some cases it can become fatal. Salt poisoning happens in two ways: either when weaner, grower or finisher pigs are deprived of water for more than 24 hours or when pigs consume excess salt (>3%) in either the feed or water or both.

25.8 FACTORS TO BEAR IN MIND WHEN YOU ARE COMPOUNDING FEED FOR YOUR PIGS

It is difficult to prescribe any one feeding strategy that will ensure a maximum return in every pig farm. Therefore, the onus is on you as a pig farmer to continually finetune your feeding programs until you get it right on your farm.

The objective of finetuning is to maximise and match the feed ingredients that are locally available in your area with your pig's dietary specifications so that your pig receives nutrients in sufficient daily amounts to support the production level and carcass quality that you are expecting.

1. When formulating a diet, it is important to consider the amount of each nutrient that is available in the feed ingredients that the pig will be able to use for maintenance, reproduction and growth processes.

2. Good pig feed should contain sufficient energy, protein, fibre, minerals and vitamins.

3. It is therefore a mixture of a number of feed ingredients that would guarantee that there are enough are sources of protein, energy, fat, vitamin, minerals. The mixture is prepared to provide all required nutrients to the pigs.

4. Combinations of a variety of ingredients is one way of balancing available nutrient requirements.

5. Farmers interested in preparing feed mix locally should understand the principle of composition of feed ingredients and pig nutrition.

6. As energy is the fuel that drives all biochemical processes, it is important that attention is given to the balance between amino acids and energy.

7. Carbohydrates such as PKC, maize, wheat, rice, etc. should form basic ingredients (about 70 to 75%).

8. Amino acid availability can be reduced in some feedstuffs due to a high-fibre content that lowers amino acid digestibility.

9. Protein supplements like oil cakes, fish meal should constitute about 15 to 25% of total quantity.

10. Requirements of nutrients to pigs varies according to age and stages of life.

11. Mineral supplement and salt should be provided in the ration about 3 to 5%.

12. The importance of providing essential amino acids in their correct levels and proportions is to maximise protein synthesis.

13. Like a human, a pig must maintain its deep body temperature at about 38°C. This becomes a problem when the ambient (environmental) temperature changes. If environmental temperatures increase above this thermoneutral zone, the pig will eat less to reduce the heat load that occurs during the digestion process and drink more water.

14. This means that in tropical countries like Africa, high temperatures will reduce pig feed intake. As a consequence, you need to increase the dietary specification of all nutrients, especially the critical essential amino acids (in reverse proportion to the reduction in feed intake).

15. High temperatures used during manufacture (such as meat and soya meal) may cause some amino acids to bind up in non-available forms, particularly lysine.

16. Concentrate feed can be prepared at home or mills by incorporating different feed ingredients (e.g. PKC, maize, rice barn, wheat bran, soybean meal, oil cakes, mineral mixture etc.) as per requirement of different categories of pig.

17. Most economic and available feed ingredients should be selected to prepare ration.

18. When concentrate feed is not available, some fish meal/ soya meal should be provided particularly during the early age, pregnancy and lactation. A small amount of

mineral and vitamin mixture should be added to the protein source to feed the pigs during these crucial stages.

19. Pure bred /high-quality cross breed pigs can grow faster if they are fed with 100% concentrate feed.

20. However, for the indigenous or popular breed, feeding 100% concentrate is a wastage.

21. Distillery waste is much appreciated in the traditional pig husbandry, especially for fattening pigs. It is advisable, however, not to include too much of this ingredient to pregnant and lactating sows and to piglets and weaners because of the alcohol contents in the waste.

25.9 SOME TIPS ON HOW TO USE LOCALLY AVAILABLE FEED INGREDIENTS

The goal is to ensure that feeds meet the animal's needs for maintenance, growth and reproduction. Good pig feed contains sufficient energy, protein, minerals and vitamins.

- Palm Kernel Cake is very suitable for pig feeding. It contains protein 10 to 12%, fat 9.5%, crude fibre 8.0 to 10.0% and carbohydrate up to 25%. It can be mixed with other feeds to 25 – 35% inclusion. PKC is widely used as a major component animal feed in areas where they are abundantly available.

- Rice Bran and broken Rice: It contains 8% protein and can be used as the main ingredient. Rice bran can be mixed with other feeds to 20 – 30%.

- Maize: is a very good animal feed. It contains up to 65% carbohydrates and 9% protein. It can be mixed and cooked with other feeds, but not more than 40% in the mix ration.

- Soybeans: is a crop which has a high nutritional value and is very good for pig feeding. It contains 38% protein (very high). It should be dried, milled or well-cooked in combination with other feedstuff like rice bran, broken rice and maize.

- Groundnut cake has a high nutritional protein value and is very good for pig feeding. It contains 30% protein (very high).

- Wheat Bran is particularly rich in dietary fibre and contains significant quantities of Carbohydrate, protein, vitamins, and minerals. Wheat Bran is widely used as a major component animal feed.

- Fruits: Fruits damaged during transportation, storage and handling can be used as supplementary feeds for pigs by boiling and mixing with other feeds such as rice bran, broken rice and maize. They can also be given fresh. Suitable fruits are: Banana, papaya, apple, pear, melons, etc.

- Banana Stem: The best way of feeding fresh green banana or plantain fruits is to chop them and sprinkle some salt on the slices since the fruits are very low in the in-organic nutrients. Pigs relish this material. Similarly, green fruits are more easily dried than ripe fruits which are very difficult to completely dehydrate.

- Vegetables: Vegetables damaged during transportation, storage and handling are used as supplementary feeds for pigs by boiling and mixing with other feeds such as rice bran, broken rice and maize. They can also be given fresh. Suitable vegetables are cabbage, lettuce, spinach, morning glory, sweet potato vine, cola-cassia (needs boiling), pumpkin, guards, water hyacinth, etc.

- Water hyacinth: it is very important to the pigs, can replace 6% feed. Effects of mixtures of water spinach and freshwater hyacinth leaves on growth performance of pigs fed a basal diet of rice bran are found good.

- Production Restaurant/Kitchen waste: needs to be properly screened and cooked.

- Slaughterhouse offal; needs to be properly screen and cooked.

- Root Crops: are being used for pig feeding, they can be mixed with other feeds up to around 10 — 20% (never more than 30%). First it should be peeled and washed and then sliced, dried and ground or soaked and fermented before use. The sliced and dried cassava can be kept longer.

- Sweet potato vine and tubers can be used as pig feed.

- Potato, yam, papaya, sweet potato, etc Maize, wheat, millet, etc.

- Different feeds are mixed and boiled to make the pig feed more palatable.

Maize stored on a pallet *Manual compounding and mixing of pig feed ingredients*

25.10 HOW TO CALCULATE CRUDE PROTEIN LEVEL IN A FEED

Protein is the usually most expensive nutrient in pig diets in many sub-Sahara countries, most of the other feeds are carbohydrates. As a consequence, protein is usually the first nutrient that is considered in diet formulation. The carbohydrate levels of the diet can then adjust to the desired level by adding high energy ingredients, which are more affordable and readily available than protein supplements.

The Pearson Square method is an easy way to determine the proper dietary proportions of high and low protein feedstuffs to add to a feed to meet the dietary requirement of your pig feed.

For example, suppose Palm Kernel Cake and Broiler starter were available as feed ingredients to feed your pig at 18 percent crude protein.

A square can be constructed and the two feedstuffs are put on the two left corners along with the protein content of each. The desired protein level of the feed is placed in the middle of the square. Next, the protein level of the feed is subtracted from that of the feedstuffs, placing the answer in the opposite corner from the feedstuff. Ignore positive or negative signs.

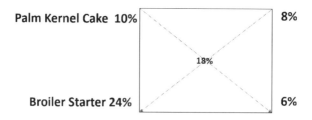

To compound the 18 percent crude protein piglets feed, we must mix 8/14 of palm kernel cake with 6/14 of Broiler starter meal.

Palm Kernel Cake 8/14 = 57.1%
Broiler Starter meal 6/14 = 42.9%

So, to make 100 kg of this feed we must mix 57.1 kg of Palm Kernel Cake with 42.9 kg of Broiler Starter meal.

If more than two feedstuffs are used in a feed, they may be grouped into basal feeds, i.e. feed with less than 20 percent protein and protein supplements that are more than 20 percent, averaged within each group, and plugged into the square method. For example, suppose Soya meal and Groundnut cake are the protein supplements and Palm Kernel cake and Rice Bran are the basal meal. The crude protein levels of in each of these ingredients are Soya meal is 44% and Groundnut cake is 40%, Palm Kernel cake is 10% and Rice Bran is 8%.

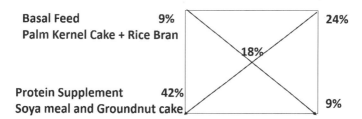

Basal feed = 24/33 = 73%
Protein supplement = 9/33 = 27%

Thus, to make 100 kg of this feed one would mix the following:

Rice bran	36.5 kg
Palm Kernel Cake	36.5 kg
Soybean meal	13.5 kg
Groundnut Cake	13.5 kg

The square method is helpful to novice feed formulators because it can get them started in diet formulation without the need to resort to trial and error.

25.11 WHAT YOU SHOULD AVOID FEEDING YOUR PIG?

- Any meat products; includes pies, sausage rolls, bacon and cheese rolls, pizza, salami and other delicatessen meats and table scraps without proper cooking and screening

- Any carcass or part of a carcass of any mammal or bird (raw and uncooked); includes any meat blood, offal, hide or feathers. Pigs that feed on carcass are also at risk of contracting diseases which are contagious to humans.

- The excreta (droppings) of any mammal or bird.

- Any substance that has come into contact with a prohibited substance via collection, storage or transport in a contaminated container such as meat trays and take away food containers.

- Household, commercial or industrial waste includes restaurant waste, without proper cooking and screening.

25.12 FACTORS AFFECTING THE QUALITY AND AVAILABILITY OF ANIMAL FEED PRODUCTION IN AFRICA

- The production and the quality of feedstuffs is often low.

- Seasonality production of feedstuff.

- Poor harvesting, processing and storage of the feed ingredients.

- Lack of appropriate feed ingredients is aggravated by persistent incidences of drought or floods that have affected the countries over the past three years.

- Low and unreliable supply of feed ingredients, especially protein sources.

- Abundant use of by-product or factory waste for livestock feed.

- Ingredients e.g. brewery waste have toxin & anti-nutritional.

- Lack of laboratory facilities for chemical analysis of ingredients.

- Inconsistent and sometimes substandard feed quality.

- Lack of trained feed technologists.

- Lack of appropriate feed processing equipment.

- Frequent interruptions in power supply to grind and compound feed ingredients.

- Lack of spare parts for maintenance of equipment which is imported from other countries.

- The need for adapted equipment that can easily be maintained using local resources.

25.13 USING KITCHEN AND MARKET WASTE TO FEED YOUR PIGS

Kitchen by-products can be from the home or from restaurants. This could also include fruit and vegetable waste from the market. Hospital waste should be avoided due to the possible contamination by human diseases and pathogens.

All feed from kitchens and market can be collected — this can include all vegetable peelings, eggshells and bones. Ideally food not containing pig meat is preferred but this option is not always available. Therefore, it is best to assume that all kitchen feed contains pork products. It is then essential — absolutely essential-- that the kitchen wastes are thoroughly boiled for at least 30 minutes before it can be fed to the pigs.

The kitchen wastes should be as fresh as possible. Ideally do not use food over 24 hours old. Boiling also helps to preserve the kitchen wastes. Prevent rodents and other vermin from eating this kitchen waste and the storage of the prepared products needs to be clean and secure.

Any feed not eaten by the pigs must be cleaned up thoroughly and disposed of. Ideally any feed not eaten should be included in the composting pile.

25.14 THE BENEFITS OF USING INDUSTRIAL WASTE TO FEED YOUR PIGS

Research have shown that the role of pig production in converting food waste or factory bye product into animal feed is the way forward to recycle food waste in sub-Sahara Africa rather than for the industrial uses such as (biofuels production) landfill or incineration that are practised by the developed countries.

There is a potential opportunity for the African government to evaluate the opportunities and improve the environmental sustainability of pork production especially in the reduction of post-harvest loss or waste which is currently very high in Africa.

Food and Agriculture Organization (2013) estimated that 45% of greenhouse gas emissions is from livestock operations that includes production, processing and transport of feed ingredients and animal feed. It is important to also note that pigs have a better carbon footprint as it produces 90% less methane than cattle produce.

Different foods and the amounts of methane they produce, the 20-year figures (Australian Greenhouse Office)

Food	kg CO2-e/kg (20 years)
Beef	111.1
Sheep meat and wool	96.3
Pig meat	10.5
Poultry	1.3

Currently, most food waste or post-harvest losses in sub-Sahara Africa are disposed in landfills, which has significant negative impacts on the environment. However, pigs have the ability not only to help Africa's food security but also improve her environmental pollution.

For example, research has shown that pigs can also extract up to 25% of the energy they need from fibre fermentation products that is produced by food factories like brewery waste and rice bran and wheat offal, etc. and can derived minerals and vitamins from expired or semi rotten fruits and vegetables from the market. There are many benefits to this, first, this means that the amount of grains and premix used in pig diets could be reduced, secondly, there is the economic benefits from using cheaper and abundantly available fibrous by-products in pig feed, thirdly, there are also environmental gains in that the waste are consumed by pigs instead of been dumped on landfills leading to water and air pollution.

I believe a better understanding of these dynamics will lead to sustainable use of fibrous ingredients in pig diets.

25.15 FEED MANAGEMENT PROBLEMS ON PIG FARMS

Though pig feed accounts for 60 — 70% of costs, research carried out on UK farms reveal that some 10 to 20 % of the feed is wasted on many pig farms.

Here are some suggested ways of reducing feed wastage on your farm:

- Always look critically at the floor of your cell, especially at the floor underneath the feeding trough, to see if excess or spill feed is wasted. This should be done early in the morning before your staff clean your pig cells.

- Make sure your feed bin or feed warehouse window is closed. If they are left open, rain may get in and spoil tonnes of feed.

- There should be proper storage of feed to prevent rat infestation waste and disease risk.

- Ensure adequate feed storage hygiene routines by making sure that feed bins are regularly cleaned.

- Water trough also needs to be regularly cleaned.

- Make sure the feed bag is not torn or to prevent feed loss during transit.

- Bag of feed should only be stored on pallets not bare floor.

- Poor milling may lead to feed being unusable and pigs cannot digest whole grains.

- Dusty feed in the feeding trough means feed is lost to the air.

- Poor placement of feed into feeding trough can result in fighting over feed.

- Inadequate feeder space for all the pigs makes variable growth inevitable.

- Ensure all uneaten food is redistributed and not wasted.

- Poor cleaning of feeders resulting in reduction in feed space availability.

- Feeders with bird and rodent contamination.

- Feed wastage under feeder do not only cost money but encourages rodents to the farm.

25.16 THE BEST WAY TO PROCESS RAW CASSAVA AS PIG FEED

The use of cassava for livestock feeding has been limited because of the fear of the presence of toxic cyanogenic glucosides in raw cassava, the deficiency of raw cassava in other nutrients apart from energy and the high fibre content of the peel.

But several researches have shown that the use of raw cassava products in cassava producing areas of sub-Sahara Africa would not only relieve the pressure on the demand for cereal grains but also guarantee abundant and year-round supply of energy for livestock feeding. This will ultimately reduce the high cost of feed in pig production.

Cassava has nearly twice the calories than that of potatoes and is perhaps one of the highest value calorie food of any tropical starch-rich tubers and roots. About 100 g of cassava root provides 160 calories.

Though it is also widely known that a freshly harvested raw cassava that is whole and unbruised has cyanogenic glucoside. However, when this is subjected to some kind of processing and the cellular structure is disrupted, the intracellular glucoside becomes exposed and is degraded to sugar which later dissociates to ketone.

For thousands of years, cassava tubers have been traditionally processed in Africa using a wide range of methods to reduce toxicity, improve palatability and convert the perishable fresh root into stable products for human consumption. These methods consist of different combinations of peeling, chopping, grating, soaking, drying, boiling and fermenting.

The challenge for pig farmers today is to find the most suitable, straightforward, scalable and cost-effective way to process cassava promptly and safely so that it can be fed to the pigs without putting too much additional activity or work processes onto the limited labour hands that is in most pig farms in the sub-Sahara Africa (or distract the farm staff from focusing the core business of taking care of pigs).

While all the methods of processing cassava mentioned above can reduce the cyanide level, a pig farmer needs to find a process that will be quick, straightforward, sustainable while also adding value to the pigs.

For example, research has shown that the cassava peel contains the highest amount of cyanide content compared to the pulp. This means that by removing the cassava peels a farmer can automatically reduce the cyanogenic glucoside by at least 50% in cassava tubers but the challenge with peeling as with other processing methods is that peeling requires additional labour and it is also time consuming. Employing extra hands to peel will reduce the cost advantage of using cassava as an alternative source of carbohydrate.

The same applies to other processes such as grating. For example, grating of the whole cassava tuber exposes and destroys the cyanide in raw cassava and about 90% of free cyanide is removed within 15 minutes of boiling fresh cassava. All these processes are also time consuming, require extra hands or machinery to be effective which a typical small pig farmer might not be able to afford.

However, when cassava is soaked and allowed to ferment, the result is great, especially for pigs. As mentioned earlier in the book, pig digestive system is well suited to benefit greatly from soaked and fermented raw cassava because pigs have an organ, known as the caecum, which allows a longer digestion period for the cellulose from plant cell walls to be properly broken down and absorbed. This organ is important in herbivore digestive system to break down raw plants, however pigs, though omnivore, benefit from this organ's presence.

Soaking of cassava provides a suitably larger medium for fermentation and allows for greater extraction of the soluble cyanide into the soaking water. Soaking removes about 20% of the free cyanide in fresh root chips within the first 4 hours and there is a huge reduction in the total cyanide in the raw cassava tuber to a consumable level after soaking in water for 3 days.

Fermentation which usually precedes soaking is the result of the action of living microorganisms. Microorganisms produce enzymes which converts carbohydrates to organics acids to create the fermented cassava product.

During fermentation, the raw cassava is literally being pre-digested for the pigs before the pig ever eats the feed. This makes it easy for the raw cassava to digest and be absorbed inside the pig thus increasing the bioavailability of nutrients and phyto-nutrients for the pig's body (in farmer's term more weight and body mass with minimal effort).

The consumption of soaked and fermented cassava by the pigs is an incredibly healthy practice as it directly supplies the pig's digestive tract with living cultures that are needed to break down food and assimilate nutrients inside the pig.

In addition, fermentation also increases the protein in cassava root, it also improves the balance of essential amino acids and makes available the valuable B-complex group of vitamins such as folates, thiamine, pyridoxine (vitamin B-6), riboflavin, and pantothenic acid vitamins content.

Furthermore, fermentation modifies the unfermented food in diverse ways, resulting in new sensory properties with enhanced aroma and flavour (which appeals to the pig), increases feed consumption and reduces anti-nutrients content.

During the soaking of roots in cassava food production, the texture of the roots also undergoes noticeable change and the roots are rendered soft and easy to eat by smaller pigs.

In practice, cassava can be loaded in a plastic tank and filled with water and left for 3 days before being fed to pigs.

However, when using soaked and fermented raw cassava to feed pigs, pig farmers should understand that the quantity and quality of protein supplementation is critical (should be higher than when using grains e.g. maize) and adding lysine and methionine will also significantly improve protein utilization in pigs. In addition, the use of palm oil with cassava will increase calorie intake of the animals and reduce dustiness of the feed.

25.17 **REDUCE YOUR PIG FEED COST THROUGH HYDROPONICS**

Hydroponic grass is young tender grass grown from a cereal grain mostly barley, sorghum or maize in just 5-7 days. This fodder can part substitute your current feed up to 50%, of your pig's feeds concentrates.

Hydroponics fodder is considered the best and most affordable livestock feed for sub-Sahara African pig farmers.

By spouting grains in your growing tray, you change the digestibility of your normal grain from 30% when in grain to 95% when in the fodder. Thus, enabling your pig to use the energy for meat production, reproduction and weight gain.

Hydroponically grown fodder also has 80% increase in essential minerals and provides 30 times more vitamin B, than milk, 22 times more vitamin C than citrus and nearly 5 times the iron of spinach. It also has a strong resistance to diseases and fungus.

Energy is the second most challenging requirement in livestock production in Africa. Pigs that are fed on ordinary grains which are not sprouted have less starch. When an animal is fed on grains, fermentation occurs in the stomach producing lactic acid which lowers pH of the stomach to the extent metabolic disorders occur, like reproductive impairment and immune suppressions.

Grains are also loaded with phytics which inhibit mineral absorption. The more enzymes you have in feed the healthier the animal. If the feed does not have enzyme then the compensation has to be made by the pancreases, meaning the animal will have to overwork the pancreas, meaning more energy requirement.

Feeding your animal with hydroponics fodder can help you to achieve the following:

- Increased digestibility
- Earlier breeding and higher conception rates
- Faster weight gain and easier weaning
- Increased longevity in dairy cows
- Higher milk production and butterfat content
- Improved hoof health

25.18 HOW TO SET YOUR HYDROPONIC FARM (EXTRACTED FROM GRANDEUR AFRICA)

Step by Step process

Step 1: Weigh the 2kgs of seed, put it in a bucket e.g. 10 litres buckets, soak them in water for not more than 4 hours. The amount of water you put in does not matter, as long as all the seeds are submerged under water.

Step 2: Drain and Incubate -After the soaking is done, drain all the water from the bucket. Ensure you drain all of it as some water is usually observed to stagnate at the bottom of the bucket. Once this is done replace the lid of the bucket. It is best if you pierce some holes in the lid as the germinating seeds require oxygen. Let the seeds incubate for 2 days in the bucket. You should inspect the seeds at least once a day and ensure they are moist. You do this by sprinkling a handful of water into the bucket. You will soon notice that they will begin to sprout. This will continue for 48 hours.

Step 3: 'Plant' on clean trays — Once the 48 hours of incubation are done, transfer the seeds to a clean aluminium or plastic tray. The tray should be cleaned first, using soap or bleach at best. Clean it well. Transfer the seeds to the tray and ensure that you spread them into an even mat with your hands. Be gentle. The trays should be placed on a slope, with the perforated end of the trays on the lower side of the slope.

Step 4: Watering — Watering should be done at least three times a day. There is no need for watering at night. Be generous with the water, as any excess water will drain out and may be recycled. Ensure that you water the entire tray and all seeds come into contact with the water.

Step 5: Harvesting — Harvest on the appropriate day. Day 6 for pigs.

Harvest on the hydroponics fodder on day 6 for pigs.

25.19 **CULTIVATING FEED CROPS IN SWINE FEEDING**

As pigs are single stomach animals, they can digest only smaller quantities of green forages/leaves than cattle. Pig farmers could cultivate some food feed crops/forages e.g. maize, sweet potatoes, cassava, water spinach etc.) at the homestead near the pig pen. Many of these crops can be cultivated as a mixed crop in a small plot of land.

Feed crops are useful for the pigs.

- It is cheaper

- It is a good source of vitamins and minerals

- It provides a major portion of the protein requirements of the animal

- It brings savings in grain consumption

- It increases profit margin

- It keeps the pigs healthier and productive

And in the absence of concentrate feed or during shortage in cash flow for feed, crops such as sweet potato, legume forages, e.g. water cress, planted can be mixed with broken rice (up to 20%) , rice bran (15%) together with some protein source (fish meal) oil cakes (vitamin and minerals from vet shop) to form a balanced feed for the pigs instead of putting the pigs on ration.

If green leaves (vegetables forages) are used, the leaves and vegetables should be chopped into pieces and be boiled to increase the digestibility of the ration as well as to reduce the chance of infectious diseases.

Food feed crops that pig farmers should cultivate

Here are some recommended food feed crops that pig farmers could cultivate for pigs. Many of these crops can be cultivated as a mixed crop in a small plot of land.

Sweet potatoes

- Sweet potatoes can be grown on a variety of soils except clay. Best suited to fertile sandy loam and deep loam with good drainage.

- Sweet potato has a relatively short vegetative cycle (4-5 months). Hence, it fits nicely into tight cropping systems and also pig production cycle.

- Sweet potatoes also produce much more dry matter per hectare than cassava.

- It requires practically no cash input and minimal horticultural practices.

- Sweet potato also competes better with weeds than other root and tuber crops,

- Cooking sweet potato increases live-weight gain and pigs grazing sweet potatoes require a protein supplement of 500 g concentrate per pig per day for optimal growth.

Cassava

- Cassava can be grown on all types of soils except saline, alkaline and ill drained soils. It grows best in hot and humid climate with well distributed rainfall (1,500 to 2,000 mm annually.

- Tapioca can be cultivated profitably on hill slopes, waste land and lands where normal cultivation is difficult. The land should be ploughed two or three times or dug to a depth of 25 to 30cm.

- April/May is the best planting season.

- It is propagated from cutting obtained from mature healthy stems.

- Cuttings are planted vertically (after smothering the lower portion).

- Planting is done in a square alignment with a spacing of 90cm x 90cm 3ft by 3ft x 3ft.

- Irrigation is not necessary for cassava when the rainfall is well distributed.

- Cassava can be utilized for animal feed as dried cassava root (chips or pellets) used as partial raw material for commercial animal feed rations.

- The use of cassava as a partial replacement for maize in young pig diets was cost effective and up to a 57% level of inclusion had no deleterious effect on the pigs.

Cassava leaves

- In Africa, Cassava is planted mostly for its tuberous root, leaving the leaves to wither after harvesting the root. It is possible to obtain from cassava leaves more than 6 tonnes of crude protein hectare year which could be directed toward foliage harvesting.

- Cassava leaf contains high level of crude protein, vitamins and nutritionally valuable minerals.

- The HCN concentration and the bitterness associated with high cyanogenetic glycoside contents in leaves decreases with the maturity of the leaves.

- Dried or ensiled cassava leaves have been used at 16.5% and 20% respectively in the diets without significant effects on performance and carcass traits of growing pigs.

- There is also a significant improvement of daily weight gain with a mixture of cassava leaves and water spinach due to increased intake and possibly the better amino acid balance of the mixture.

Cocoyam

- The best soil is sandy loam and should be ploughed 2 to 3 times after applying adequate quantities of organic manure and wood ash.

- Spacing needed is 60cm from row to row and 45cm from plant to plant.

- When plants grow to about 30cm high, the soil around is loosened and the earth level around the plant is elevated (the process is called earthen up).

- Cocoyam intended for pig feed needs to be cooked prior to drying and feeding to ensure removal of the toxic substance (oxalic acid) present in the corms, leaves and petiole of the plant.

- It is also recommended that cooked dried cocoyam can be fed to sows in gestation and late lactation but not to starter pigs or those in the early grower phase.

Maize

- Well-drained soil should be selected.

- One ploughing is followed by 2-3 harrowing

- Nitrogen should be applied in two split doses. The first split dose should be applied along with the full dose of phosphorous and potash at sowing time. The second split does of nitrogen should be applied 4 to 5 weeks after sowing,

- Irrigation is important to maintain optimum soil moisture conditions. Frequency of irrigation will depend upon rainfall intensity. Water logging should be avoided.

- One cutting in a year after 70 to 90 days of sowing yields optimum level.

Banana and Plantain

- Both bananas and plantains are crop plants found mostly in the humid tropics where they are used as staple foods for humans. The banana plant produces bunches with varying numbers of small, fleshy fingers, sometimes up to 200 fingers, while the plantain produces bunches with fewer but bigger fingers.

- Bananas are the type normally exported around the world, while plantains are rarely exported but are used locally in various forms by humans. Plantains in fact are often regarded as the "cooking bananas".

- According to FAO statistics, the total production of bananas in 1988 was 41.9 million tonnes while that of plantains was 24.0 million metric tonnes. We can assume that about 30–40% of the total production of bananas and plantains are potentially available for livestock feeding as a result of their being rejected for export, accidentally damaged in the field, domestic wastes, etc.

Every part of the banana and plantain plant can be used to feed pigs. The following materials have been fed with varying degrees of success to various types of livestock:

i.   Fresh, green, chopped or unchopped green banana fruits with peels.

ii. Ripe, raw whole banana or plantain fruits.

iii. Dehydrated, sliced, milled, whole, green bananas or plantains.

iv. Cooked, green, whole banana and plantain fruits.

v.   Dehydrated, milled, green and ripe plantain or banana peels.

vi. Chopped, fresh, green plantain and banana fruits ensiled with molasses, grass. legume, rice bran or any other products that will increase their feeding value.

vii. Whole, fresh, green leaves, fed directly to pigs fresh or after being ensiled with an easily fermentable carbohydrate such as molasses.

viii.Banana and Plantain stalk or pseudostem, chopped and fed raw, or ensiled with easily fermentable carbohydrates, e.g. molasses.

Cooking the different raw materials together to improve digestibility and to break- down toxins from some feeds as raw banana stem, maize and soya grains, beans, kitchen waste, forage crops, etc.

26. Marketing your pig profitably

A market is a place where buyers and sellers interact to trade goods and services based on supply and demand. It can also be defined based on a location, a collection of buyers and a season for buying.

Marketing is a process in which businesspeople such as pig farmers sell a product (pig or pork) to customers (in exchange for money) in order to make a profit. Marketing involves promoting or offering a product or service that meets the needs of or is expected to satisfy a customer in exchange for money or something of value.

According to Adam Smith, "Consumption is the sole end purpose of all production: and the interest of the producer ought to be for promoting that of the consumer."

Marketing is therefore not an activity that farmers should turn to after production, rather it is an ongoing process of understanding customers' needs and striving to fulfil those needs better than the competition.

To a pig farmer, marketing should feed into every decision from the location and construction of a farm, through to stocking, raising and selling of pigs and what happens after the sale. Pig marketing therefore entails the performance of all business activities involved in the movement of pig and pig products from your farmgate through to the consumer. From all these statements, it is obvious that a good knowledge of the pig industry sector and how your product fits the market has a direct impact on overall business success.

In rural areas, most buyers and sellers are in immediate contact with each other and as a result they are able to determine what each other needs and values, however, as society becomes urbanised and sophisticated, there comes a large chasm between farmer and end consumer, as a consequence, pig farmers now have to rely on others to supply their products to the customer.

As we will see later in this chapter, pig marketing in many African countries is entirely in the hands of traditional middlemen. Government involvement is limited except in the areas of disease surveillance, or collecting livestock quarantine fees.

26.1 THE PIG MARKETING CHAIN

A market chain describes the linkage of all the activities required in transporting or supplying the product from the farmgate to the final consumer.

This pig marketing chain shows not only the various stakeholders that are involved in moving our pigs from the farmgate to the consumer but also how this relationship affects the final market price of our product.

This section is based on the authors 20 years' experience of dealing with various stakeholders both from our farm and partner farms, most of which are based in the southwest of Nigeria. Our experience was similar to some degree (but not all) the findings made by M.K. Ajala and A.O.K. Adesehinwa in the paper that they wrote on "the role of participants in pig marketing in Northern Nigeria".

Farmer

The majority of pig farms in sub-Sahara Africa are small farmers with less than 100 pigs and the farms are also scattered around the rural areas especially in the villages. Most of the farms have almost no tangible coordination among themselves. They mostly dispose their pigs at the village level to local assemblers because they have no connection with the middle men nor transporter that could take their pigs to larger markets. In addition, because they are small farms, they sell only a few pigs at a time to meet their urgent cash demands. As a result of all of these factors, most pig farmers are price takers and are not in a good position to bargain very effectively for the price of their pigs.

Local Assemblers

At village level, itinerant local traders are local indigene who knows where most of the local pig farms are situated locally and their capacity. They visit the pig farms regularly to monitor the availability and quantity of market size pigs that are available in each of these farms. Most of these farms only have between one and ten pigs to sell at a time. Local assemblers tend to pay some deposit (or give their word depending on their creditworthiness with the farmer) to secure the pigs and they keep on going from farm to farm (village to village) until they are able to gather enough pigs that will fill the middle men truck (this is usually between 20 to 50 pigs). Some of the assemblers are pig farmers themselves but they have the connection to the middlemen and they understand their pig specifications. They are also able to communicate with both the farmer and the middlemen in their individual language. Once they have successfully assembled the agreed number of pigs at the right market size, they will then call on the middlemen and guide them to each of the farms.

Under certain circumstances, especially during the festive season when there is an acute shortage of pig supplied than the demand, ownership of pigs may change hands two or three times before reaching the middlemen (with each new owner placing a small mark up in the selling price). However, in most cases, it is usually direct supply from buyers at the village farmgate to the middlemen market.

The middlemen

The middlemen are usually from the pork consuming community of Nigeria, usually Edo state especially from Warri or Ughelli etc. Once they are notified by the local assemblers, they will come down to southwest Nigeria with truck and will be guided by the local assemblers to each of the potential farms. After negotiating the price, they weigh the pigs on scales per kg and pay for the total weight of the pigs at the farmgate. The middle men are responsible for the transportation costs of moving the pigs from the farmgate through to their own state (about 400 km) and on the way they also pay the local or quarantine tax for each state that they travel through until they get to the final destination where the pigs will be sold at the central pig market.

Local assemblers' commission can range between N10 to N20 per kg of pigs, and they are usually paid by the middlemen. To the middlemen commission is an essential link with the local assemblers because of their role in sourcing of the right quantity and quality (i.e.. right size) of pigs from their locality, for bargaining and arranging livestock sales. However, this suggests that local assemblers will do their utmost to make sure the middlemen get a good price so that he can afford their service.

Most of the middlemen themselves rarely own vehicles for transportation; they use the services of other transporters. Transportation of pigs to subsequent markets is usually by trucks of varying sizes and capacities depending on distance and number of animals involved. For example, the journey from the southwest of Nigeria to Edo State can take as long as 8 to 10 hours on the road. Transportation costs average N0.25 per head per kilometre (km) based on distances ranging from 400 km. The trip usually take place overnight to reduce the heat stress on the pigs. At the destination, the pigs are then displayed at the central pig market.

Pig market

The middlemen deliver the pigs to the major pig market at the city centres in the south and south east of Nigeria

In most of this centre, there is just enough facility to provide shelter for the pigs before they are sold or slaughtered. The pigs are paraded and at this market there is usually no weighing, weight determination is by visual estimation, price depends on estimations and buyer's bargaining power. Payment is made mostly by cash.

The municipal slaughterhouse (abattoir) is usually very near to these centres. These slaughtering facilities are grossly inadequate. Standards of hygiene are very low and lack of chilling facilities determine the very small numbers of pigs that can be sold on a daily basis as meat is highly perishable. Slaughtered pigs are hanged as a whole or half or quarter pig for sale.

Retailers (Butchers)

Retailers are the people who buy the pigs from the pig market at the city centres and take the live pig to their little communities throughout Edo State and other nearby states where the pigs are slaughtered and dressed as pork meat, converting them into meat to meet the consumers' need. The pork is chopped into half or quarter pieces and also in lots of 20kg and are carried in a tray covered with cloth (to prevent flies) about by hawkers and local meat sellers on their head. The retailers then sell in convenient units to consumers in 1 to 2kg. Pork is sold fresh and without refrigeration after slaughter. Occasionally, meat is cut into small pieces and roasted as suya or fried and boiled meat pieces.

Hotels and restaurants and fast food outlets

Some farmers also supply pork directly to hotels and restaurants. Hotels and restaurants buy pork in bulk (e.g. half or whole slaughtered pig) to prepare meals for their customers. By creating and maintaining good relationships with the hotels and restaurants, farmers can end up having long-term contracts with them. This will create predictable income and stability for the farm. The price for supplying pork to hotels and restaurants is usually higher than for retailer and for abattoirs.

Butcheries

New and modern butcheries are springing up in Nigeria, they use modern and sophisticated slaughtering machines and equipment that are made of stainless steel or plastic that are easy to clean and sanitize. The slaughtering process includes stunning the animal before slaughtering, hoisting (lifting up and suspending) the animal carcass immediately after killing and moving the carcass along an overhead rail or line, throughout all the subsequent slaughtering and dressing procedures, after processing and dressing the animal will be hoisted into the cold room. For example, Master Meat is the meat for ShopRite, a large Retail outlet in Africa.

Butcheries buy quality pigs directly from small scale and medium scale producers. They usually come to inspect farm hygiene and their animal feed as they only buy from farms with good quality lean pigs and as a result farmer can negotiate for good payment terms.

Individuals

Farmers also sell pigs to individuals or organizations. Individuals do come to the farm and buy pig or pork in bulk for various reasons, including for parties and family functions. And some pork consumers purchase pigs cooperatively for slaughter and distribute among the group members.

In some cases, when one or two pigs are sold locally at farmgate by individual, pigs are carried by motorbike (okada) from the farmgate or neighbouring villages directly to the local butchers (retailers) who slaughter for fresh pork sales in open markets

Selling direct to consumers allows producers to set a price that covers costs and provides a larger profit.

In conclusion, the marketing chain for pigs in most African countries is a long chain with the pigs passing through many market participants (intermediaries) and a succession of markets before reaching the final consumers. The longer the chain the higher the price the consumer will have to pay.

However, it is important to note that despite the disparity in the farmgate price and the final consumer price, which is sometimes double, a large proportion of pig farmers especially in the southwest prefer selling their animals at farmgate through the local assemblers to the middlemen because it guarantees quick payment for their pigs. It also reduces the risks associated with transportation of live pigs to the market.

While payment for most pig purchases is usually made in cash at the farmgate, at times some farmers sell on credit to some customers that they consider to be credit worthy from successful previous transactions. And vice versa, some middlemen do give some credit to farmers to raise pigs for them, especially if there is an anticipated pig shortage and the farm is of a reputable size and quality. They only do this to guarantee steady supply of animals from the farmer. The credit is paid back through supply of pigs to the merchants.

26.2 FACTORS THAT AFFECT PIG PRICES ON THE MARKET

As mentioned earlier, pig prices are seasonality and festivals.

Firstly, pig prices are generally low in the southern part of Nigeria during the dry season because during this period the Fulani herdsmen usually move their cattle away from the north towards the southern part of Nigeria so that the cattle can graze on the remaining wet areas that are still available in the southern part of the country. This creates abundant supply of cattle and affordable beef in the south, leading to lower demand and lower prices of pig and pork. When the Fulani herdsmen return to the northern part of the country at the beginning of the rainy season, prices of cattle and goat increase due to short supply and the demand for pork meat increases.

Secondly, in the months of November, December and April, pig prices are high as these months correspond to the festive periods of Christmas and Easter respectively. The seasonality of pig demand in Nigeria means pig pricing can easily be manipulated by market participants, especially sellers.

According to Ajala and Adeshinwa, "With the absence of standardization and poor pricing of pigs in Africa, it is easy for traders to collude on price or number of animals to be sold and as a result pig prices most of the time do not reflect the source prices. This eventually results in higher gross margins to traders than the farmer who did the hard work of raising the pig".

Thirdly, no rail transportation is used to transport pigs. Transportation is mainly by truck despite its high cost. Transportation cost is further complicated by the poor roads and incessant increase in fuel prices contributing to the high cost reported by the traders.

26.3 TIPS TO HELP YOU SELL PIGS PROFITABLY IN NIGERIA

Sell your pigs using a digital scale — Every time you sell using a manual digital scale you lose at least 2 kg per pig. Sometime in a tonne of pig sold there is a cumulative loss of 85 kg which is same value as giving away an additional 1 pig for free. During my many experiences of witnessing or participating in farmgate pig sales, I have seen lots of conflicts and fierce disagreements springing up between the buyers and sellers over the popular manual dialogue scale as this scale is easy to manipulate by either party. I strongly recommend that every farm should have either a digital hanging scale or digital cage scale as this is more difficult to manipulate by either the seller or the buyer.

Maintain your seller bargaining power — There is an African adage that says, "do not negotiate on an empty stomach", this makes sense when you combine it with the Jewish quote that says, "To a hungry man everything bitter is sweet." Proverbs 27:7.

Start promoting your pig long before you need to sell them i.e. reach the market weight, ensure that you have sufficient feed and cash to keep your animals an extra 30 days after maturity. This is relevant because middlemen buyers sometimes delay responding to local assembler sales request when they have other assemblers or farms that are closer or have a better deal. Sometimes the buyers also do this deliberately to create anxiety and weaken the seller's power. This might take between 1-4 weeks delay to your initial sale request. Most middlemen might not immediately agree to the terms of your sales if your farm is in a remote area and, as a result, you might need to wait longer.

I noticed the timing of these delay tactics by the middlemen in the pig industry in Nigeria around the month of August and September when many parents (especially women) are prepared to sell their pigs to pay for their children's school fees. Many buyers do take advantage of the desperation of some of these pig farmers especially women around this period by using delay as a tactics to coerce them to sell at a cheaper price.

Money First — Ensure buyers pay completely before weighing your pigs. You achieve this by making sure you have an average weight estimate of your pigs before calling the buyer and before they arrive on your farm (or before they start weighing) they made 80% payment to your account and once they have weighed and loaded the pigs, they pay the remainder in cash on the farm.

A lot of buyers will deliberately weigh more pigs than they have cash to pay for in order to ask for credit and once they have loaded your pig onto their truck it is not biosecurity safe for you to unload such pig back to your farm . They bank on the farmer's reluctance to reintegrate an already stressed pig back into the herd after weighing hence they walk away with part of your money which you might never redeem. Always ask how much they wish to spend and make sure you only load the kg of pig worth.

Don't Start too Small — while we have advised you throughout this book to start your farm small, you should not start too small. The majority of the buyers will only take you seriously if they can buy at least 2 to 3 tonnes (40 pigs) from you at a time. This makes their transportation and logistics smoother. For example, if you are only selling 10 pigs that means that they will have to travel to 4 or 5 farms to load their truck before they can start travelling back to their state. All of these increase the transportation cost and stress to the animal.

Size Matters — Majority of your buyers would prefer to buy pigs weighing 70 kg plus and some may even pay a little premium for such pigs for the following reasons: Buyers have to pay a specific "tax" while transporting through each state or when slaughtering pigs, most of this tax is levied per head of pigs regardless of the size of the pig, hence they would pay less per tonne if the pigs individually have more weight.

Another reason is that the smaller the size of a pig, the bigger the proportion of the unwanted parts e.g. the offal. This is a disadvantage to the abattoir because for smaller pigs, the proportion of unwanted parts of pork per tonne of pig slaughtered is higher.

26.4 ALTERNATIVE TO MARKET CHAIN

In light of the complexity of the current market chain mentioned above, a commercial farmer needs to find the most effective and efficient means of getting its products to these markets profitably.

While you may start your pig enterprise by depending on the market chain e.g. you may decide to sell your first batches of pigs produced on your farm to middlemen, so as to test the market etc. but as an enterpreneur, you must begin to contemplate as soon as possible the potential of bypassing traditional marketing chain by turning to direct marketing and using a value chain approach.

A value chain approach deals with aspects of adding value along the chain of activities from production to consumption.

These are the different kind of value adding that you can do to you pigs:

- Transforming the product from one form to another (e.g. from live pig to pork meat).

- Modifying the geographic location of the product (extending the market from local market e.g. the southern and south east or Nigeria to exploring the regional market and making use of new ECOWAS treaty i.e.. the neighbouring countries e.g. Togo, Republic of Benin and Ghana).

- Sorting and processing the product to different target market (from fresh pork meat to roasted meat or suya for city dwellers).

- Packaging—no matter how basic to make the product more appealing to buyers.

However, to achieve a successful value chain, you need to answer the following question.

26.5 WHAT DO YOU WANT TO SELL AND WHO IS YOUR TARGET CUSTOMER?

Product type:

As a farmer, you are already (or about to start) producing live pigs on your farm. This is a good starting point to start looking at all the products that you could sell as live pigs on your farm, they include piglets, finisher, gilts, pregnant sows and boars.

The notion of developing a market for your farm product is to identify the total consumer base (or different sub-sets of customers) that is more likely to purchase each of your product and then "targeting" them using specific marketing tactics.

For example, the live pig produced on your farm will attract the following group of customers:

- **Informal markets** include new farmers who are stocking up their farm for the first time and those replacing their old/sold stock or their poorly performing pigs on their farms. This group tends to buy one or two pigs and most transactions are cash payment

- **Formal markets** include non-government, commercial and government organizations, those working on poverty alleviation and agricultural development programs. This group tends to buy large number of pigs, their interest is usually advertised in the media, Internet (websites, etc.), tabloids, radio, TV, etc. Most of these transactions are usually formal involving quotations, invoices, receipts, etc., payment is usually by cheque or bank transfer and payable after delivery.

- **Target abattoirs** (slaughtering houses), Pigs are usually transported by the farmer to the abattoirs, pigs are weighed, slaughtered, and pay against kilograms recorded. All risks (e.g., rejected carcasses due to health issues, death during transportation, etc.) are taken by the farmer, however, premium is usually paid for quality and quantity delivered.

- **Live pigs traders** — this is when middlemen come to the farm and buy live pigs, in most farm pigs are weighed and sold, payment is made at the farmgate for the whole pig and from the farmgate all risks are taken by the trader.

However, if you decide to sell pork meat product as opposed to selling live pig, you will need to have a small slaughter facility and probably start out small and work up to a profitable size as the market demands and dictates.

Alternatively, you may want to consider bringing in other farmers or join with others to form cooperatives. But from our experience, it can be very difficult to keep everyone engaged with the requirements needed to make a cooperative slaughtering process work. In addition, getting into complex slaughter business with other farmers requires adequate skill and knowledge of the business and capital to build the slaughter facility, not to mention meeting the regulations imposed upon any facility processing food for human consumption in your country.

However, if you are new to value adding, we recommend that you start small, for example, start by selling fresh pork meat to the people in your neighbourhood or town.

Please note if you are slaughtering and selling 2 pig a day, 40 pigs a month, you will need to have (40 pigs a month x 7 months (cycle) pig of different sizes + 20 sows +2 boars) = 302 pigs at given any time on your farm just to fulfil just this order. Along with this, you may decide to sell chops, package them for a premium price or sell them as fried pork meat.

From this you may progress to establishing a pork joint. Pork joints are springing up everywhere. You can offer raw pork as well as ready to eat meat. You can also serve other cooked foods and beverages together with the barbecued or fried pork. Pork is also cut into small pieces and roasted as Suya or tsire.

Don't underestimate the amount of pigs it will take to supply a pork joint. For example, a typical pork joint in a good location sell between 100 to 200Kg (equivalent to about two to four pigs) per day. For your pig farm to meet the supply of 1 or 2 pigs daily to your pork joint, you will need to have at least 600 pigs on your farm at all times.

Furthermore, if your ultimate goal is to add value to pig, you do not have to wait to raise the pigs on your farm (to the size and the quantity of pigs mentioned above) before you start the value adding aspect of your business. You can easily purchase live pigs from other farms and add to the pigs while waiting for the pigs on your farm to mature. This will serve as a pilot test for your niche market.

Finally, selling your slaughtered pigs directly to consumers and operating your own pork joints alongside your pig production will position you to enjoy up to 200% profits compare to farmgate price without sharing with middlemen in the distribution chain.

26.6 HOW DO YOU KNOW IF THE CUSTOMER WILL BUY THE PRODUCT?

At the beginning of the profitable pig farmer training, I always reinforce this statement to our participants that:

"You are not a pig farmer until you sell your pig in exchange for money. Until you sell, you are just a zookeeper".

Over time I have added to this statement that *"A person is not really your customer until they make a repeat purchase or become regular buyers of your farm produce".*

To identify and translate a "potential" customer to your customer, you need to divide your buyers into smaller groups based on their characteristics such as income, geographic location, season, product type and behaviour.

Income:

According to Kotler and Armstrong (2013) *"people change the goods and services they buy over their lifetimes as their wealth increase, adding to their taste in food, clothes, furniture and recreation are often agerelated"*.

In your sales offering you need to position your products so that all your target customers can afford your products.

While the Gross National Income, or GNI, which represents the sum of a nation's Gross Domestic Product (GDP) for sub-Sahara Africa is very low. However, underneath the GNI figure is the fact that like any culture there are people who are poor, working class, middle class and upper class.

This variations in income levels and the size of each group will affect the quality and quantity of the product that will be demanded by each of your customers and this may necessitate selling a wide range of products to target different groups within the population of various income levels.

For example,

- Poor and low-income people may only be able to afford just the head, hoofs, legs or offal of a pig because they are cheaper but a good source of animal protein.

- While working and lower middle class may want to buy general pork cuts.

- The upper middle class and expatriates may prefer to buy packaged pork primal cuts, gammon sausages, bacon etc.

- Pork joints and meat can be designed and packaged to cater for the city dwellers .

Geographic location:

Customers located in distant areas may require you to deliver the pigs or pork to them or demand that you reflect the transportation cost on your farmgate price. For example, in Nigeria, farms where most pigs are produced is far away from pork consuming communities, pigs will have to be bought and transported to those places by the farmer or the middlemen.

There are also several risks that are associated with transportation such as quality deterioration in case of pork especially if they are not stored in a chilled or frozen van and in case of live pigs, vehicle breakdown or even road accidents. Transportation of live pigs requires additional costs for inspection and movement permits but so also is the reward for the farmer that dares to take the challenge.

As we mentioned earlier most of the neighbouring countries surrounding Nigeria prefer pork meat, however to meet the demand of the regional customers pigs, you will not only need to pass through customs and your animal could also be quarantined before entering such countries and you will also need to meet the regulatory requirements of such countries.

Season:

As mentioned earlier, you need to know the seasonal variation of pig or pork sales in your country and position your product to take advantage of it. For example if you are aware that during the months of November, December and April, pig prices are high as these months correspond to the festive periods of Christmas and Easter respectively, you can start raising your fatteners 6 months earlier so that they can meet reach good market weight at this period.

Other seasonal factors include the fact that the demand for piglets also increases after the festive season because some farmers will be restocking their farms for the next festive season, this should inform the time that you will start breeding

Also note the price of pigs tend to fall slightly in August and September because of over supply from parents that want to quickly sell their pigs to raise money to pay school fees of their children. You can plan your farm away this time of low price.

Behaviour;

Consumer buying behaviour involves the study of individuals and the method they employ to choose, utilize and set out products and services to fulfill their wants and the effect these methods have on the consumer and society as a whole. It includes all the thoughts, feelings and actions that an individual has or takes before or while buying a product, service or idea as well as answers such questions as what, why, how, when and where an individual makes a purchase.

Religion is a key component of culture and has the strongest influence on people's lives and behaviour.

The Jews and Christians are forbidden from eating pork in the Old Testament by the quoting of Deuteronomy 14:8 and Muslims are forbidden by God to eat meat of pig.

In addition, some customers have conditional requirements that affect their ability to buy. For example, government and non-government organizations rarely buy from informal businesses, only businesses that are registered with the government, they also buy a specific quality of pigs and their payments are often delayed.

People that eat pork meat at pork joints tend to eat pork for refreshment and entertaining friends, as a result they prefer to eat pork with alcohol or other beverages.

26.7 THE MARKETING MIX

Marketing is the process used by farmers to attract customers to buy their products in order to make a profit. The goal of marketing is to increase sales.

As a commercial pig farmer, you need to thoroughly understand the characteristics of your products, understand what product attributes are marketable to specific target customers and highlight these characteristics in product packaging and image.

In this section, we will use the concept of 'Marketing Mix' to design a marketing plan for your pig farm.

The Marketing Mix can be summarized as the four Ps (4Ps): Products, Price, Place, and Promotion.

The PRODUCT itself (i.e. live pigs):

What do customers want? (what will appeal to them?) e.g.,

What do your customers want your pigs for? This may sound a strange question, but there are various possibilities, each of your customer have a specific usage for your product for example, if they want:

- Piglets and weaners — your customers might want to buy piglets and weaners to raise on their farm to market weight so as to provide fatteners for sale, that means they want castrated weaner male. As a supplier, you need to produce piglets that can grow fast and with good quality carcasses with a high percentage of meat and a small quantity of fat. For example, by adding castration to your farm routine at 2 to 3 weeks, you will produce a good batch of castrated male pigs that can grow fast and also not have the tainted smell.

- Breeder pigs — your customers might want to buy and raise pigs for breeding. They will desire weaner male (not castrated) and weaner female, gilt or boar. To supply breeder pigs to other farms you will need to start your farm with boars and gilts from prominent and popular breeds that are used in your area, such as the Landrace and Large White etc. They need to come from a farm known to have pigs of good quality and where the management and standard of hygiene are excellent. Your farm will need to keep accurate records of growth and feed conversion. And also keep the performance record of the breeder pigs and their parents.

- Finisher — Local assemblers might want to buy mature finisher male for middlemen or for pork processors, etc. you will need to raise a lean pig with good quality carcasses with high percentage of meat and a small quan-tity of fat. While the middlemen they prefer good percentage of meat and some fat in their pigs.

In summary, the live pig that you sell will be determined by your customer's demand and it should be of high quality, and also healthy. This can be archived through the quality of feed, good bio security and the tender loving care with which you raise your animal. Your pigs' appearance should be very clean, well nurtured and attractive. Your business should operate on the assumption that it will do whatever is reasonably necessary to keep the customer happy.

The PRICE at which your pig will be sold:

Compare your selling price to your costs,

- To be a profitable pig farm, you must sell your pigs at the price that enables you to cover your costs and then add the profits.

- There are two categories of cost on your pig farm, they are the direct costs and indirect cost.

- Direct costs are costs that are directly related to the products, e.g., cost of buying breeding stock, feeds, drugs, staff cost, transport etc.

- Indirect costs are all other costs for running the business, for example rent, security, etc.

- To calculate your selling price of your pig, you need to consider the total product cost (direct and indirect) Total costs + Profit = Price.

- Then you also need to consider the amount of money customers are willing to pay, to determine this you need to consider the price of substitute products e.g. the price of poultry, beef and fish. Your price per kg should never exceed this alternative meat because pork is regarded as the cheapest alternative to them. Research has shown that in Nigeria most people prefer beef more than any other meats, however, there is cross price elasticities between other meat types apart from beef.

- Then you need to consider the competitor's prices. Your competitor's price is important however, you should consider your profit margin but do not compromise quality or deceive about the product because you want to sell at a lower price than that of your competitors.

- There may be need to offer special prices to attract new customers, quantity discounts (e.g., for customers buying more than twenty weaners) and seasonal prices (e.g. special Christmas prices for pork and special weaner prices when demand is lower.

In summary, you should try and minimize your production costs so that you can offer a more competitive price on the market. You should consider using feed concentrates and mix it with our locally available feed ingredients e.g. PKC, Soya mill, Rice bran , Groundnut cake and brewery waste to reduce feed costs. The prices of your products will ultimately be determined by the market forces; however, you should not try to lower your prices below the industry's average as that will affect your profitability. By using the market's prices and all that you have learn in this book to improve your own production efficiency, all your products will be bought, so there is no need to lower your prices unnecessarily. As you progress in your business, you should continually identify and target premium buyers that are ready to pay for quality and offer discounts to those who buy in bulk to gain customer loyalty.

The PLACE where it is sold:

- Decide where to sell your products (farmgate, pig market away from competition, local market, etc.).

- You might have to consider the transport costs (from your farmgate to place of sale).

- You also have to consider the quantities and price customers are willing to pay, whether it is worth the transportation risks such as death of live pigs during transportation, quality deterioration for pork and others.

- Ultimately you might decide whether to sell your products through middlemen or directly to consumers.

The PROMOTION (that is, the means and style of advertising and selling):

You should use various method of promotion to gain more customers and increase general awareness of your farm and the products you offer.

Word of Mouth

Word of mouth advertising via quality products can be used to market your farm and the product. You should spread the word of your pigs in the community and use your personal networks to identify new customers.

You should join farmer's cooperatives, as they are a source of potential customers. They may have a list of buyers that they might share with you.

Community Involvement

You should maintain and enhance your reputation within the community, through joining the pig farmer's association and other pig farmer chat rooms to understand the pig market.

Fliers

Your marketing strategy will include the use of fliers which are going to be distributed to butcheries, abattoirs, schools, churches, supermarkets, hotels and fast food outlets. These fliers will be well designed, attractive and very informative, containing our prices, contact details and products which we sell.

Social media

You should place adverts and promote your farm on Facebook, Instagram and YouTube. Placing your advert in the weekly social media will ensure that your advert will be seen by as many people as possible.

Internet Marketing

Your company's website is a dynamic marketing tool for the company. The website should provide information about your products for target customers. As the company grows, its recruiting needs can be addressed by posting carrier opportunities and Frequently Asked Questions about the company. With time, you may consider ecommerce, whereby you will integrate your website with PayPal, the online payment system, which will allow customers who want to pay for your products online to do so.

You should link your website to your social media accounts on Facebook, LinkedIn and Twitter and regularly update your website with latest information, promotions and discounts.

27. Reference

1. *https://www.smallstarter.com/get-inspired/how-to-start-pig-farming-in-africa/*

2. *https://university.upstartfarmers.com/blog/starting-a-modern-farm*

3. Economic Efficiency of Pig Production in Oyo State .... *http://www.journalrepository.org/media/journals/AJEA_2/2012/May/1337836987-Adetunji-Adeyemo_2011AJEA746.pdf*

4. Economic Analysis of Swine Production in Nigeria: A Case *https://pdfs.semanticscholar.org/1889/0e2a35e4c1cbeaed5cf2e25aebcb538c4507.pdf*

5. History of pigs, pork, and bacon | Quatr.us Study Guides. *https://quatr.us/food-2/history-pigs-pork-bacon.htm*

6. Pork Production — Growth Industry in Morocco | The Pig Site. *https://thepigsite.com/news/2008/04/pork-production-growth-industry-in-morocco-1*

7. Tried and True Ways to Fail in Farming — Running a Small Farm. *http://sportsmansvintagepress.com/read-free/five-acres-independence/tried-true-ways-fail/*

8. Why You Should Invest in Pig Farming ? | ITS TRIPPING. *https://www.itstripping.in/invest-pig-farming/*

9. Would You Tell Me Please Which Way I Ought to Go From Here *https://me.me/i/would-you-tell-me-please-which-way-i-ought-to-3820003*

10. How to start a commercial pig farming business — sandalili.com. *http://sandalili.com/pig-farming-business/*

11. Modern pig production technology. A practical guide to profit by John Gadd 2011

12. General Information on Pig Trending now — Agriculture Nigeria. *https://www.agriculturenigeria.com/farming-production/livestock/pig*

13. Who Invented the Piggy Bank and How Did Piggy Banks Get .... *https://zippyfacts.com/who-invented-the-piggy-bank-and-how-did-piggy-banks-get-their-name/*

14. Reasons Why People Like You Are Starting a Modern Farm. *https://university.upstartfarmers.com/blog/starting-a-modern-farm*

15. Pig production & Marketing Uganda Limited. *http://www.globaleducationmagazine.com/pig-production-marketing-uganda-limited/*

16. History of pigs, pork, and bacon | Quatr.us Study Guides. *https://quatr.us/food-2/history-pigs-pork-bacon.htm*

17. General Information on Pig Trending now — Agriculture Nigeria. *https://www.agriculturenigeria.com/farming-production/livestock/pig*

18. Important Reasons To Invest In Agriculture In Nigeria Or .... *http://startuptipsdaily.com/invest-in-agriculture-in-nigeria-now/*

19. Pig farming — Smallstarter Africa. *https://www.smallstarter.com/get-inspired/how-to-start-pig-farming-in-africa/*

20. Natural Pig Farming: — tebatt.net. *http://www.tebatt.net/PROJECTS/PROJECT_HOMEFARM/Garden_Diary/LIVESTOCK/PIGS/Pigs.html*

21. Untitled1 [www.nda.agric.za]. *https://www.nda.agric.za/docs/Infopaks/pigs.htm*

22. Social Behavior of Swine — Behavior — Merck Veterinary Manual. *https://www.merckvetmanual.com/behavior/normal-social-behavior-and-behavioral-problems-of-domestic-animals/social-behavior-of-swine*

23. Are Pigs Clean Animals? | Reference.com. *https://www.reference.com/pets-animals/pigs-clean-animals-edb095acf23425c5*

24. Who is Likely to Succeed at Farming? — Small Farming. *http://sportsmansvintagepress.com/read-free/five-acres-independence/likely-succeed-at-farming/*

25. Charles R. Swindoll Quotes (Author of The Grace Awakening). *https://www.goodreads.com/author/quotes/5139.Charles_R_Swindoll*

26. Tips on How to Be Optimistic — Personal Growth Ideas. *https://www.personalgrowthideas.com/blog/7-tips-on-how-to-be-optimistic/*

27. Quote by Steve Jobs: "You've got to find what you love *https://www.goodreads.com/quotes/903982-you-ve-got-to-find-what-you-love-and-that-is*

28. SIX LEADERSHIP PRINCIPLES TO LEARN FROM AN EAGLE. BY .... *https://www.youtube.com/watch?v=K1ColskZoh0*

29. Housing — nda.agric.za. *https://www.nda.agric.za/docs/Infopaks/housing.htm*

30. Rules for Starting Your Own Farm | The Art of Manliness. *https://www.artofmanliness.com/articles/9-rules-for-starting-your-own-farm/*

31. Advantages and disadvantages of using your own money to .... *https://www.nibusinessinfo.co.uk/content/advantages-and-disadvantages-using-your-own-money-start-business*

32. Raising finance from friends and family | nibusinessinfo.co.uk. *https://www.nibusinessinfo.co.uk/content/raising-finance-friends-and-family*

33. The Most Important Rule of Investing. *https://www.thebalance.com/the-most-important-rule-of-investing-357325*

34. The challenges of agricultural lending — Rural Finance and .... *http://www.ruralfinanceandinvestment.org/sites/default/files/1164410190454_AgLend_Lesson1.pdf*

35. Choosing a Farm Business Structure? Start here. — Upstart .... *https://university.upstartfarmers.com/blog/farm-business-structure*

36. Sole Trader Advantages and Disadvantages. *https://www.smallbusinesspro.co.uk/small-business-finance/sole-trader.html*

37. 1.5.4 Forms of business — Business. *http://businesswithmredwards.weebly.com/154-forms-of-business.html*

38. Why Is Organizational Structure Important? | Chron.com. *https://smallbusiness.chron.com/organizational-structure-important-3793.html*

39. What is the role of the Managing Director? | Institute of .... *https://www.iod.com/news/news/articles/What-is-the-role-of-the-Managing-Director*

40. Swine Human Resources: Managing Employees — eXtension. *https://articles.extension.org/pages/27276/swine-human-resources:-managing-employees*

41. Maslow's hierarchy of needs — Wikipedia. *https://en.wikipedia.org/wiki/Maslow%27s_hierarchy_of_needs*

42. Staff training and education | The Pig Site. *https://thepigsite.com/husbandry/herd-management/staff-training-and-education*

43. General Information on Pig Trending now — Agriculture Nigeria. *https://www.agriculturenigeria.com/farming-production/livestock/pig*

44. LESSON 2 BREEDING & SELECTION AIMS Select appropriate pig *https://www.acsedu.com/download/samples/PigsLesson2.pdf*

45. conformation — carrsconsulting.com. *http://www.carrsconsulting. com/thepig/health-farm/productionmgt/breeding/giltmanagement/ conformation.htm*

46. How You Can Start a Profitable Pig Farming In Nigeria .... *https:// howng.com/how-you-can-start-a-profitable-pig-farming-in-nigeria/*

47. Getting Gilts Ready for the Breeding Herd | Pork Business. *https:// www.porkbusiness.com/article/getting-gilts-ready-breeding-herd*

48. Housing, equipment, and supplies for raising swine. *http:// waynecounty4hlivestock.weebly.com/uploads/1/9/2/2/19220499/ masterstockman-swine.docx*

49. Farmers Handbook on Pig Production — SlideShare. *https://www. slideshare.net/growelagrovet/farmers-handbook-on-pig-production*

50. Basic Pig Husbandry — The Boar | The Pig Site. *https://thepigsite. com/articles/basic-pig-husbandry-the-boar*

51. Transport and Care of Pigs | Pigs | Livestock .... *http://agriculture. vic.gov.au/agriculture/livestock/pigs/transport-and-care-of-pigs*

52. CHAPTER 6: Transport of livestock — fao.org. *http://www.fao. org/3/X6909E/x6909e08.htm*

53. Basic Quarantine — American Mini Pig Association. *https:// americanminipigassociation.com/interactions-with-pigs/basic- quarantine/*

54. Basic Pig Husbandry — Gilts and Sows | The Pig Site. *https:// thepigsite.com/articles/basic-pig-husbandry-gilts-and-sows*

55. PigProgress — Delayed Puberty. *https://www.pigprogress.net/ Health/Health-Tool/diseases/Delayed-puberty/*

56. Estrus or Heat Detection — Pork Information Gateway. *http:// porkgateway.org/resource/estrus-or-heat-detection/*

57. MANAGING THE SOW FOR OPTIMUM PRODUCTIVITY. *https:// projects.ncsu.edu/project/swine_extension/healthyhogs/book2000/ see.htm*

58. Synchronization of estrus in swine — Pork Information Gateway. *http://porkgateway.org/resource/synchronization-of-estrus-in-swine/*

59. Ensuring a successful mating | The Pig Site. *https://thepigsite.com/ genetics-and-reproduction/insemination/key-points-to-a-successful- mating*

60. Breeding Management in Pigs — Management and Nutrition .... *https://www.merckvetmanual.com/management-and-nutrition/ management-of-reproduction-pigs/breeding-management-in-pigs*

61. The Length of the Gestation Period in Swine — animals.mom.me. *https://animals.mom.me/length-gestation-period-swine-3417.html*

62. MANAGING THE SOW FOR OPTIMUM PRODUCTIVITY. *https:// projects.ncsu.edu/project/swine_extension/healthyhogs/book2000/ see.htm*

63. Managing Sows In Gestation | National Hog Farmer. *https://www. nationalhogfarmer.com/mag/farming_managing_sows_gestation*

64. Care & Management of pregnant Sow — KVK Mokokchung. *http:// www.kvkmokokchung.in/index.php/2012-04-03-12-21-17/2012-04- 03-12-34-32/leaflets/32-care-management-of-pregnant-sow*

65. Livestock Kenya — Farrowing and care of new-born piglets. *https:// livestockkenya.com/index.php/blog/pigs/174-farrowing-and-care-of- new-born-piglets*

66. Farrowing and Lactation in the Sow and Gilt — Animal Genome. *https://www.animalgenome.org/edu/PIH/prod_nursing.html*

67. Induction of Labor at 39 Weeks — ACOG. *https://www.acog.org/ Patients/FAQs/Induction-of-Labor-at-39-Weeks*

68. Care of the Sow During Farrowing and Lactation — eXtension. *https://articles.extension.org/pages/31077/care-of-the-sow-during- farrowing-and-lactation*

69. Baby Pig Management — Birth to Weaning — Pork Information .... *http://porkgateway.org/resource/baby-pig-management-birth-to- weaning/*

70. Read e-book Pigs From Down Under — Part 1 — Life On The Farm. *http://www.stringrecordings.com/img/dragon/pigs-from-down- under-part-1-life-on-the-farm.php*

71. Basic Pig Husbandry — The Weaner | The Pig Site. *https:// thepigsite.com/articles/basic-pig-husbandry-the-weaner*

72. carrsconsulting.com. *http://carrsconsulting.com/thepig/normalpig/ behaviourhabits/behaviourhabits.htm*

73. Vector borne infections infections transmitted through .... *https:// www.coursehero.com/file/p1q8d44/It-is-occurrence-in-a-community- or-region-of-a-group-of-illness-of-similar/*

74. T-Cells | Ask A Biologist. *https://askabiologist.asu.edu/t-cell*

75. Farmers Handbook on Pig Production — SlideShare. *https://www. slideshare.net/growelagrovet/farmers-handbook-on-pig-production*

76. How To Start A Hog Raising Business — businessdiary.com.ph. *https://businessdiary.com.ph/1076/how-to-start-a-hog-raising-business/*

77. Pig Husbandry Distance Education | Study Pigs Online. *https://www.acsedu.co.uk/Courses/Agriculture/PIGS-BAG209-232.aspx*

78. Mycotoxins in pig production | Agriculture and Food. *https://www.agric.wa.gov.au/feeding-nutrition/mycotoxins-pig-production*

79. Full text of "Feeds and feeding;" — archive.org. *https://archive.org/stream/feedsfeeding00henr/feedsfeeding00henr_djvu.txt*

80. HSH-10K-6.30.2013 — SEC.gov. *https://www.sec.gov/Archives/edgar/data/23666/000002366613000014/hsh-10kx6302013.htm*

81. Feeding pigs in Africa is expensive. Changing their diets *http://theconversation.com/feeding-pigs-in-africa-is-expensive-changing-their-diets-is-the-answer-65171*

82. The role of functional fibers in piglet feeds — WATTAgNet. *https://www.wattagnet.com/articles/22227-the-role-of-functional-fibers-in-piglet-feeds*

83. Nutrient needs | Department of Agriculture and Fisheries .... *https://www.daf.qld.gov.au/business-priorities/agriculture/animals/pigs/feed-nutrition/nutrients-diets/nutrient-needs*

84. The importance of water for pigs | Knowledge center .... *https://www.impex.nl/en/knowledge-center/the-importance-of-water-for-pigs*

85. Nutritional Requirements of Pigs — Management and .... *https://www.merckvetmanual.com/management-and-nutrition/nutrition-pigs/nutritional-requirements-of-pigs*

86. Salt poisoning or water deprivation in pigs | Agriculture .... *https://www.agric.wa.gov.au/feeding-nutrition/salt-poisoning-or-water-deprivation-pigs*

87. Nutrition basics | Department of Agriculture and Fisheries .... *https://www.daf.qld.gov.au/business-priorities/agriculture/animals/pigs/feed-nutrition/nutrients-diets/basics*

88. PROTEIN SOURCES FOR THE ANIMAL FEED INDUSTRY. *http://www.fao.org/3/y5019e/y5019e03.htm*

89. The role of energy | The Pig Site. *https://thepigsite.com/husbandry/feed-and-nutrition/the-role-of-energy*

90. Recycled food waste in pig diets can reduce environmental .... *https://www.nationalhogfarmer.com/nutrition/recycled-food-waste-pig-diets-can-reduce-environmental-footprint*

91. Roots, tubers, plantains and bananas in animal feeding. *http://www.fao.org/3/T0554E/T0554E17.htm*

92. Feed wastage — carrsconsulting.com. *http://carrsconsulting.com/thepig/health-pen/healthmgt/feed/commonprobs.htm*

93. Chapter 15. Fish Feed Formulation — fao.org. *http://www.fao.org/3/X5738E/x5738e0g.htm*

94. Concept — Hydroponics Kenya. *https://hydroponicskenya.com/resources/concept/*

95. The 'step by step' of how to grow hydroponic barley/wheat .... *https://www.grandeurafrica.com/the-step-by-step-of-how-to-grow-hydroponic-barley-wheat-fodder/*

96. The Use of Cassava, Sweet Potato and Cocoyam, and Their By *http://article.sapub.org/10.5923.j.food.20120204.02.html*

97. The Role of Marketing in Pig Production in Nigeria Part 4 .... *https://www.youtube.com/watch?v=H5XE6pxsHTQ*

98. Marketing tips: The fresh produce supply chain — African .... *https://www.africanfarming.com/marketing-tips-fresh-produce-supply-chain/*

99. Developing a Niche Market for Pork — Purdue Extension. *https://www.extension.purdue.edu/extmedia/AS/11-04-04.pdf*

100. THE INFLUENCE OF CULTURAL FACTORS ON CONSUMER BUYING .... *http://www.eajournals.org/wp-content/uploads/The-Influence-of-Cultural-Factors-on-Consumer-Buying-Behaviour-A-Case-Study-of-Pork.pdf*

101. List down their answers d Marketing Marketing is Finding *https://www.coursehero.com/file/p291nidi/List-down-their-answers-d-Marketing-Marketing-is-Finding-out-what-the-customer/*

102. Pigs: how to get started — Part 2 | Farmer's Weekly. *https://www.farmersweekly.co.za/animals/pigs-2/*

103. Good Practices for Biosecurity in the Pig Sector | The Pig .... *https://thepigsite.com/articles/good-practices-for-biosecurity-in-the-pig-sector*

104. paper GOOD PRACTICES FOR BIOSECURITY IN THE PIG SECTOR FAO *https://docplayer.net/10116035-Paper-good-practices-for-biosecurity-in-the-pig-sector-fao-animal-production-and-health-issues-and-options-in-developing-and-transition-countries.html*

28. A glossary of technical terms in pig production

Absorption	to take in or assimilate substances e.g. into tissues.
Acronym	Word or term formed from the initial letters of other words (PRRS, FCR)
Acute	Of recent onset — rather than depicting severity
Ad libitum (ad lib)	without restraint
Adipose	fatty
Adjuvant	a material that aids another, i.e. in a vaccine to increase antigen potency
Adsorption	attracting and holding other substances onto surfaces
Aetiology	the science dealing with the causes of disease
Aerobe	aerobic) a micro-organism which needs oxygen to function fully
Agalactia	partial or complete lack of milk
Ambient (temperature)	temperature close to the pig's body
Amino-acid	protein building block
Anabolism	anabolic) the formative stage of metabolism
Anaerobe (adj anaerobic)	a micro-organism which can grow in the absence of oxygen
Analgesia	absence of sensibility to pain (analgesic = painkiller)
Anaphylaxis	anaphylactic) severe or unusual allergic shock reaction

ANFs Anti-Nutritional Factors.	Materials present in certain feed raw materials which interfere with digestive or metabolic pathways
Androgen	male hormone
Anoestrus	no oestrus, lack of oestrus
Anoxia	anoxic) interference with (lack of) oxygen supply
ANS Automatic Nervous System,	involved in 'Flight or Fight' stress
Anterior	towards the front
Anthropomorphism	attribution of human characteristics to animals
Antibody	specialised proteins produced by lymphocytes (white blood cells) in response to presence of an antigen (qv)
Antigen	any substance foreign to an organism (i.e. a pig) reacting with an antibody so as to produce an immune response within the organism
Antioxidant	material which inhibits the oxidation (qv) of compounds e.g. prevents rancidity of fats
Arthritis	inflammation of a joint
Aspirate	Suck out. (However, aspiration can mean inhalation)
Astringent	causing contraction
Ataxia	muscle incoordination
Atresia	closure of a structure
Atrophy	wasting; shrinking
Attenuation	reduction; thinning (diluted) Attrition wearing away
Audit	a systematic review
Autogenous	self-generating; originating within the body
Autonomic	not subject to voluntary control (e.g. Autonomic Nervous System)
Bacterin	a vaccine made up from killed bacteria
Bacteriocide	substance which destroys bacteria
Bacteriostat	substance which inhibits but does not destroy bacteria
Batch farrowing	farrowing sows in deliberately formed groups to facilitate workload and supervision, also to make disease in the offspring easier to contain
Bile	fluid produced by the liver which breaks up large fat globules for digestion by enzymes. Stored in the gall bladder

Billion	one thousand million
Biopsy	removal (for microscopic examination and testing) tissue from the living body
Biosecurity	all the measures taken to preserve health and defend against disease, not just sanitation measures
Birthweights	Target 1.5 kg piglet. Action level <1.2 kg
Blastocyst	early stage of embryo formation (from 'blast', a bud)
Bloat	(gastric) distension with gas, common with feeding (hot) whey
Blood poisoning	common term for blood infected with bacteria or their toxins
Born alives	those piglets which drew at least one breath, confirmed by the bucket test — did the lungs float or sink quickly?
Breech foetus	buttock-first at parturition
Brewer's grains	feedstuff residue after starch fermentation Brewer's yeast brewing by-product after harvesting and drying saccharomyces cerevisiae yeast
Brooder	substantial cover over heat source used early-on in wean-tofinish housing
Brown fat	fatty tissue which gives off heat.
Bulk density	the density of a granular substance (e.g. animal feed) calculated as the unit volume of the substance including the spaces between the particles/grain (see density)
Caecum	a small pouch between the small intestine and colon containing cellulose-splitting bacteria. Present in pigs and poorly developed in humans
Calorie	the amount of heat needed to raise 1 gramme of water by 1°C (1 calorie = 4.187 joules)
Carbohydrate	the simplest carbohydrates are the sugars (saccharides). More complex are the polysaccharides (e.g. starch and cellulose). Sugars (e.g. glucose) are intermediates in the conversion of food to energy; polysaccharides serve as energy stores in plants and seeds, cassava, etc. Cellulose, lignin etc provide supporting cell walls and woody tissue in plants thus are not very digestible.
Carcinogen	cancer-causing substance
Cardiovascular	to do with the heart blood vessels

Casualty	any pig slaughtered in an emergency due to disease, injury or distress. Casualties must be distinguished from culls
Catabolism	procedure within the body where complex structures are broken down into simpler compounds with the release of energy
Catalyst	a substance which assists/speeds up a reaction but which is not used up during the process.
Cellulose	see carbohydrate
Celsius	0°C freezing, 100°C boiling. Centigrade = 100 steps. Celsius to Fahrenheit (qv) °F = (°C x 9/5)+32 i.e. °C x 9 ÷ 5 + 32 = °F.
Centimetre	(cm) 100th of a metre, 0.3937 ins
Cervix	(vet) (adj cervical) neck, or narrow part of an organ. In the female between the uterus and the vagina. A safety valve to protect the uterus from foreign bodies.
Chromosome	contains coiled DNA. In animal cells, determines sex and transmits genetic information
Chronic	in existence for a long time and causing less of a reaction than acute
Cilia	tiny hair-like substances which move the cell or move mucus over it
Cohort	a group of animals with similar characteristics used in a research trial
Colitis	inflammation of the colon
Colon	the large intestine between the caecum and rectum
Colonisation	the ability of bacteria to adhere to a living surface and then multiply
Condensation	it the change of a vapour into a liquid
Conduction	the movement of energy (sound, heat or electricity) by the agitation of molecules
Congenital disease	present at birth Congenital evident from birth
Consultant	an ordinary guy a long way from home, or who has left salaried employment on grounds of economics or age, and whose quality of life improves markedly thereafter.

Convection	the movement of heat through a liquid or gas. Heat expands portions of the material, they become less dense and rise; their place is taken by colder portions, thus setting up convection currents.
Correlation	the degree of association of variables. Linkage, i.e. age of the pig can be correlated or linked to increased fat cover
COSHH	Control of Substances Hazardous to Health. UK regulations (1989) providing one set of stipulations for all occupational health risks
Cost/benefit analysis	taking account of social costs/benefits as well as purely financial ones
Crude fibre	the non-digestible cellulose, hemi-cellulose and lignin portions of a feed (see also Fibre) Cycle not the same as parity (qv).
Cycle	denotes a time from event to event e.g. birth to birth or breeding to breeding
Cystitis	inflammation of the bladder
Deadweight	carcase weight dressed to a specific standard
Deamination	processing of surplus protein to waste material
Denature	to produce a structural change in a protein which causes it to reduce its biological properties
Density	the ratio of the mass (weight) of a substance to its volume
Dermal	to do with the skin.
Dermatitis	= skin disease
Deviation	a measure of dispersion, indicating variability from the Standard deviation (SD) average.
Dewpoint	the temperature at which water vapour present in the air saturates the air and begins to condense to form water deposits, i.e. dew begins to form
Diagnosis	the identification of disease. Clinical diagnosis is the identification from clinical signs during life backed by by laboratory tests (see also prognosis)
Dietetic	to do with the diet
Differential diagnosis	using the differences in diseases derived from symptoms backed up by epidemiological (qv) tests to select a diagnosis most suited to the evidence

Digestible Energy	the gross energy eaten less that voided in the (DE) faeces. 1 MJ (megajoule) DE = 239 Kcals.
Dilation	stretching Discrete separate. (Note: discreet = tactful
Diuretic	increasing urine amounts, also a product to do the same
Diurnal	day to night/night to day
Dressing percentage	(Killing Out % : Expressed as a percentage of liveweight shortly before slaughter.
Dynamics	(e.g. thermodynamics) the reaction of bodies to force
Dyspnoea	difficult breathing
Dystocia	abnormally laboured farrowing (foetal d. = due to the foetus; maternal d. = due to the sow)
Ectoparasite	a parasite living on the host's body, e.g. fleas (endo = inside the body, e.g. worms)
Electrolyte	a substance, normally a mineral salt, which allows the intestine to insorb water at the same time it may be exsorbing it (i.e. during diarrhoea) thus deterring dehydration.
Embryo	from the time the organism develops a long axis to the time the major limbs etc have started to develop, when it becomes a foetus
Empty days	(Open Days; Non-productive days) the number of days per year or per litter the sow is not carrying or feeding piglets.
Endemic	present at all outermost skin layer(s) times
Endocrine	hormonal
Endometrium	the lining of the womb
Enteritis	inflammation of the intestine
Enzyme	a protein which acts as a catalyst. A chemical 'go-between' facilitating metabolism. The pig contain 13,000 different enzymes.
Epidemic	disease attacking many subjects at the same time
Epidemiological	the study of diseases and their causes
Epithelia	to do with cell formation in the body (see epithelium
Epithelium	the cell covering of external and internal body surfaces
Epizootic	1 widely diffused and rapidly spreading 2 concerning an epidemic
Ethology	study of animal behaviour

Exogenous	outside the body
Exponential	(growth) (stats) ever-increasing
Expression	1. to squeeze out 2. The manifestation of a heritable trait (q.v.) in an individual carrying the gene or genes which characterise it
Emetic	used to induce vomiting
Encephalomyelitis	inflammation of both brain and spinal
Extrapolation	(extrapolated from) inferred or deduced from the data presented
Extrinsic	outside (opp: intrinsic)
Exudate	fluid emanating from a wound or irritant
F1	First filial generation or first cross, terms used in genetics
F2	Second filial generation
Fahrenheit scale	Freezing point is at 32°F and boiling point of water at 212°F. Fahrenheit to Celsius °C = (°F – 32) x 5/9
Farrowing index	number of farrowings a sow achieves per year.
Farrowing interval	Time between farrowings Target 152 days in normal circumstances
Farrowing fever	MMA syndrome
Fermentation	enzyme conversion of carbohydrates etc to simpler substances (like lactic acid). Done artificially, i.e. for the animal, it helps digestive efficiency
Fibre crude	fibre is today considered a largely meaningless term.. Fibre quality and amounts offered can be deficient in modern sow diets (constipation; lack of gutfill; stress
First litter sow	female pig between the date of the first effective service and the date of the next effective service
Fixed costs	labour, contractors' costs, buildings and rent, machinery and equipment, finance charges, stock leasing, feeds, insurance, sundries
Fructose	a sugar found in fruits and honey (lactose = milk sugar; mannose = yeast sugar
Gastritis	inflammation of the stomach lining Gastroenteritis (vet) inflammation of the stomach lining and intestine

Gene	unit of heredity comprising a simple segment of DNA molecule that makes up a chromosome. Two copies of each gene, one from each parent, are present in every cell.
Genome	correctly; the complete inventory of hereditary traits contained in a half-set of chromosomes, all the genes in an organism
Gestation	110-116 days in the sow, from fertilisation to birth
Gilt	correctly, a young female pig which has not yet had a litter of pigs, rather than one before first conception.
Gross margin	net output minus total feed costs and other variable costs (qv)
Habituation	an aspect of learning in which repeated applications of a stimulus results in decreased responsiveness
Haemoglobin	component of blood which transports oxygen to and from muscles.
Header tank (env)	water reservoir at the top of a gravity water line
Hepatitis	inflammation of the liver Heterogeneous not uniform: dissimilar Note: pronounced heterogeneous
Heterogenous	from another source; not originating in the body e.g. 'foreign body',
Hormones	a wide variety of chemical messengers with specific functions. Work via the bloodstream
Humidity	the amount of moisture in the air (see Dewpoint) Humoral processes carried out by the body's fluids
Hybrid vigour	heterosis (qv) better performance and viability in the first generation from matings of parents of different breeds. The advantage is quickly lost if hybrids are then interbred
Hydrochloric acid	secreted by cells lining the stomach, vital (especially in the weaned pig) to 'sanitise' the ingesta prior to it being passed on to the duodenum (qv)
Hyper- and hypo	'hyper-' indicates extremeness, excessivity, e.g. Hyperactive; while 'hypo' indicates deficiency, beneath or under, e.g. Hypoglycaemia (low blood sugar) and hypodermic (under the skin)
Hypertrophy	increase in size of an organ due to excessive cell production
Immunity	the condition of being secure from a particular disease

Immunoglobulins	a specialised protein usually produced following exposure to an antigen
Implantation	the attachment of the fertilized egg to the womb wall (endometrium) usually between day 10 to 30 after service
In vitro	seen in a test-tube or artificial environment (e.g. laboratory work/research)
Incremental	added or increasing costs
Infarct	area interrupting the blood supply
Inflammation	the normal healing reaction of the body to an injury i.e. protective walling off of an injured area from the cause Ingestion eating/swallowing material (ingesta)
Integrity	e.g. tissue integrity. Condition/soundness of tissue
Intrinsic	inside
Lard	commercially rendered pig fat
Latent	concealed, not obvious
Laxative	mild = aperient, strong = purgative/cathartic
Lesion	wound, ulcer, sore, tumour, bite, scratch, etc. A deviation from the normal in a body
Lipids	fats, greases, oily and waxy compounds Lipoproteins how fats are moved in the blood e.g. HDL = high density lipoproteins and conversely
Lymphocyte	white blood cell, T cell
Medulla	the inner portion of any organ
Melatonin	hormone released by the pineal gland (q.v.) controls the development of follicles and ovaries
Meningitis	inflammation of the lining of the brain, the meninges
Metabolism	all the processes which lead to the build-up of the body (anabolism) and the breakdown of body molecules to provide energy
Metritis	inflammation of the uterus
Microgram	one millionth of a gram or one thousandth of a milligram.
Micronutrient	element (nutr) a trace element, e.g. Se, Fe, Cu, Zn, etc
Mould	common name for a fungal organism/fungus
Mummified	degenerate (discoloured and shrivelled) piglets which died before farrowing

Mycotoxin	fungal poison
Necrosis	cell death (adj necrotic)
Nematode	roundworm
Neonatal	just born (usually up to one week).
Neonate	Neoplasm a tumour
Net energy	(Net Energy, NE, considers the amount of energy used in digestion and deducts this from ME (q.v.) to leave the amount available for growth and maintenance. NE thus provides a more accurate estimation of 'true' energy in a feed ingredient. Net or nett (econ & nutr) total amount (remaining) e.g. net energy. No further deductions made
Net margin	gross margin (qv) less fixed costs (qv)
Net output	sales plus credits, less purchases plus valuation charge (closing valuation minus opening valuation)
Neuritis	inflammation of a nerve
Nervous system	Central Nervous System involves the brain and spinal cord. Autonomic Nervous System is not subject to voluntary control
Objective	(as distinct from subjective) based on sound evidence. Realistic
Obstetrics	science of pregnancy and birth Occluded (vet) closed (or sometimes, severely obstructed)
Oedema	build up of fluids in a body (e.g. Bowel Oedema)
Oesophagus	the throat to the stomach passage (i.e. gullet)
Oestrogen	female hormone
Oligosaccharides	complex carbohydrates which act as prebiotics (q.v.) and stimulate the growth of probiotics (q.v.)
Olfactory	by smell
Oocyst	the highly resistant stage of a coccidia's life cycle
Opportunity cost	earmarking money put by for one project to be be spent on another should it appear opportunely
Overheads	fixed costs
Oxytocin	hormone which acts as a stimulant towards pregnancy and releases milk (together with the suckling stimulus) in lactation
Oxidation	replacement of negative charges (electrons) on a molecule by positive charges (protons). The opposite of reduction. (See also anti-oxidant)

Palpate	examine by touch
Pancreas	organ which produces enzymes to break down proteins, carbohydrates and fats (pancreatic 'juice')
Parity 1	similarity; 2 in the sow, the number of times a sow has farrowed e.g. a gilt is in parity 0 and a sow which has farrowed 4 times is in her 4th parity
Parturient	giving birth or related to birth
Passive	external stimulus (as distinct from 'active' where the animal responds spontaneously / originates the response))
Pathogenic	disease producing (pathogenicity = level of disease
Peripheral	near to the edge (of). (Periphery = outer edge or outside the central object)
Phenotype	the outward appearance of an animal in expressing its inheritance (as distinct from genotype = its whole genetic make-up)
Power	(to the power of) mathematical symbol to simplify the display of very large (or very small) numbers, e.g. 1000 = 103 or 1 x 10 x 10 x 10 (kilogram, kilowatt).
Prebiotics	act on gut conditions or precondition nutrients or capture hostile organisms e.g. oligosaccharides. Different from probiotics (qv
Precursor	forerunner, usually leading to another more active result
Premature	before day 110 of pregnancy but where some foetuses farrowing have survived, nevertheless, for 24 hours
Probiotics	beneficial organisms which colonise the gut surface rather than pathogens e.g. lactobacilli. Competitive exclusion
Prognosis	a forecast of the likely effects of a disease and its cure prospects. Diagnosis is the identification of a disease
Proliferation	increase, multiplication
Prophylaxis	fending off disease, prevention (adj prophylactic)
Prosthesis	an artificial body part replacement Protocol an action plan, set of guidelines
Provitamin	a substance from which an animal can form a vitami
Pulmonary	pertaining to the lungs (or pulmonary artery)
Quadrant	one quarter of the circumference of a circle
Qualitative	non-numerical description, e.g. colourful, small, etc

Quantitative	numerical description e.g. fourth, two kilometre, 1000, etc
Quartile	one fourth of a dimension plan or structure. Mainly used in ventilation design
Random	unplanned (random variable, see variable
Radiant	emitting heat from a surface Ratio the relationship between two quantities
Reagent	material used to produce a chemical response so as to detect and measure other materials
Recessive	a gene which only functions when it is provided by both parents
Reduction	see 'oxidation', its opposite reaction
Sterotypies	abnormal behaviour(s) characterised by rapidly-repeated
Stereotypic	actions to no fixed purpose/directed at inappropriate objects
Sternum	the breast bone
Stillborn	correctly, piglets which did not draw breath once expelled, as with born-deads. Can be confirmed by the 'bucket-test'. (see born-alives)
Strain	the outward manifestation of stressors (fright, aggression, vices etc)
Stress	1. conditions and reactions (stressors) affecting the wellbeing, mental and physiological, of the pig 2. compression, tension (structures)
Subcutaneous	under the skin
Subjective	an unconfirmed, personal, opinion. The opposite of objective
Temperature;	Lower Critical Temperature (LCT) is the ambient temperature below which the pig needs to divert food energy into keeping warm. Evaporative Critical Temperature (ECT) is the ambient temperature at which panting occurs and urgent cooling action is needed. Respiration rate is usually more than 60 breaths per minute. Upper Critical Temperature (UCT) is the ambient temperature which, when exceeded, the animal's life could be in danger
Terminal	continuing breeding from a first cross without crossbreeding crossing further

Therapeutic	treating disease, curing, alleviating (n therapy) Therm heat required to raise 1000 kg of water 1°C. 1 therm = 1000 Kcal = 106 megajoules (MJ)
Ultrasound	used in pregnancy diagnosis by equipment capable of emitting radiant energy at over 20,000 cycles per second
Variable (stats)	different measurement(s). Random variable(s). A group or quantity which exhibit various values, each of varying probability
Variable costs	costs which are likely to vary frequently
Vascular	to do with the blood vessels / blood supply
Vector	an effluent sprayer covering a defined area
Vegetative	its most common meaning is resting i.e. vegetative state
Vein blood	vessel leading from various organs back to the heart in contrast to an artery which carries blood from the heart to various organs and the extremities
Velocity speed	air movement) vital in correct air placement in a piggery
Wet-dry feeding	technique where a small amount of meal is nudged by the pig into a receptacle which is then moistened once the pig activates a drinker nozzle over it. Also called (inaccurately) Single Space Feeding
Wet feeding	pipeline feeding (qv). Also known as Liquid Feeding
Weaning to service	the time between the date of weaning and date of interval first mating. Date of weaning is day 0.
Yield	dressed carcase weight
Zoonose	an animal disease transmissible to man
Zygote	(gen) the fertilised ovum just before first cleavage

Made in the USA
Middletown, DE
18 March 2023

27032330R00286